T5-CVC-815

Breaking
The
Secretary
Barrier

Breaking The Secretary Barrier

How to Get Out from Behind the Typewriter and Into a Management Job

Janet Dight

McGRAW-HILL BOOK COMPANY
New York St. Louis San Francisco Hamburg Mexico Toronto

The case histories in this book are based on real people and real events, but the names of the participants, as well as some of the details—industries, job descriptions, titles, and time frames—have been changed so that actual identities will not be recognized.

Copyright © 1986 by Janet Dight

All rights reserved. Printed in the United States of America. Except as permitted under the Copyright Act of 1976, no part of this publication may be reproduced or distributed in any form or by any means or stored in a data base or retrieval system, without the prior written permission of the publisher.

1 2 3 4 5 6 7 8 9 DOC DOC 8 7 6 5

ISBN 0-07-016905-5

LIBRARY OF CONGRESS CATALOGING IN PUBLICATION DATA

Dight, Janet,
    Breaking the secretary barrier.
    1. Secretaries. 2. Women executives. 3. Management.
I. Title.
HF5547.5.D54   1986   658.4'09'024042   85-11360
ISBN 0-07-016905-5

Book Design by Judy Allan

To Rick, who makes everything possible

Contents

Acknowledgments

I want to thank all the women who shared their stories with me over the past few years—I hope their experiences will be inspirational and educational for secretaries everywhere.

I also want to express my appreciation to:

- Dick Clancey, who helped me break the secretary barrier.

- P J Haduch, my editor, who believes in this book, and who provided the extra support and guidance this neophyte author needed. And to her assistant, Barbara Kastner, who handled the administrative end of this project, while on *her* way to breaking the secretary barrier.

- Alysa L. Drew, who, under considerable time pressure, critiqued the rough parts.

- Denise Faulkenbury and Sherri Few, who were good sports about being used as bad examples.

- R. C. Smith, Jr., whose management insights were a valuable addition to this book.

Introduction: It Ain't Gonna Be Easy

Despite all the progress women have made in the past 20 years, we have a long, long way to go. The men running the corporations and government agencies today were born and raised in an era when women stayed home, cooked, cleaned, and played hostess to their husbands' friends and business associates. Wives were responsible for removing the aggravating details from their husbands' lives and reducing the level of distraction. At the office, secretaries functioned the same way. They were "office wives" whose purpose was to create a pleasant, efficient atmosphere for their bosses to work in.

Unfortunately, not much has changed since the "good old days." Secretaries still have the role of helping hand around the office and they do it well, but somehow that role has become confused over the years with low IQ and lack of motivation. Secretaries were not then and are not now regarded as full-fledged members of the corporate team. They are not considered promotable.

The corporate team is still male-oriented. Most men born before 1950 (and a few born after) regard *all* women as less than equal in business. Women executives make them uncomfortable, and the higher the woman is in the organization, the more uncomfortable they become. The problem is that those men will be around for up to 30 more years, holding down the top, most influential jobs, and continuing to cast a wary eye on ambitious women.

Men born *after* 1950, most of whom have a more enlightened attitude, and women who have achieved management status, won't be totally in charge for several more decades. That means it isn't exactly going to be smooth sailing for secretaries trying to work their way up.

Essentially, you have two choices: you can wait until the world is a better place (and make your mark in a nursing home somewhere in the future), or you can take advantage of the progress that's been made so far, and make your own way.

It isn't going to be easy. Making the transition from secretary to manager will have its share of headaches, and worse, heartaches. The business world is cold and cruel at times, and you'll need a thick skin to get through it.

You'll find the obstacles to your success are many and varied. Your boss and other members of management have no real interest in your getting ahead. Other secretaries will resent you when you try. People you thought were friends may turn against you. You'll have to overcome your lack of management experience and your shaky self-confidence. You may have to slog your way through a number of assistantships and apprenticeships before you land a *real* management job. Your children, if you have them, won't be happy about the extra hours you spend at the office. Your husband, if you have one, may not only be unhappy about the extra hours, he may also be threatened by your new interest in your job and your improved self-esteem. You will have to adjust everything you do and rearrange everything you are; you will have to look different, talk different, work more hours, be more aggressive, and take more risks.

It's going to be a huge task—and a difficult one. But if you play your cards right, you can break the secretary barrier. And when you do, the rewards are fabulous. The sense of accomplishment, the feeling of prestige, and the respect you receive are some of the best feelings in the world. You will get a job that pays better, that makes you feel better about yourself. You'll have more intellectual stimulation and a more challenging environment. You'll make new friends who are exciting to be with. And you'll realize that there are no limits—you can go as far as you choose.

The purpose of this book is to show you how to push for that promotion, how to lay out a strategic plan for success, how to do everything you need to do to get out from behind that typewriter.

I'm not going to pull any punches. In many cases, secretaries have helped dig the hole they find themselves in. They don't know how to create opportunities and capitalize on them, or they don't recognize a helping hand when their boss extends one. Some secretaries who have tried to get ahead have failed and just given up.

I won't kid you or play to your illusions or fantasies, because kidding yourself is a sure road to failure. I'll show you what you are doing wrong and how to correct it, and I'll show you how to use your talents and abilities to their maximum advantage. I won't give you management theories that only an Einstein could put into practical use. I'll give you information you can start using today.

Because the business world is predominantly male—at least at the top—the case histories in this book usually refer to secretaries as "she" and bosses as "he." That has some practical value: "he/she" and "him/her" on every page of this book would make both you and I crazy, and using "she" for secretary and "him" for boss makes for clearer examples ("She scheduled a meeting with her" doesn't tell you who scheduled with whom). But it also has basis in reality. According to the Bureau of Labor Statistics, 99 percent of the secretaries in this country are women, and 74 percent of the managers are men.

We've got a long way to go. But you can make it. I'm convinced of that because I made it. In 1973, just out of college with a degree in English, I was hired as an assistant/secretary in the marketing research department of Borden, Inc.'s Consumer Products Division. In only 4 months, I convinced my boss to hire a secretary for us. After 9 months, I was promoted to assistant product manager for the Krylon Spray Paint brand—the first female executive in that division. It wasn't easy, particularly in those days, but I did it. Today I'm a consultant specializing in developing marketing and advertising plans for new products and new businesses in the computer industry.

Other women have made it, too, and more are making it every day. They are all glad they did, and you will be too. So no matter how far you want to go—to that copywriter job in the advertising department or all the way to the president's office—this book is for you.

Let's go.

Janet Dight
Colorado Springs, Colorado

1. Enough is enough

Today you typed yet another letter for your boss that you could have written better yourself. By the end of the week you will have taken fourteen phone messages that he should answer but won't, and by the end of the week, those callers are yelling at *you*, not him. You make coffee three times a day while your boss stands around watching and telling you about the ski trip to Vail he and his wife have planned. You worked until 7:00 last night (without asking for overtime), and this morning, your boss glared at you for being 10 minutes late. You've worked your tail off for the company for years, and last month they hired a kid fresh out of high school at only $100 less a month than you're making.

Had enough?

Of course you have. But what can you do about it? Tell your boss that from now on you'll do all the letter writing because his communication skills are so weak? Walk into his office and say, "Herb, I don't think that interdepartmental policy you issued yesterday is going to fly around here. Let's get together at 2:00 and talk it over?" Tell him to make his own coffee, you've got more important things to do?

Not hardly. (Well, you could, but you'd be unemployed moments later.)

You're smart, talented, and you have ambition, but you're stuck. You're in a job that goes nowhere—you're a secretary.

To the corporation, you are an accessory, a part of the equipment issued to each executive. You are an extension of your typewriter, a piece of office furniture. You are lumped together with the files and the paperclips and the back issues of *Business Week*—doing your job but never getting noticed.

You want to get ahead, but you're not sure if you can make it over that high, wide, and well-guarded barrier between the secretaries and the executives.

WHAT EXECUTIVES BELIEVE

Managers in almost every organization regard secretaries as unpromotable. They think women become secretaries because they aren't capable of doing anything better—or aren't interested in anything better. It rarely occurs to them that you want to do more, to be more—that being a secretary is a fine starting place, but you want to move up, be promoted, get ahead. Managers are genuinely and universally surprised when their secretaries sit them down for a heart-to-heart chat about career development. It always comes as a shock that their secretaries don't want to stay in the same job with the same meager 6 percent raise every year. And managers are especially surprised by how angry their secretaries are when they finally get around to the "how the hell do I get ahead in this company" discussion.

All this surprise comes from the fact that once you're hired as a secretary, your boss assumes and expects that you'll stay a secretary—for life. When a manager is hired, it is taken for granted that he will move up in the organization. Promotion is a key element of an executive's life; it's the yardstick by which his success, or lack of it, is measured. A manager who is hired to supervise production and 10 years later is still in the same job, is considered a failure, because he didn't move up. Because he tried to get promoted and failed, or worse, he didn't try at all. Not *trying* to get ahead is an even greater stigma for managers than trying and not succeeding.

This same philosophy doesn't apply to secretaries. Not only are you *not* expected to get ahead, but managers are taken aback when you try.

Secretaries are not perceived as a pool of talent that the company can draw on to augment their current managerial strength. As far as promotions go, you literally don't exist. When a management or supervisory job opens up, the company goes out and hires someone to fill the job. They don't look at the secretaries and ask if one of them could do the job. Management doesn't consider how your job responsibilities could be expanded; they don't worry about your career path; and they are not concerned about how you can grow as an employee of the company. They aren't deliberately trying to hold you down; they just don't know you're there.

Because most executives believe:

Secretaries aren't career-oriented (or why would you have taken such a lowly job in the first place?).

Secretaries aren't motivated (when was the last time you told your boss you want a better job?).

Secretaries lack ability (have you shown them you can do more than type and file?).

I have a male friend who is the head of a major department in the local city government, and when I told him I was writing this book, he was impressed. But he added a word of caution to his encouragement. "You have to realize," he said, "that most secretaries simply don't have what it takes to get promoted."

That's what you're up against. That attitude is pervasive among the management ranks.

THE INVISIBLE WOMAN

Your nonexistence problem is most clearly visible on the company's organization chart. Have you seen that organization chart lately—or ever? Can you find your job nestled in a neat little box somewhere? Are you there right under your boss's job? Of course not. You're not on the organization chart, and as a secretary, you never will be.

If you don't have a copy of the organization chart, get one. Try looking through the files; there's probably one attached to the annual report or the business plan. Or ask your boss for one. If you're afraid he might question what motivation you have for wanting it, or even what right you have to see it, tell him you want to get a better overview of how the company works and that the organization chart will help you do that.

Organization charts are very enlightening. The first thing you notice is that you'd have to get promoted just to appear on it. Organization charts show management positions only. And see those little vertical lines connecting one level to another? Those lines show a promotional path from one management level to the next. Since there are no secretaries on the organization chart, you won't find any lines, that is, any promotional path from secretary to manager. Though that may seem depressing at first glance, it's actually good news, because it means that once you break the secretary barrier, you can move up readily from there. You'll find moving around the management field is greatly facilitated by being in the game in the first place. Finally, in a large organization—obviously you don't need a copy of the organization chart if you work for a four-person company—the corporate structure may hold opportunities you hadn't considered, and the organization chart can show you departments you should be investigating.

THE HIDDEN SECRETARIAL ORGANIZATION CHART

Though secretaries don't appear on the official organization chart, there is a hidden organization chart, a pecking order if you will, among secretaries. The assistant vice president's secretary carries more weight than a loan officer's secretary. The general manager's secretary has more status than the property manager's secretary.

But the secretarial organization chart functions *only among secre-*

taries. As far as the managers and executives are concerned, a secretary is a secretary. They are all indistinguishable.

If you're the executive secretary to the president of a division or the administrative assistant to the chairman of the board, you may be tempted to believe you are somehow elevated in the corporate structure, just because your boss is way up there. Don't. Your boss's status matters only to you and the other secretaries. Compared to any junior executive or fledgling manager, *you* have no status at all. The 23-year-old assistant production manager in the Tulsa plant holds a more distinguished position in the company than you do.

So don't kid yourself. Take another look at the organization chart—secretarial boxes no more appear under the president's box than they do under the assistant accounting manager's. To management, all secretaries are equal.

There is a real danger in assuming that the secretarial organization chart affects your status in the company and your chances for promotion. Considering yourself more important because you're a vice president's secretary can generate serious repercussions from both managers and other secretaries.

In a large consumer products firm, the vice president of marketing's secretary quit, and Marian, secretary to the data processing manager, was "promoted" to fill the opening. Although Marian had never been one of the friendliest people in the office, she underwent a drastic personality change as soon as she accepted her new job. She refused to engage in small talk with anyone for any reason. She was all business, all the time. She was not only condescending to the other secretaries, but she became very authoritative with the executives. She acted as if becoming the vice president's secretary had conferred some special power on her.

When her boss asked her to check on a monthly sales report he hadn't yet received, she stormed down to the sales manager's office, interrupted a meeting, and announced, "Mr. Hadley would like to know why he hasn't received that monthly sales report yet." When the sales manager, obviously irritated, informed her he would have it in by the end of the week, she replied haughtily, "Well, I'm sure you're aware that it was due last Friday. You're keeping Mr. Hadley waiting." Then she went back to Mr. Hadley and reported how uncooperative the sales manager had been.

This is self-defeating behavior of the first order. By overestimating her status, Marian managed to accomplish all of the following:

- She seriously misrepresented Mr. Hadley, who wasn't particularly concerned about the report. He had thought she would just pass on a cordial reminder.

- She misrepresented the sales manager, a usually congenial man, by telling Mr. Hadley that he had been uncooperative, and introduced a strain into the two men's relationship.

- She generated the sales manager's immediate and permanent dislike with her inexcusable faux pas of dressing down an executive—in front of other people.

- She earned herself the nickname "the Assistant Vice President." Whenever she walked down the hall, secretaries and managers alike would whisper, "Look out, here comes the Assistant Vice President!" And everybody would break up laughing.

- She ruined any chance of getting promoted out of the secretarial ranks.

Marian failed to realize that, as a secretary, every manager and executive in the division had a higher status than she did. She also forgot that people with higher status invariably demand respect. If you are below them on that infamous organization chart, whether you're a secretary or a vice president, they expect you to act in a respectful manner. The more levels between you, the more respect you're expected to show. Even if they are unethical, incompetent, and socially unacceptable, you are still obligated to assume a deferential attitude. That doesn't mean you have to grovel or take abuse, but it does mean adhering to commonly accepted mores: not interrupting meetings unless it's an emergency, addressing superiors in a polite manner, not criticizing someone in front of other people, and so on.

Violating corporate behavior standards can only hurt you. And confusing your boss's status with your own is a sure road to disappointment. All you will do is damage your reputation and diminish your chances of promotion.

SECRETARIAL EXCELLENCE—THE CATCH-22

Secretaries who aren't good at their jobs, of course, have no hope of getting promoted. No one would promote somebody who couldn't handle a simple secretary's job, would they? If you can't type and file properly, how could you ever manage departmental communications or develop a quarterly budget? To get ahead, you must be very good at the job you're doing now. You have to demonstrate that you have more than mastered the skills needed in a secretary's job and that you're ready to move on to bigger and better things.

But that can become a Catch-22. If you're good, there is actually a *dis*incentive for your boss to consider you for promotion. A good secretary (like good everything else) is hard to find. A good secretary can make the difference between a smooth, efficient operation and one that never seems to be hitting on all cylinders. A good secretary can substantially increase her boss's productivity by taking over administrative tasks, keeping him organized, and managing the paperwork flow in the office. A good secretary is every manager's dream.

More often than I care to think about, I have heard male bosses say wistfully to their female executives, "You know, you would have made a hell of a secretary." (Female executives always show remarkable restraint in responding to this remark.) Men, of course, don't recognize the condescension in that comment, the inherent regret that all women aren't still secretaries and they of course can't imagine their own bosses saying that to them.

Your boss has no real motivation to let you move on, even though it means a better job and more money for you. You're making him look good and function well, and that's what's important. What's best for him and his department is a much higher priority than what's best for you. That isn't malicious; it's just practical on his part. If you get promoted, he has to hire a new secretary, and training a new secretary is a tedious, time-consuming process (do you realize how much you really know about what's going on in your department?). And it's risky—she could turn out to be nowhere near as good as you are but he'd be stuck with her.

If your boss's letters are typed error-free, if his appointment calendar is accurately kept, if the coffee is always ready, he's perfectly happy with the status quo. What you have to do is shake up the status quo. You have to let him know that you don't want to be a secretary until you're 65 and doddering toward retirement. And you have to convince him that promoting you will be good for him.

When I got my first management position, my boss, the director of marketing, said to me, "I really wouldn't mind if eventually I ended up working for you, because it would establish, beyond any shadow of a doubt, my ability to select and train good people." That's a terrific attitude, but it's a rare one—and one your boss probably hasn't considered. You need to suggest this possibility, and point out that your success is his success as well.

REWARD IS INEVITABLE

Difficult though it seems, it is possible to get promoted, because even the most dyed-in-the-wool "good old boy" respects talent, ambition, and hard work. You have to have all three to overcome their preconceived notions of what a secretary can (or can't) do, but you can get ahead. Because in business, if you do a good job, you get rewarded. That's almost a guarantee. What isn't guaranteed is the form that reward will take. It may be just a handshake and an attagirl, or it can be a promotion, a new title, a raise.

Believe it or not, what you get is up to you. *You* determine what reward you get for a job well done, because you only get what you ask for. And that's all you get. Most managers give secretaries the minimum reward possible—and get away with it—because the minimum is what secretaries expect and accept. Why give you a $100 a month raise, if you don't complain when you only get $50? Why give you a raise at all if you're content with a bouquet of flowers and a thank-you card?

Secretaries take what they can get and almost never ask for more. They are traditionally timid about making demands. After all, we "girls" were raised to make people happy, not make waves. We're supposed to go along with the program, and never flagrantly disagree with anyone—especially if that someone is the boss.

At home, we were always rewarded for being nice and cooperative. But at the office, nice and cooperative is expected behavior for secretaries; it doesn't lead to promotion. In the business world, there are no handouts. What you achieve, you must achieve for yourself. No benevolent boss is going to appoint you customer service manager because you sound so nice on the phone. The chairman of the board isn't going to wander by your desk one day and "discover" you.

If you don't ask and keep pushing, you'll never get it.

ATTITUDE ADJUSTMENT—YOU CAN'T SAVE THE WORLD

Attitudes are very difficult to change. And the larger the group or area the attitude covers, the more difficult it is to change. Women who have made it into management didn't try to change anyone's mind about "women in business." They didn't try to convince everyone that all women were capable, competent, motivated individuals. Instead, they concentrated on conveying the impression that *they* were qualified *as individuals* to handle their jobs well. They didn't worry about anything but their own image.

Similarly, you won't be able to convince management that it is suddenly a good idea to promote secretaries. You can't change their attitude about all the secretaries in your organization—that way causes frustration. What you can do is convince them that *you*, as an individual, are an exception. That you are head and shoulders above the rest of the secretarial crowd, that you are so outstanding that it would be a shame *not* to promote you.

You can't single-handedly break down the promotion barrier for all secretaries, but you can break it down for yourself. Then once you move up to management, you'll have the means to help other women up coming up behind you.

LAYING OUT A PROMOTION PLAN

You have to develop a concrete plan for getting ahead. Wishful thinking, half-hearted attempts, and poorly thought out strategies will never get you promoted. You have to lay out a plan of attack that covers every possible activity you need to do to make yourself promotable. Then take it one step at a time, and be willing to do what it takes.

BE WILLING TO DO WHAT IT TAKES

That's one of my favorite phrases, because it's the key to getting what you want. Make it your motto. Be willing to stick to your plan, no matter how tough other people try to make it for you. Be professional when others around you are petty and unfair. Rise above the detractors and the roadblocks. Make allies of the people who can help you, and learn how to fight the people who would stop you. Analyze everything around you and learn to use it to your advantage. And most importantly, never forget your goal.

You need to:

Look ready for success. Could you pass for a manager the way you currently dress at work? Would someone who didn't know you be able to tell you're a secretary just by looking at you?

Develop a calm and confident manner. A mousy attitude and intimidated behavior mark you as someone who ought to stay a secretary, someone who doesn't have the emotional fortitude to play in the big leagues.

Build the skills needed in every management position. Good communication skills, a facility in budgeting and analysis, an aptitude for seeing "the big picture," and an adeptness in dealing with people are essential for any manager.

Understand the game. Business, whether it's profit, nonprofit, or government, is not a life or death matter—even though some people treat it that way. It's a game, and if you understand the game, the rules, and the individual players, you can play it well yourself.

Learn to make your own breaks. The secretary who waits for success to come knocking on her door will wait a long time. You have to create your own opportunities.

Starting with Chapter 2, this book outlines each of these steps and how to accomplish them. Every step is important and every detail counts, because as a secretary, you're starting the race from way behind the starting line. But if you can put the whole package together, and I'm certain you can, you've got it made.

It's like the Army. If you are an enlisted soldier, you ordinarily can rise only so far in the organization. Under normal circumstances, you don't get promoted from sergeant to captain; it just isn't done. But in wartime, under exceptional circumstances, it can and does happen. Well, this is war, ladies, and in combat, battlefield promotions happen all the time. The key is being heroic enough to earn that promotion.

2. Can you make it from where you are?

Every secretarial position can be expanded into a better job, even if it's still secretarial, and many secretarial positions can be turned directly into management jobs.

You should believe that, but you probably don't. Over the course of your career (not your job, your *career*), you may have come to agree with all the managers, executives, bosses, and other secretaries who said you couldn't get promoted, who said that becoming a manager was an unrealistic goal for a secretary. They pointed to your lack of management experience, to the corporate training program that required a college degree, or to all the secretaries in the company who hadn't gotten promoted, and they said you wouldn't make it. You believed them. You decided promotion was the impossible dream, and you gave up trying.

Well, it's time to start believing in yourself again. It's time to give it one more try—only this time the right try, the right way.

THE STANDARD LIST OF EXCUSES

Secretaries have developed a long list of reasons, out of self-defense and self-protection, why they can't get promoted. Rather than face the real reasons they're stuck behind a typewriter, they place the blame somewhere else. They get themselves off the hook by saying that since it's not their fault, there's nothing they can do about it. They claim to be defeated by circumstances beyond their control.

That long list of reasons why promotion is impossible includes:

1. This company is run by male chauvinists who wouldn't promote a woman if their lives depended on it.

2. We have women executives, but they're hired from outside. Our company never promotes secretaries.

3. I can't get past all the menial work long enough to show them I can do anything else. I don't have time to take on more responsibility.

4. My boss and I don't get along. He'd *never* help me get a better job.

5. In my company, there's nowhere to get promoted to.

6. I don't have a college education—typing is the only skill I've got.

FEAR—YOUR GREATEST ENEMY

These aren't reasons; they're excuses. And what these six excuses boil down to is fear. Fear that if you try to get promoted, you won't make it, and you'll have to live with that failure. Fear that you'll look foolish trying to play the game *their* way. Fear that all the condescending things said about secretaries over the years are true—that deep down you just don't have what it takes.

Horse feathers.

I have met very few secretaries who weren't capable of handling more responsibility. Secretaries have much more ability than it takes to type a letter or answer a phone. The skills that make you a good secretary—organization, communication, problem-solving, decision-making, and assertiveness—are the very qualities that good managers have. If you are a good secretary, you can be a good manager.

As excuses, the ones above just aren't very good. Here's why:

EXCUSE #1: THE EVIL SPECTER OF MALE CHAUVINISM

Strident women's libbers have made male chauvinism the root of all evil for unsuccessful women. Anything that's wrong with your career, your personal life, or the world in general can be traced directly to men oppressing women. Very convenient. Whenever you fail, you can just point a finger at the nearest male. You always have a scapegoat—*he's* to blame, not you. You may have a bad attitude, you may have given up trying, you may be putting in the minimum time and effort possible on your job, but, hey, it's not your fault. It's that nasty male chauvinist over there.

Sure, there are instances where honest-to-God male chauvinists are refusing to promote women. But they are fewer and farther between than women would like to believe. In fact, many women who are successful today had help at some time in their careers from a male mentor. These women quickly and gratefully accepted the assistance when it was offered—they didn't regard men as the enemy; they weren't afraid or suspicious of a helping hand.

The long-standing tradition of women being subservient to men, in business and at home, hasn't faded away completely. But it's no longer the 1950s—it's the 1980s, and if you allow yourself to be subservient, you do so by your own choice. You permit it, and you have to take some of the blame when you get treated, or *think* you get treated, this way. I've worked with and for men who had no use for "female businessmen," but I never let them hold me back. Don't you, either.

I heard the male chauvinist complaint most frequently, oddly enough, from a woman named Marcie who had been promoted from secretary to computer programmer trainee to an assistant in the marketing department. Her responsibilities were continually growing, but she was still convinced that she was being slighted as a woman. She hadn't been made a vice president, so obviously the guys running the company hated women. Every time I heard this refrain from her, I pointed out that there were other women executives with the same company, and they were treated quite well by the same management. She'd sigh and say, "Yes, but they're different."

Marcie was blinded by her belief that there was a male chauvinist skulking down every corridor. When advancements came in small increments (though come they did), it wasn't enough. She felt that a truly liberated management would have given her a high-level executive post and wouldn't expect her to work her way up. She didn't want to face the fact that success takes a lot of time and effort. Instead of being appreciative of her past accomplishments, optimistic about her future progress, and realistic about earning her way up, it was easier to believe she was being held down.

In the latter half of the twentieth century, in the largest democracy in the world, nobody is holding you down—nobody but you. Men aren't stopping you, *you* are stopping you. That is not to say that the men of the world won't make it difficult for you. They will. In fact, some *women* will make it difficult for you. But they won't make it impossible. You can achieve the success you want, if you're willing to work for it. There's no question that you can make it, but you'll have to, as the saying goes, work harder, smarter, and longer than a man who's trying to get ahead in the business world.

Not fair? Of course it's not fair. Most of what goes on in the world is not fair. But complaining or giving up doesn't change anything—it just wastes energy you could put toward your own progress. Refusing to make an effort because the system isn't totally equitable is childish and immature.

The system isn't fair, but it isn't the major roadblock unsuccessful women want to believe it is. Men have recovered from the shock of finding women executives in their midst. The 1970s were a time of orientation for men, of getting used to the idea that women were becoming equals at work, that staff meetings and sales calls and company-paid lunches were going to include women. Most of them got over saying "excuse me" every time they said a swear word. They stopped worrying about standing up when a woman executive walked into the room (something they never did for secretaries anyway). They are no longer astounded by a woman project manager, a woman lawyer, or a woman vice president. That doesn't mean they're all thrilled by this new state of affairs. But the ground has been broken, and to claim that men are the cause of your failure is an outdated attitude.

Most of the time, believing you can't get ahead is what's holding you back. The fatalistic attitude of "I can't get ahead because I'm a woman" is a put-down of yourself and your abilities. Women all over this country are successful. That *you* are not has nothing to do with the fact that you're female. It has to do with lack of career planning, lack of self-confidence, lack of assertiveness, and lack of the strategic plan for promotion we talked about in Chapter 1.

EXCUSE #2: SECRETARIES NEED NOT APPLY

Some companies get their women executives from somewhere else, anywhere else, than their own secretarial ranks. They hire young college co-eds with degrees in business, or they hire other companies' female managers. They ignore their own secretaries as a possible source of talent, and the secretaries, seeing the handwriting on the wall, say "we can't get promoted here."

Where women executives work, but secretaries don't get promoted, it may be more the secretaries' fault than the company's. Take a hard look at the secretaries you work with. Take a harder look at yourself. Do any of you dress like managers, act like managers, show an enthusiastic attitude toward the company and your future in it, work with your bosses to plan career paths? Or do you sit at your desks, glumly doing your job, scrambling to stay on top of all the work your boss throws at you, discouraged because they're paying you hardly anything, and wondering why everybody acts like you're not there?

Don't give up. And don't let anybody talk you into giving up. If you make yourself stand out, if you develop a managerial attitude and appearance, if you do a top-notch job, *you can get promoted*. But as long as you continue to blend in with the rest of the secretarial ranks, you have no chance. Management is blind to secretaries—they just don't notice them. And most secretaries act in a way that reinforces that attitude. Until you draw attention to yourself, until you demonstrate your potential, *they won't see you*. And if they can't see you, they can't promote you.

This entire book is written for women who believe that being a secretary is what's holding them back. Being a secretary isn't the problem, it's what most women do as secretaries and how they act as secretaries that are the obstacles to success.

EXCUSE #3: SWAMPED BY THE LITTLE THINGS

"I don't have time," one secretary said, "to take on additional responsibility. My entire day is a roller coaster ride from one emergency to another."

I'm always amazed when I hear this statement from secretaries—*because no one is in a better position than they are to expand their jobs into managerial positions.*

But they see no time available to accomplish this: the phone rings a hundred times a day, a dozen reports have to be written, and the boss has one letter after another that has to go out ASAP.

Secretaries in this actually enviable position should do two things immediately:

1. Read up on time management and organization, then make some well thought out recommendations to your boss on how to better handle the workload. Prove to your boss that you're working at maximum efficiency.

2. Then because there's no doubt still too much to do, recommend that your job be split into two jobs, an entry level secretarial job for the menial stuff, and a supervisor or assistant manager position for you. And keep selling that concept (gently, of course) until your boss buys it.

Randi, secretary for a small computer software firm, did everything. Besides all the typing, filing, and regular secretarial chores, she handled the bookkeeping, order processing, and supervised the part-time production workers. As the company and the workload grew, Randi became increasingly aggravated, overworked, and frustrated. When she finally told her boss that she couldn't handle it any more, he agreed to hire another person, and asked Randi which part of her job she wanted to give up to someone else. Randi's first instinct was to give up the order processing. It was time-consuming and exasperating, because something was always going wrong. But splitting off order processing would still leave her with the secretarial work. She decided she needed more time to think about it, and asked her boss if she could have a day or two to develop a plan for reorganizing her job.

She spent hours listing all the elements of the job and how they could be arranged. She realized that with fewer distractions, she would have time to manage the order processing properly. She could incorporate her own ideas on how to streamline the operation and get orders out faster. But she enjoyed the bookkeeping/financial part of the job more and didn't want to give that up. Besides, both order processing and bookkeeping offered upwardly mobile tracks in management, and until she could determine which had more potential, she knew she should hang on to both.

But how could she work it out? Because she hadn't been thinking like a manager, it hadn't occurred to her that she could keep the *management* portion of the order processing and bookkeeping and delegate the rest. As soon as she made that connection, she saw how she could split the job to her best advantage. She made detailed job descriptions for each position, including salary ranges.

The next day she presented her plan. Her new position would be Order Processing Manager, with responsibility for bookkeeping and financial matters, and a new secretary/receptionist would be hired. Her boss bought it. Randi's plan and overall presentation convinced him that Randi was ready for a management job.

Randi didn't get quite the raise she was looking for, but she knew after she'd had a chance to prove herself in the new job, more money would follow. And since Randi's first love is really numbers, she began an evening program in accounting at the local university. As the company grows, Randi is planning to grow with it.

If you can't find the time to take on better assignments and set yourself up for a promotion, you're showing that you're not *ready* for one. Are you, like the secretary who described her day as a roller coaster, constantly frazzled, running around randomly trying to get everything done and keep everyone happy? If so, no wonder you haven't been promoted. In your boss's eyes, you're barely coping with what you've got now, why would he expand your responsibilities? He has no reason to assume that you could handle any additional assignments at all, let alone do them well.

The excuse of ''no time'' is the worst excuse of all, because it's one of the best conditions for getting ahead. Get control of your job. Demonstrate that you have the ability to manage a difficult situation and the time to handle greater responsibilities, and you may find yourself in a much better job.

EXCUSE #4: THE BOSS AS SPOILER

Many secretaries, in fact many people, have poor relationships with their bosses. They are convinced that their boss would never help them get promoted and that he has no desire to see them get ahead. And they're absolutely right. When your boss is unhappy with your work or you personally, his only desire is to see you quit and go somewhere else.

But your boss is the single most important factor in your getting ahead—and that means a workable relationship is essential.

Fortunately, most bad relationships seem worse than they really are, and they can often be improved substantially with a little effort on the secretary's part. Even if you feel you are completely blameless, take it on yourself to make the first move. Be adult enough to schedule a meeting with your boss, and behind closed doors, see if you can come to some agreement on what the problem is and how to rectify it. The mere fact that *you* bring it up and make a sincere effort to improve relations may be enough to push the relationship in a positive direction.

Diana, secretary to a bank assistant vice president, worked for a man who continually made snide remarks about her work. If she was 10 minutes late, he'd say sarcastically, "Had a rough night last night?"

If she made a personal call from the office, he'd wonder out loud if they should install an extra line to handle her personal business. He always walked off quickly before she could reply. She made a couple of attempts to discuss his remarks, but he claimed that he was just kidding and that she was overly sensitive. He obviously wasn't happy, but he refused to talk about it.

As a last resort, she told him they needed to have a long talk. She feared he might fire her for telling him she was uncomfortable with his behavior, but at this point it was a risk worth taking. In their meeting she said she felt he was unhappy with her performance and that his comments upset her, even though they were supposedly just jokes.

She said she'd really like their relationship to improve, because she enjoyed her job and wanted to continue to work there. She asked if he was willing to work on the relationship, or if he would prefer that she find another job or transfer to a different department.

"To my surprise," Diana said, "he told me exactly what was bothering him. He was unhappy with some of what I was doing, and there were specific changes he wanted made. He just hadn't had the nerve to tell me. It wasn't easy for me to sit there and take the criticism, but I did. I even made some suggestions on what *he* could do to improve our relationship, like dropping the snide comments and keeping me better informed of what he wanted done, deadlines, and such. It has really made a difference."

You *can* improve your relationship with your boss, if you make a commitment to improving it, decide on a course of action, and act on it. You've got nothing to lose. And you may be surprised how far a little effort goes.

EXCUSE #5: ALL DRESSED UP AND NO PLACE TO GO

The secretary in a one-person office. The secretary in a company that is laying people off. The secretary to the chairman of the board. The secretary to a group of very specialized research scientists. They all say the same thing: there's no place to get promoted to. The organization is too small or too technical, the company is in financial trouble, or the boss is too high in the organization. The list goes on and on. Secretaries in these situations assume that there's just no place to go. But that's not the case. There's always somewhere to go, always some way to improve your position in the organization.

"Sure," you say. "I'm the police chief's secretary. What can I do— get his job when he retires eight years from now?"

Nope. And if you work in a doctor's office, you're not going to be promoted to physician. And if you work for a genetic engineering company, they won't make you head research biologist. But don't assume because you can't get promoted to your immediate boss's job that you can't get promoted at all.

The police chief's secretary didn't become chief, but 6 months later she was able to expand her job into an office manager position. She was put in charge of the three secretaries who worked for the deputy chiefs and the two data entry clerks who handled the input of police reports into the computer system. She got a raise because of her new position, and she's keeping her eyes open for even better management jobs that she can apply for in the city government.

In any organization, especially private industry, new jobs are created all the time, and new opportunities continually arise. Pay attention to these changes, and you'll find ways to expand your job or transfer into another department. You can increase your responsibility for nontechnical management in technical companies. Even companies that are in financial trouble may give you the opportunity you need.

Anne, secretary to the owner of a small business forms company, talked to customers frequently on the phone when her boss was out of the office. The company desperately needed a full-time salesperson, but costs were higher than expected, and there was no money in the budget for a sales representative's salary. Because the company was so small and unstable, they had been unable to hire a sales rep who would work on commission.

During one of her boss's regular harangues about the horrible state business was in, Anne got up the courage to suggest that her boss give *her* the sales position on a trial basis, and that they hire a part-time secretary to handle the basic typing and filing. Anne would retain her same salary, but a commission would be added. Her boss was desperate enough to take a chance on her. She gave the job her all, and proved to have a knack for selling—she generated a 20 percent increase in business the first month.

Today, the company is doing well, and Anne handles all the selling. She has the title of director of sales, two commissioned sales reps reporting to her, and a secretary of her own.

EXCUSE #6: TYPING YES, COLLEGE NO?

Secretaries who claim to have no skills other than typing are putting themselves down unnecessarily. As a secretary, you are competent in communication skills; you have organizational ability and an ability to translate requests into action. As a woman, you have an instinctive feel for working with people, for dealing with sensitive situations, and for getting people to cooperate.

But the fact that you've never developed a profit and loss statement, never written an employment policy, or don't have a college degree makes you feel inadequate. In your mind, you're not as well qualified as other people in the office who have that experience or that diploma. That you feel inadequate is understandable, that you *are* inadequate is mistaken.

This area is so important and so touchy for secretaries that Chapter 4 will describe in depth what education you really need—or *don't* need—to get ahead. We'll also discuss what skills, background, experience, and abilities you need to get a promotion—much of which, you'll be surprised to find, you already have.

THE REAL REASONS YOU HAVEN'T BEEN PROMOTED

All these excuses aside, there *are* some good, solid reasons why you haven't been promoted. There are no good reasons why you *can't* be promoted, just some why you haven't. One or more of these may be what's holding you back:

1. Inability to control your job and demonstrate your managerial abilities.

2. Failure to demonstrate your problem-solving ability.

3. Lack of the self-confidence and assertiveness that executives must have.

4. Failure to actively expand your job responsibilities.

5. Failure to develop a "big picture" perspective.

6. Lack of knowledge about your boss's job, your company, and your industry.

7. Failure to enlist your boss's help in your promotional endeavors.

8. Lack of a career-oriented attitude.

9. Failure to establish yourself as part of the "team."

10. Lack of a managerial appearance.

11. Failure to communicate in an executive manner.

12. Failure to develop the appropriate professional relationships at work.

13. Failure to doggedly pursue a promotion, no matter how many setbacks you encounter.

This list isn't meant to frighten you—it's meant to show you areas of competence you have to master to get promoted. You can't overlook any of them and get ahead.

BELIEVE IN SUCCESS

Some of the most successful people in this country have had to overcome educational, social, physical or professional obstacles to succeed. But they all shared one thing in common—they all believed they could make it, and this belief is what made it possible. *You* have to believe you can succeed, and if you believe it and work at it, it will happen.

You may have some setbacks along the way. (One secretary said, "I'm a secretary; I'm *starting* with a setback.") But setbacks are part of life, and they are especially part of a manager's life. If you let yourself give up the first time things don't go your way, you will never make it as a manager. There'd be no need for managers if things went smoothly all the time. If everyone did their jobs as they were supposed to, if products were never defective, or if suppliers were never late with deliveries, managers would be an unnecessary drain on the payroll. Managers are necessary because people call in sick, machines break down, and orders get lost. Managers don't give up when things go wrong, they get to work.

When you get set back, that's when you really need to gather all your strengths and abilities together and fight your way into a more successful situation. Don't give up without a fight. Rocky Marciano, the great heavyweight boxing champion, reportedly said it's not important that you get knocked down—everybody gets knocked down—what matters is what you do *after* you get knocked down. The winners get up and keep fighting. It's an attitude you'll need throughout your managerial career.

WAYS UP THE CORPORATE LADDER

You have five possible avenues of promotion open to you:

1. Move into your boss's job.
2. Apply for other established management jobs in your department.
3. Create a new position directly above yours to move into.
4. Transfer to another department, either into a more responsible position or into a secretarial job with more potential.
5. Look for a better job somewhere else.

Evaluate your situation to decide which option is the best one for you to pursue.

MOVE INTO YOUR BOSS'S JOB

Many of you are in a position where you could move into your boss's job if it's vacated. Whether you can get your boss's job depends on:

Your boss's position in the organization. The higher your boss is in the organization, the more difficult it is to move into the job directly above you. If your boss is the chairman of the board of a

Fortune 500 company, forget it, but if you work for an office manager, getting her job is a very real possibility.

The size of the organization. Large organizations have more layers than small ones, and are not usually flexible about personnel making big jumps. You climb the corporate ladder one rung at a time. Small companies, on the other hand, are usually less rigidly structured and may let you jump several levels.

A word of advice: don't assume that because you can *do* your boss's job that you can *get* your boss's job—especially if that job has one or more managerial levels under it. Upper management believes that people should work their way up through the chain of command (superachievers are an occasional, but rare, exception). If your boss is the food and beverage manager for a major hotel, you might have to go through the steps of catering sales representative, banquet supervisor, and restaurant manager before upper management would consider you qualified for your boss's job.

Remember, too, that nobody but you (and maybe the other secretaries) knows you could do your boss's job—he certainly isn't telling everyone a secretary could handle it.

OTHER ESTABLISHED MANAGEMENT JOBS IN YOUR DEPARTMENT

You can and should apply for any and all of the lower management positions in your department when openings become available.

If the job directly reports to your boss, don't be shy about submitting your application for it. Don't wait for your boss to approach you—he may never do it.

If the job reports to someone else in the department, tell your boss you're interested and ask him to put in a good word for you. If he's the head of the department, he may be willing to exert a little pressure on your behalf.

You may have to take a few rejections before they'll take you seriously as a management prospect, or you may get the job only to find it downgraded because it's being filled by a "former secretary."

But persevere—and as long as it's a management job, take whatever you can get.

CREATE A NEW POSITION FOR YOURSELF

Creating a position that you, and only you, can fill is the best way to move up. Expand your job and your responsibilities until they're too big for just one person to handle. Then lop off the secretarial part of the job, and give it to a new person you hire, and with some luck, you get that person to report *to you*. Your new job is a hybrid between your boss's job and the managerial parts of your old job.

This expand-and-divide technique is actually a variation on moving into your boss's job, because the primary way you expand your job is by cannibalizing his—moving things he doesn't want to do into your job description, taking over things he doesn't have time to do, handling things you do better than he does.

The best part of this approach is that you are the only one qualified to take the job.

TRANSFER TO A BETTER JOB IN ANOTHER DEPARTMENT

This takes some subtle, often difficult, maneuvering. You have to find out about the openings and apply for them without alienating your boss. You may have to rely on other people from other departments to get information for you, and you have to prevent your boss from thinking you are disloyal to the department you're working for. But with a cooperative boss, this is a real possibility. (Don't assume that because you have a less than ideal relationship with your boss now that this option isn't open to you. Chapter 13 will give you more information on how to get an uncooperative boss back on your side.)

Transferring to a different department, though, gives you a big advantage over leaving the company for another job. Before you transfer, you can determine whether the job, if it's still secretarial, has more potential than the one you have now. And because you're familiar with the company and the people, you won't have to get "broken in"—you can hit the ground running.

ABANDONING SHIP

Your fourth option, and the one course of action I *don't* recommend you take—at least right away—is leaving the company you're with now. You know the environment where you are now. You are familiar with the company, its products and services, your boss, the other people in the organization, and your current specific duties. All these factors are unknowns in a new job. Trading in your present secretarial job for another one may put you into a situation even less conducive to promotion. Unless you have firm commitments from your new employer about opportunities for getting ahead, that new job could turn out to be a dead-end.

You have also already paid your secretarial dues where you are now. If you quit and go elsewhere, you may set your timetable back as much as a year, maybe more. Once you accept a secretarial job, you are obligated to fulfill those secretarial responsibilities for a reasonable amount of time before you begin pushing for a promotion.

So before you jump to the conclusion that there's nowhere to go in your company or organization, look closely at your current situation. Can you move into your boss's job, can you expand your job, or get transferred? Make sure the answer really is "no" before you leave to take another secretarial job.

BEING REALISTIC

So what's realistic? If you're not going to be appointed vice president the second day on the job, what can you expect? Determining what expectations are realistic depends on three criteria:

1. Timing
2. Next-job possibilities
3. Your abilities

WHEN IS THE TIME RIGHT?

If you have been a secretary for at least a year with your present employer, it's time, probably past time, to start making your move. If you've been on your present job less than a year, be subtle about any moves you make. Start setting up your opportunities, but don't expect any real advancement right away.

It is always a mistake to take a secretarial job and immediately begin harassing your boss for a better job and more money. You sabotage your chances for future promotion if you demand one the first day on the job. Your boss will wonder why you took a job you didn't want; you'll be labeled a difficult employee; and your boss may even consider firing you.

Unless, of course, you were hired as an assistant, albeit with secretarial duties, or the secretarial job was described as a "growth" position, then push for results as quickly as you can. Your efforts to expand your job will meet with acceptance and much less resistance than the average secretary faces. You must still fulfill the job duties you were hired to do, but you can expect faster results, because the company hired you with promotion in mind.

Michelle, fresh out of college with a journalism degree, took a job with a small advertising agency as a receptionist. Because the agency was expanding, her job expanded. She got more secretarial responsibilities and some media-buying responsibilities. But the increases didn't come as fast as she wanted. After 6 months, she looked around and saw an office manager who refused to delegate anything, a bookkeeper who spent most of the day on the phone with her friends, a new accounts manager who did little else but play golf, and she got mad. The situation was ripe, if properly handled, for Michelle to make some real headway, but instead, she decided to try to bully her way into a better job.

"I've got twice the ability of most of these people," she said, "but they won't let me do anything important, because they're all afraid I'll take their jobs away from them." She made an appointment with Glen, the owner of the agency, and demanded to know how long she would have to wait for a better job. "I let him know," she said proudly, "that I wasn't going to stick around forever typing and answering the phones."

I asked if she'd made any progress with Glen (knowing she couldn't have with that attitude). "Well, no," she said, "but now he knows how I feel."

What she didn't know was how Glen felt. He had hired Michelle, knowing she was overqualified for the job, but planning to bring her along, gradually giving her more responsibility, and letting her learn the advertising business from the ground up. If she had been paying attention, she would have realized that was exactly what was happening: her job was steadily expanding. But now, after only 6 months, she was complaining about the job she had willingly and, because of a long and frustrating job search, gratefully accepted. By telling Glen she didn't like the way he was running his agency and the way he was managing "her career," she was actually telling him that he had made a mistake in hiring her. Because rather than developing and growing with the agency, rather than building her job in any and every way she could, she was demanding a handout.

Glen was impressed with Michelle's ability, so despite her pushiness, he kept her on, worked with her, helped her pace herself, and taught her how to get along better with the other people in the agency. A year and a half after she started, she was in charge of the media department at almost twice her original salary.

Michelle was lucky. She had a boss who was not only progressive and interested in the long-term potential of his employees, but sympathetic to the problems women have in getting ahead. Other women have not been so lucky. Harassing your boss for more money and more responsibility when you haven't proven yourself in your current position can lead to your being ignored, reprimanded, or even replaced. It isn't a bad idea to accept a secretarial job to get your foot in the door, particularly in an industry like advertising that's difficult to break into—what *is* a bad idea is kicking the door down once you get it open, and demanding to be ushered into the nearest executive suite.

NEXT-JOB POSSIBILITIES

What should your next step be? What *can* it be? Outline all the possibilities. Can you expand your job and split off the more menial tasks? Or is there a position right above you, like office manager, or customer service representative, that you could move into when there's an opening? Is your organization large enough that a transfer is possible? How amenable is your company, and specifically your boss, to transfers? Could you move into a first-line management position or would you have to transfer as a secretary?

Determine what is a realistic first step in your climb up the corporate ladder. Don't set your sights on becoming customer service manager and be disappointed if you achieve anything less. Be open to any and all management or supervisory positions, because the goal, first and foremost, is to get out from behind that typewriter.

EVALUATING YOUR ABILITIES

In deciding what the next step should be, take an objective look at your abilities:

- What areas are you strong in?
- What areas give you trouble?
- Do you have a way with words?
- Are you known for your organizational skills?
- Are you uncomfortable talking to people you don't know?
- Does math give you a headache?

Chances are, if you've been working for any length of time, you already have a fix on what type of work you'd like to be doing and what you'd be good at. You know whether a promotion to the finance department would be an exciting challenge or a prison sentence, whether the sales department offers a great future or continual frustration for you.

I won't waste your time with job-skill surveys. Consultants always want you to fill out surveys, answer questionnaires, and keep time/activity logs to show what you do, how often you do it, and how well you like doing it. Besides being boring, all those wonderful surveys are not very effective, because:

1. Done right, they take up a lot of time you may not have (particularly time/activity logs). Done wrong, via quickie questionnaires and tests, you don't get accurate information.

2. You know what you want already, what you enjoy, and what you're good at. Maybe you don't have this information quantified down to four decimal places, but you've got it close enough to know what jobs you'd be interested in pursuing.

3. You may not have much choice about which management job you get. Surveys and questionnaires that show you should be in sales are irrelevant if they're not hiring in the sales department but there's an opening for an assistant manager in administration.

As a secretary, you can't afford to hold out until the managerial position you're ideally suited for and have always dreamed about opens up. You need to get into management any way you can and as quickly as you can. Naturally, you don't want to take a management job that will make you look incompetent, or you'll end up being a secretary again. But do take any one that you can handle. The management job you *really* want can be reached more easily from another management job than from where you are now.

3. If you must go elsewhere...

Despite my advice against quitting, you may indeed be in a situation where staying on is futile. A few cases really are dead-ends:

- *You work in a one-person office, such as a medical or legal practice, and business is slow.* In a growing practice, even though it's a one-person practice, it's possible to increase your responsibilities, becoming an assistant or an office manager or a paralegal. In less technical fields, like management consulting, you can work yourself into a full-blown executive position. But if the business isn't growing—and there's nothing you can do to help it grow—it's time to move on to greener pastures. Make sure before you go, though, that your boss doesn't have future plans to expand that might make it worth your while to stay.

- *You have a terrible relationship with your boss, and you refuse to try to correct it.* The key here is *you refuse to try to correct it.* I strongly recommend that you spend at least two months trying to correct a bad relationship with your boss before you give up and start looking for another job. A *minimum* of two months. If you're not willing to make an effort to establish a good working relationship, you won't make any progress where you are now. Promotion is out of the question, and you probably can't even get transferred (unless you're in a civil service position). You're pegged as someone who can't get along with other

people, and many companies don't want to transfer "problem employees" from one department to another. No matter how friendly you are
to everyone else, when you don't get along with your boss, you are
considered difficult to work with.

   Another word of advice: I've never seen a bad working relationship
where both people weren't at least partially to blame. If you aren't
willing to make an effort, you may have a stubborn streak that is part
of the problem.

- *You are already practicing all of the advice in this book, and you still
  can't get promoted.* After you finish reading this book, if you can say
  with complete confidence that you aren't lacking in any area, and you
  still can't get some kind of a promotion, move on with my best
  wishes.

PREPARING TO MOVE ON

If you do finally decide that there's no way out but quitting, do the
logical thing, and *don't* quit. No rational person, of course, quits
before she has another job, but there's more to it than that.

   Problems at your current company can be hidden as long as you
are still employed there. You have the right to ask prospective employers not to call your current employer for a reference or employment verification—this protects you from getting fired for job-hunting. Always mention in an interview that your boss is unaware you
are looking for another job, and ask that your résumé and interview
be treated confidentially.

   In addition, your current job, no matter how much of a dead end,
can provide material for your résumé that will help you find another
job with more potential.

   Don't even start looking for another job, until you've milked your
present job for every management-related activity you can get your
hands on, and every possible experience that will look good on your
résumé. Get involved in the office computerization before you quit,
see if your boss will let you handle some client liaison work, or ask if

you can develop next week's production schedule. (Of course, if you get assignments like this, you may not want to quit after all.)

BEEF UP YOUR RÉSUMÉ

What can you put on your résumé that will show a prospective employer you have management potential? Your primary job may be typing and answering the phone, but secretaries always do more than that. They talk to customers, collect data, work with computers, write reports, process personnel information, and much more. All these activities should be included on your résumé.

For example, if you occasionally answer customer inquiries for your boss, include it on your résumé: "Handled customer inquiries and problem resolution." It shows that you are capable of dealing with people, that you can follow through, and that you are used to dealing with problems—all very marketable skills.

If you make all the travel arrangements for your department, and you've been instructed to keep costs as low as possible, your résumé should read: "Managed department travel budgets."

Anything you've done, whether you did it once or you do it daily, can be included on your résumé. Don't lie and say you've done things you haven't, even if you think you could handle them—you might get caught by an inquisitive interviewer who wants lots of details you can't deliver. But do include anything you have done and could do again. If you made all the lodging and food arrangements for the sales force meeting 2 years ago, include it on your résumé. You only did it once and may never do it again in your current position, but it's something you know how to do. It shows you had increased responsibility. You can say, "Responsible for organizing and coordinating national sales meeting." That may imply you did it every year, but prospective employers don't need to know it wasn't a regular portion of your job. And unless the interviewer specifically asks if you handled it every year, you don't need to clarify that it was a one-time job. You've done it once, you could do it again, and that's all that counts.

POWER WORDS

Any activity—bookkeeping, filing court documents for an attorney, sorting out the customer mailing list, or calling the newspaper to place local advertising—can improve your image in the job market, *if* it's properly described on your résumé.

Secretaries tend to describe the *tasks* they do rather than the *responsibilities* they have. That's always a mistake, because it demeans the work you do. Don't say, "I send the sales report to our branch offices every month," when you can say, "I'm responsible for monthly communications with fourteen branch offices." You don't just perform tasks—you have responsibilities.

One way to shift your emphasis from tasks to responsibilities is to use what I call "power words" to describe your work:

Responsible for

Managed

Supervised

Administered

Handled

Maintained

In charge of

Coordinated

Functioned as

Work hard to incorporate these words into descriptions of your job. They build your image as someone ready to move into management. Use them when you talk about your job, even to other people in the company, and in particular, use them on your résumé. If you're looking for a new job, they could mean the difference between just another secretarial job and a first-rate, first-line manager's job.

Here are some examples of how to beef up your résumé with power words:

Task Description

Sorted mailing list for obsolete addresses and change-of-addresses. Supervised two part-time high school students who processed mailings.

Collected weekly sales reports from salesmen, tallied total number of calls and gave a summary to product managers.

Took training course on new word processor, and taught other secretaries how to use it. Will probably teach new secretaries as they are hired.

Responsibility Description with Power Words

Managed direct mail activities, including mailing list maintenance and supervision of mail-room personnel.

Responsible for weekly collation and report of national sales activity. Functioned as liaison between sales and product management departments.

In charge of word processing training company-wide.

THAT CRITICAL FIRST IMPRESSION

Countless books, articles, seminars, and counselors exist to tell you how to create a professional-looking résumé, how to have a successful interview, and how to negotiate for the best possible starting salary. When you decide to go elsewhere, make use of those resources. I won't try to cover everything you should do, but I can give you a few tips from the viewpoint of a prospective employer.

First, a professional-looking résumé *and cover letter* are critical. They are your introduction to the company, and the first cut will be made on what the résumés convey about the candidates.

Remember that résumés and cover letters are *business* documents. What they look like is an indicator of how much business sense you have. They should be on the best quality paper you can get: a 20-to 25-pound stationery stock with a laid or text finish. If you're not sure what that means, go to any instant printing shop and they'll be happy to show you. Type an original of your résumé—good, dark print on white paper—and the printer can reproduce copies on the high quality stationery. Buy envelopes and extra blank sheets to use for your cover letters and any follow-up correspondence.

If you want a fancier effect, you can purchase personalized business-size stationery at most department stores. Watch for sales during the year.

Stationery stock comes in a variety of colors, but white, cream, or buff are the only acceptable ones for your cover letters and résumé.

THE COVER LETTER

The cover letter gives you an opportunity to do two very important things:

1. *Describe skills not covered in your résumé.* Your job experience may not show that you have excellent written and verbal communication skills, that you enjoy working with people, and that your interpersonal skills are outstanding. If you're applying for a customer service job, these skills are important. Talk about them in your cover letter.

2. *Emphasize skills or experience pertinent to the job you are applying for.* If the position reports to the vice president of acquisitions, you might want to call attention to your legal secretary background, and point out that your familiarity with contracts could be very valuable to the company.

Don't waste your cover letter by saying only that the enclosed résumé is in response to the ad they ran and that you would welcome an interview. That's obvious—why else would you have sent the résumé in the first place? Use your cover letter as the marketing tool it can be. The sample cover letter on page 39 shows how.

2967 Murray Road
Columbus, Ohio 43222
December 2, 1985

Ms. Roxanne Conrad
Director of Personnel
Promotions Unlimited
75 North Main Street
Columbus, Ohio 43231

Dear Ms. Conrad:

I read with interest your ad for an assistant contracts administrator in last Sunday's issue of the Gazette. Because of my
background, I feel I am well qualified for the position and would
welcome the opportunity to discuss my qualifications with you in
person.

As the enclosed résumé indicates, I have an extensive legal
secretary background, and my current position with the Fulcher
Polytechnical Institute has given me broad administrative experience. I'm sure my experience in both areas would be of benefit
to Promotions Unlimited.

My written and verbal communication skills are excellent, and I
have the ability to work well with people at any level in an
organization. I believe in taking the initiative in solving
problems and making decisions.

I'll look forward to hearing from you.

Sincerely,

Jean D. Collier

Enclosure

THE RÉSUMÉ

For years, I have collected résumés, and I suggest you do the same. Anytime I see a quality résumé, one that handles something the way I'd like to handle it on my résumé, I make a copy or ask the owner for a copy, and put it in my résumé file. When I start a job search, I pull all these out and review them. I invariably find ways to make myself more marketable.

By way of telling you what *not* to do, let me tell you about the last time I hired a secretary. We received eighty résumés in response to the first ad we ran. Only *six* were even marginally professional enough to consider scheduling interviews, and only four of those had good cover letters. The other seventy-four were a mess. All the no-no's you can imagine showed up:

- Cutesy note paper ("From Donna!").

- Copies of copies, so faint you could hardly read them.

- Résumés with strikeovers and typos (typos—for a secretarial job!).

- Handwritten résumés on notepad paper.

- Shocking pink paper to draw attention to the résumé.

- A five-page résumé outlining everything the applicant had done since birth.

- A job-objective statement that said the applicant was looking for work as a medical technician (then why is she applying for our secretarial job?).

Make sure your résumé has none of that working against it. The sample résumé on page 41 is a widely accepted format—don't deviate from it thinking you'll make your résumé look more "interesting." Employers don't want to see "interesting;" they want to see professional.

JEAN D. COLLIER
2967 Murray Road
Columbus, Ohio 43222
(614) 555-5054

PROFESSIONAL EXPERIENCE

February 1983
to Present

Development Assistant/Secretary, Development
Office, Fulcher Polytechnical Institute,
Columbus, Ohio

Assisted Director of Development in all areas
of fund-raising. Managed direct mail campaigns, and coordinated fund-raising activities among the Development Office, the Alumni
Office, and the President's Office. Supervised two-person clerical staff responsible
for tracking donations and endowments from
receipt to disbursement.

August 1978 to
February 1983

GMA Chemical Corporation, Legal Division,
Pittsburgh, Pennsylvania

Legal Secretary, December 1979 - February
1983. Handled extensive secretarial responsibilities in the area of labor negotiations.
Managed cost-accounting and interdepartmental
billing for three senior attorneys; acted as
liaison between legal and personnel departments; and managed document flow and record/
file organization.

Receptionist, August 1978 - December 1979.
Handled switchboard responsibilities for 300-
member Legal Division.

EDUCATION

September 1976
to May 1978

University of Pennsylvania, Pittsburgh,
Pennsylvania

Majored in Business Administration. Grade
point average: 3.4, of a possible 4.0.

PROFESSIONAL AFFILIATIONS

National Association for Collegiate Fund-Raising

I advise against using a job-objective statement on your résumé. A vague one doesn't tell anybody anything, such as:

Objective: To obtain a challenging position with an opportunity for advancement.

A very specific one limits the use of your résumé. You can't respond to an advertisement for an assistant contracts administrator if your objective statement says:

Objective: To obtain an entry-level management or creative position in a progressive public relations agency or department.

That tells the prospective employer that if they hire you, you'll still be looking for a PR job. They have no reason to think you're signing on for the long-term.

Some other things I think you can leave off:

- Don't write "Résumé" at the top of your résumé—the format makes it obvious what it is.

- The phrase "References available upon request"—that goes without saying. And *never* include the names and phone numbers of actual references, or letters of recommendation—you look like you're trying too hard.

- Personal information, if you're uncomfortable including it. "Personal information" means marital status, age, health, height, and weight. It does not mean a list of your hobbies or favorite social activities.

- Early jobs, or the date you graduated from high school or college, if either makes you seem too old. You don't need to go back more than 15 years on your job history.

- "Junk" jobs that you had as a college student or a housewife, or that you took during a "transitional" period in your career.

THE THANK-YOU LETTER

Thank-you letters following an interview are certainly not necessary—I've never made a hiring decision based on one—but they're a nice gesture, and they give you a chance to make one last pitch for yourself. Almost everybody, after leaving an interview, thinks, "I wish I had remembered to mention, . . ." or "I really should have put more emphasis on my . . ." You can make those points in a thank-you letter.

An important note: a thank-you letter, like a cover letter or a résumé, is a *business* document. It is not a 3" × 5" flowery card with "Thank You" in gold script across the front. It is a business letter expressing appreciation for a business meeting—the interview.

The sample thank-you letter on page 44 shows what one should look like.

THE INTERVIEW

Going back to my stack of eighty résumés—we scheduled interviews with the six women whose résumés we liked. Surprisingly, only two had a good personal appearance and a professional demeanor. They were asked back for a second round of interviews, and we ended up hiring both of them.

The other four had problems. One made a good verbal presentation, but she was extremely overweight and wore a stark navy-blue suit two sizes too small and no make-up. Two of the others were almost mute, answering my questions with as few words as possible in quiet little voices. The last one grilled me about working hours, lunch hours, raises and vacations—which told me she wanted a job with as much money and as little work as possible. It's conceivable that any of these four might have turned out to be excellent secretaries once they were on the job. But their appearance or presentation was so bad that they were never even considered.

```
                                        2967 Murray Road
                                        Columbus, Ohio 43222
                                        January 5, 1986


Ms. Roxanne Conrad
Director of Personnel
Promotions Unlimited
75 North Main Street
Columbus, Ohio 43231

Dear Roxanne:

It was a pleasure meeting you last week.  Promotions Unlimited
seems like a fine organization, and I hope you will seriously
consider my application for the assistant contracts administrator
position.

You mentioned during the interview that this position requires a
certain amount of "quiet diplomacy."  My current job at Fulcher
also requires a well-developed ability to get cooperation from a
number of different departments, and I'm sure my experience in
that area would be an asset to the contracts department.

Thank you for taking the time to talk with me, and please don't
hesitate to call if you need any additional information.

Sincerely,


Jean D. Collier
```

Don't let that happen to you. Write professional, look professional, and talk professional. Have answers ready for those tough questions like, "Tell me about yourself," and "What skills do you have that would benefit our company?" If you're interviewing for a secretarial job, look for signs that this new job could be expanded or that it has room for advancement:

- Is the company growing rapidly?

- Is this particular job a growth position?

- Do the initial job responsibilities include more than just typing and filing?

- Is your prospective boss overworked?

- Does he need help managing that workload?

- Is more than a 9 to 5 commitment expected?

- Is this a new job? If not, what happened to the secretary who had it last? Was she promoted? Did she quit? If so, why?

Ask all these questions straight out. Don't be timid, afraid that you will offend the interviewer and not get the job. If they want timid people, you don't want their job.

Ask questions that will give you clues about the job's potential for advancement—questions that make you sound eager for responsibility but not anxious to get out of the secretarial work. That's a fine line—you don't want your prospective boss to think you'll be pushing for more money and your own office as soon as your 30 days probation is over, but neither do you want him to assume that being a good typist is your highest aspiration.

Good questions to use are:

- "I'm the type of person who works well independently, and I enjoy taking on additional responsibilities. How does that fit with the job you have open?"

- "Do you foresee this job staying the same over the next several years, or will it expand, with additional responsibilities being added?"

Listen carefully to what the interviewer says. Is he surprised that you ask? Does he claim the job will expand, sensing that's what you want to hear, without giving any specifics? Those reactions are warnings that there might not be much substance behind the lip service. If your questions get a negative reaction, or if they are met with indifference, go elsewhere.

DON'T BE AFRAID TO APPLY FOR MANAGEMENT JOBS

Go after entry-level management or supervisory positions—your beefed-up résumé can help you get one. But don't be discouraged if you don't land one. For management jobs, employment is still a buyer's market. In some areas of the country, the job market for managers is so tight that employers can specify the exact qualifications they're looking for, practically down to the color of the applicant's eyes, and get what they want.

Secretarial jobs are a different matter. Good secretaries are always in demand, and if you must take another secretarial job, it's not a defeat. It just means that you put your promotion plan into effect at your new location.

When I was first hired by the Borden Chemical Company, the job was marketing research assistant/secretary. The title didn't mean much to me until I was told that the previous secretary had left because the job was expanding, and she didn't want to do anything but secretarial work. The message was clear: this job had potential.

I didn't get the salary I wanted, and I wasn't thrilled that, after 4 years of college, I was starting out as a secretary, but I knew I could move in the job. I was right. In less than a year, I became the assistant product manager on Krylon Spray Paint and was the division's first woman executive.

INDUSTRY SHOULDN'T BE A CONSIDERATION

Don't worry too much about what industry you're getting into. Unless you have extremely specific career goals that you refuse to compromise, such as becoming an accountant or an art director, don't restrict your job search. A manager is a manager. Management skills are transferable, and you can move into your desired industry or profession once you become a manager. That glamour industry you've always had your eye on will quickly lose its appeal if you get into it via another dead-end secretarial job. The not-so-glamorous industries in not-so-glamorous sections of town can offer the opportunity you're waiting for. Don't pass them by.

4. What qualifications do you really need?

Some secretaries think they can't get promoted because they lack experience or education. They despair of ever getting a good managerial job, because they don't know how to develop a national marketing strategy, arrange financing for a major acquisition, or forecast cost trends in raw materials. They can't program a computer, they haven't passed the state bar examination, and they don't have a Ph.D.

DO YOU NEED A COLLEGE DEGREE?

Don't forget that all executives start their careers with no experience, and some of them start with no advanced education. Stories abound of the chief executive officer or the multimillionaire who barely finished high school, but went on to become a huge success. In every large organization, you can find middle and upper-management executives who never graduated from college. Yet secretaries place some kind of mystical belief in the value of a college education—they believe they can't get ahead without one.

College helps, there's no doubt about it. Even if you've taken only a few courses, you can put a college reference on your résumé, and that improves your image. In fact, if you plan to change jobs, college courses are worth taking just for the résumé value they have.

A full degree gives you even more credibility and eliminates the "you don't have a college education" criticism. But as any secretary who already has one will tell you, a college degree is not a golden passkey to a great future, and it's no one-way ticket to the president's office. Once you become a manager, a college degree, an M.B.A., or another advanced degree can help further your career. But right now, your efforts are better spent getting into management in the first place.

Whether you should go to college, if you haven't already, and whether you need to earn a degree once you're there, depends on these factors:

1. How technical your job interests are.

2. The length of time you've been working.

3. Your age.

4. What college experience you already have.

With one exception: if you recently graduated from high school and have just started your first secretarial job, *quit, go to college, and get a marketable degree*. Not a degree in history or philosophy, but one that will get you into management, one in hospital administration or business or computer science. If you can't afford to quit, go to night school, or get a night job and go to school during the day. With the right college degree, you won't have to fight your way through the secretarial morass to get to a management job. You can *start* in one.

TECHNICAL CAREER = COLLEGE REQUIRED

The more technical your career goals, the more crucial college becomes. If you want to get into medicine or law, one or more college degrees are obviously mandatory.

If you want to get into data processing, engineering, or accounting, some college work is necessary, and a full degree is advisable. In these fields, you may be able to learn some technical skills on the job, but college is a better, faster, and more thorough way to learn. On-the-job training is generally unstructured and suited only to the job you're training for, and in the technical fields, lack of proper credentials will reduce your chances of reaching middle and upper management.

Proper credentials are more than just a diploma. *Which* college you go to can impact your success. The more technical the subject, the more important it is which college you attend. A top-notch school with high standards and a good reputation will get you a better job in a more prestigious company when you graduate.

Conversely, taking courses or getting a degree from a school with a bad reputation can keep you from getting a job, because nobody wants to hire poorly trained students. People in technical management positions are very aware of the caliber of education provided by schools in their area. They know who provides quality education and who doesn't, and they steer clear of graduates from second-rate schools.

Be particularly careful of computer science programs. Because of the lucrative employment opportunities in data processing, computer schools are springing up all over the country, and every college, junior college, vocational school, and technical institute is adding a computer curriculum. To capture tuition money, schools are hastily throwing together programs with carelessly developed course materials, obsolete equipment, and inadequate instructors. A computer science curriculum is notoriously expensive to set up and maintain, and very few schools have the resources to put together quality programs.

When it comes to technical education, it's strictly caveat emptor. So take these precautions:

Interview managers in your field of interest. Get their recommendations on which school in your area has the best program. Also ask if there are any schools whose graduates they *wouldn't* hire.

Investigate the school you're considering. Ask to see a list of placements, and evaluate who's hiring their students. Call some of the employers for references.

Be wary of the "advice" you receive at for-profit schools. Many private schools are operated for a profit. Admissions counselors are on commission and earn a portion of your tuition when they enroll you. They are there to *sell* you, not advise you. That doesn't mean the school is bad—it may be the best in town—but it does mean you have to take anything the counselor says with a grain of salt.

COLLEGE FOR NONTECHNICAL CAREERS?

It's possible to get by without a college education in marketing, sales, administrative management, customer service, production supervision, and other nontechnical areas—but college courses or a degree will certainly improve your performance and your ability to get promoted.

Don't expect, however, that taking courses in those areas will automatically improve your image. You may be very proud of yourself for taking that Principles of Salesmanship course, but don't expect to be smothered with praise and admiration at work.

There's a peculiar problem of perception with nontechnical management jobs. Because they aren't "scientific," they get less respect. Because there are no hard-and-fast rules for making sales, no esoteric formulas for determining the quality of an advertisement, and no "right way" to motivate assembly line workers, people don't believe these jobs are difficult. Many managers in other technical jobs are convinced that they could do marketing, sales or purchasing with their eyes closed. Everybody in the engineering department knows exactly what the sales department is doing wrong (because as they'll tell you, anybody with an IQ over 65 can sell), and anybody in maintenance, given half a chance, could square away the company's administration problems in a week.

On the other hand, the marketing, sales, and purchasing managers are convinced that their jobs are an art that requires outstanding judgment and years of experience—something you can't pick up in a college course or two. So when you enroll in Intermediate Business Principles 201 at the local junior college, don't be surprised if nobody is too impressed.

BACK TO REALITY

This is compounded by the theoretical nature of college-level business courses, especially at the introductory level. They are designed for students who haven't been exposed to the sobering realities of the business world. They spend 3 months deriving a 12-variable formula that describes how the economy works, but they don't tell you what to do when a large corporation tests a new product so long that it becomes an old product before it even reaches the marketplace; or what to do when you submit a new benefits package proposal to upper management, and 18 months go by without an answer; or what to do when a vice president demands that a branch office be opened in Zimbabwe, despite the costs, because his son is a missionary there.

As a secretary, you need practical, useful information. You need to know the law of supply and demand, but you don't need to spend a semester in class proving it mathematically. You don't need to be loaded up with academic theories on the sociological implications of excessive disciplinary procedures and the resultant high turnover. You just need to know that if you're too hard on people, they quit.

You can learn what you need to know on the job and by reading the trade books and publications in your field. These are aimed at practitioners, not students, and they contain solid, applicable information. Combined with your day-to-day observations, trade journals can provide an excellent education for you. Start reading them. Your boss probably subscribes to the most important ones already, but if not, try to arrange a company-paid subscription for yourself.

THE VALUE OF EXPERIENCE

The farther away you are from being college age, the less you need college to establish yourself as a contender for a management job.

If you've been a secretary for 5 years or more, you can forego college (again, unless you're headed into a technical area). The longer you've worked, the more your experience compensates for the lack of a college education. You're mature, you've been in the work force for a few years, you understand how business works in general and how your organization functions in the specific.

Struggling through college—and it's a struggle if you work full-time and have a family—to earn a degree in, say, sociology won't do you a bit of good when you try to get promoted.

Andrea, secretary to a distribution manager, fell into the need-a-degree trap. Her boss was overworked and desperately needed an assistant. Andrea should have been in line for the job, but she felt she wasn't qualified. After 8 years as a secretary, she had plenty of experience and ability to handle the assistant's job, but she didn't see that as a credential. She was convinced she needed a college degree to get promoted. She had enrolled in the local university and was obsessively pursuing an English degree at night. She talked about nothing but her school work, she studied during lunch hours, she even arranged to leave early on Tuesdays and Thursdays so she could make an afternoon class. She felt she was really on her way.

In reality, she was on her way to nowhere. Her love of literature and her English degree had no relevance whatsoever to any management job in the company. Andrea's obsessive behavior convinced her boss that she was interested in a college education, not a professional career. When the decision was made to hire an assistant, Andrea was only briefly considered, then passed over.

Three years later, she is still going to school. The assistant (whose job Andrea should have had) is now a manager, and Andrea is still sitting behind a typewriter.

WORKING AGAINST THE CLOCK

As in Andrea's case, pursuing a college degree can actually be detrimental to your career ambitions. Getting a bachelor of arts degree at age 35 will not launch you into a management career—it will just make people wonder why you're wasting your time going to school when you could be putting that effort into your job. A bachelor's degree, even in business, is too little too late if you've been a secretary for years. Sure, at 22, a business degree can get you into the company's management training program, or make your first job managerial instead of secretarial. But at 30 or 35, it won't help.

If you're over 25, time is no longer on your side. You don't have years to spend getting a degree. Working your way through college on a part-time basis can turn a 4-year degree into an 8-, 10-, or even 12-year degree. You just don't have that kind of time.

For specialized training, like accounting or data processing, don't waste your time with a full degree program. The first 2 years of most degree programs consist of general requirement courses like basic English, psychology, and sociology—courses for kids just out of high school who are supposed to get a well-rounded education. These courses aren't worth the time and effort you'll have to put into them. Try to enroll as a special student, not a degree candidate, and take only the courses you need.

THE ALMOST DEGREE

Two or three years of college can be almost as good as a degree. On your résumé, prominently put the college you attended, what your major was, and your grade point average (if it's good)—just don't mention that you didn't graduate.

You don't need to broadcast that you never finished, nor do you need to rush out and finish off those last few requirements. And you don't need to be embarrassed that you didn't graduate. Feel free to discuss your college education: "When I was studying French at North Carolina State University . . ." If someone tries to pin you down about when you graduated, simply say you were a few courses short. I'm always reminded, when this issue comes up, of an episode of the old "Mary Tyler Moore Show." It came out that Mary never finished college, but had put on her résumé that she was a graduate, to get her job at the TV station. She was terrified that she'd lose her job, which of course she didn't.

PAYING FOR IT

Don't forget to check out your company's tuition assistance program. Most companies will pay your tuition if the courses you take are to improve your job performance. If they don't have one, talk to your boss or the personnel department—they may be willing to reimburse your tuition anyway, if you can show your education is job related.

Pauline, a secretary in a small, but growing real estate firm, thought she would be good at sales, but wasn't eligible for promotion without a real estate license. She couldn't afford to pay for it herself, so she made a deal with her boss: if the company would pay her tuition, she would take a reduced commission for the first year or until the tuition was paid back, whichever came first. Her boss agreed. Twice in the first year after she received her license, she was named Salesperson of the Month, and gave her boss a very nice return on his tuition investment.

With the growing number of adults going back to college, student loans and financial aid are plentiful, and they are no longer just for impoverished students. You can probably qualify for some type of financial assistance, if you need it. Your college of choice can give you all the details.

CONTROLLING YOUR EDUCATIONAL ENTHUSIASM

If you take college courses, handle your new-found knowledge with subtlety. Use it in every way possible to do a better job, but don't lecture everyone in the office about what you've just learned. Imparting your wisdom unsolicited annoys people, and being enthralled by newly learned theories or strategies only underscores your previous ignorance.

Tim, a 45-year-old engineer, wanted to be more well-rounded professionally, so he enrolled in a college business curriculum and began taking marketing and advertising courses. The head of the advertising department thought, great, Tim will be more accommodating about giving us product information once he understands what we're doing (even though, she pointed out, they'd been trying to explain that to Tim for years).

Those were famous last words—or famous last thoughts. Several times a week, Tim raced into the director of advertising's office with his new revelations: "My class last night was really great. The instructor explained how important it is to have visual consistency in your company's ads, so that customers can recognize them month after month. He said it builds brand recognition. Have you ever thought of doing that?''

The company's ad campaign had always followed that principle, but Tim didn't know that. He didn't realize he was touting a basic, fundamental concept as if it had just been invented. He was unaware he was insulting the director of advertising by assuming she had never heard of it. And he didn't notice that everyone in the advertising department wished he'd go back to spending his evenings in the office instead of in the classroom.

Don't make the mistake of assuming that because *you* didn't know it until yesterday, nobody else did either.

THE BIG FIVE MANAGEMENT SKILLS

Regardless of whether you go into advertising, computer programming, or automobile design, there are skills that all managers must have—and most of them aren't skills you can learn in college. They cut across the boundaries of technical or nontechnical jobs, because they apply to *being* a manager, not to what you manage. They are:

1. Written communication.
2. Verbal communication.
3. Dealing with people.
4. Math and finance.
5. Problem solving.

These skills will determine your future success as an executive. Before you can become a manager, you will have to demonstrate that you are adept at all five. Managers capable of promoting you will evaluate you in each of these areas before they decide whether to give you the nod.

WRITTEN COMMUNICATION

Writing in an intelligent, concise, and professional manner is important to your credibility as a manager, and equally as important to getting you into management in the first place. Managers spend a tremendous amount of time writing. They write everything from handwritten notes to long-range business plans, and they write to everyone—upper management, their employees, customers, suppliers, and other managers. As society becomes increasingly information-oriented, writing clearly and succinctly is an increasingly valuable skill.

Although secretaries are immersed in written communications every day, they often allow themselves to function at the lowest possible level. They act only as transmitters—transcribing, typing, and only occasionally polishing their boss's output. They fail to maximize the opportunities they have to influence or control their department's communications, and thereby increase their own visibility.

VERBAL COMMUNICATION

Although poor writing can tarnish your image (how many times have you laughed at a boss who couldn't spell or put a decent sentence together?), people will forgive you. But they won't tolerate poor verbal communication. If you can't make your point clearly and concisely, if your speech is hostile, confused, or incomprehensible, you're in trouble.

If you find that people often don't seem to understand what you're saying, start listening to yourself. Make outlines before you discuss a topic with someone. Review conversations after you have them: what exactly did you say and what wasn't understood? Attach one of those inexpensive recording devices to your phone and analyze your conversations until you discover the problem. Verbal communication skills are critical because people will remember what you *say* long after they forget what you write.

Because communication is such a vital area, Chapters 9 and 10 are devoted to showing you how to develop your written and verbal skills to get yourself noticed and promoted.

ABILITY TO DEAL WITH PEOPLE

Management means working with people. You manage the people working for you, and even if you have no employees, you work with other executives, both inside and outside your organization, to establish and accomplish goals. Dealing with people is easy when those other people are friendly, cooperative, and in agreement with your ideas. It's not so easy when those people don't like you, feel threatened by you, disagree with you, or have no ability to deal with people themselves. How proficient you are at working with the latter group will be a major factor in your managerial success.

Secretaries think dealing effectively with people means being sociable and well-liked. They think it means that everybody stops by your desk to say hello, or that all the other secretaries ask you out to lunch, or that you never have a disagreement with your boss. It doesn't. Dealing effectively with people means that you get maximum cooperation, productivity, and support from the people you work with—which includes *all* of the following:

1. Working as a team member with other people of equal rank.

2. Delegating responsibilities and tasks to people who work for you or who are lower on the corporate ladder than you are, and motivating those who work for you to do a good job. (This is called working well *down the line.*)

3. Getting assistance and support from the people above you. (This is called working well *up the line.*)

MATH AND FINANCE

You don't have to be fluent in calculus, but you must be able to work with numbers and do basic math. As a manager, you will be constantly working with figures—developing budgets, preparing cost estimates, approving expense reports, or even just keeping track of your employees' unused vacation days. If you can't total up your lunch order at McDonald's, let alone balance a checkbook, run—don't walk—to the nearest remedial math course.

Once you've mastered fundamental math, take a course or seminar on the basics of accounting, or do some reading on your own. Regardless of your area of expertise, how high you rise in the organization, and how big that organization is, you will eventually be working with a number of standard financial/operating documents. You will need to develop them, defend them, or at the minimum, read and understand them. You can't afford to stare blankly when someone asks what you thought of last month's P&L.

At this stage of your career, you don't need to be able to produce an income statement off the top of your head, but you should know what one is for. Here are some important documents to be aware of:

The operating budget shows a detailed projection of sales or income, and gives an in-depth breakdown of the costs and expenses a company will incur making sales (or providing services if the company is a government agency like a fire department).

The income statement (also called a profit-and-loss statement or a P&L) shows income and expenses, too, but very generally. The emphasis here is on the difference between the two—is it a profit, a loss, or breakeven? The P&L usually shows four levels of profitability—gross profit, net operating income, pre-tax profit, and net income—which are figured like this:

$100	Sales/revenue
− 45	Cost of goods
$ 55	**Gross profit**
− 35	Administrative and overhead expenses (including marketing and sales)
$ 20	**Net operating income**
− 9	Direct expenses (such as interest payments)
$ 11	**Pre-tax profit**
− 4	Taxes
$ 7	**Net income**

Net income is also called after-tax profits, or the bottom line. It's pure profit—all costs and expenses, including taxes, have been deducted.

A balance sheet is a snapshot of the company's financial condition at any point in time, such as of December 31, or the end of the first quarter. It shows assets and liabilities, which must always equal each other (hence the name "balance" sheet). A value is assigned to the stock or owners' investment to make the equation come out right.

Accounts receivable reports show what money is owed to the company. An accounts receivable *aging* report shows how old those debts are.

Accounts payable reports are listings of what money the company owes to its suppliers. An accounts payable *aging* report shows how old those obligations are.

A break-even analysis determines what sales level a company must reach to cover its costs and begin making a profit.

A capital expenditures budget plots expenses over time for major physical purchases like buildings or equipment.

Performance indicators are the "instant analysis" tools of business. These quickie statistics—like gross margin, return-on-investment, or inventory turnover—don't give the whole picture, but they do tell executives if the company is on the right track. Understand which performance indicators are important to your business, and you, too, can know where the company's headed.

These documents are used in every profit-oriented business. Non-business and nonprofit organizations have other specialized forms, as do highly technical or financial companies. Get to know the financial documents that are commonly used in your department and the ones that your company uses. Familiarity with the financial condition of your organization will convince the right people that you know what's really important.

PROBLEM SOLVING

Managers do two things: they plan what's going to happen, and then they make sure it happens as planned. But even the best laid plans run into problems, and nothing grinds an operation to a halt faster than a manager who can't or won't make decisions and solve problems.

The ability and willingness to solve problems is the most important quality a manager can have. Intelligent and aggressive problem-solving will get you promoted faster than anything else you can do. Chapter 8 will show you how to develop your problem-solving abilities and how to use them to your advantage.

EXPERIENCE VERSUS ABILITY

Having the right skills and abilities makes up for a lack of management experience. Many secretaries see that lack as a serious detriment to their career development. "I don't know how to be a manager; I've never done it before," is a frequent refrain. But most people are in the same boat. No one, male or female, would ever scale the corporate ladder, if they had to have experience in a job before they could be promoted to it.

The reason people get promoted, and the same reason *you* will get promoted, is that someone above them believes they can do the job—someone believes in their ability. People will believe in *your* ability if you have demonstrated it in the job you have now. Demonstrating your ability tells them that you have the qualifications to do a higher-level job, and the capacity and desire to learn what you need to know to do that job well.

NATURAL MANAGEMENT ABILITY

The only real difference between you and the people with jobs above yours is the respective levels of job-specific knowledge. The people above you do not automatically have more natural management ability than you do. Your boss may have 10 years experience in production and be very knowledgeable about how to manufacture things, but he may or may not be a good manager. His decisions about production will be better than yours, because you lack a background in production, but *that does not mean he is a better manager than you could be.*

George was an absolute wizard at the production side of advertising. He could get graphic houses, typesetters, and printers to give him top quality work and meet almost any deadline. But he was the world's worst delegator. He managed every detail of every project himself. He hand-delivered copy to typesetters; he typed his own production schedules; he even mailed production materials himself, just to make sure they arrived on time. The workload was so overwhelming that he was on the verge of an ulcer, a nervous breakdown, and a divorce. Under pressure from his boss, he finally hired an assistant, but it didn't help, because George couldn't delegate. The assistant did little but sit around and watch George continue to work himself into a frenzy.

George's secretary, on the other hand, had all the delegation ability he lacked. She was able to get people to do all kinds of things for their department. She'd arrange for the account executive to take the latest ad to the client for approval, so that George didn't make a special trip. She'd write up status sheets for jobs that passed over her desk, so George would know their progress. She'd call copywriters who were past their deadlines and remind them, politely, that their copy was due.

George never seemed to notice this help (he was too frantic most of the time), and the secretary never mentioned it. She didn't realize that she was functioning as a manager. Had she pointed that out to George, and told him how she could help if he'd give her more authority, *she* would have had the assistant's job. George had the job knowledge, but his secretary had the management ability. She just didn't realize it.

Marge, a data processing manager, could program a computer to do practically anything, but she couldn't get her team members to cooperate. Her projects were always late and over budget, because she didn't know how to motivate people to work *with* each other instead of *against* each other. The projects she managed were known for their delays, infighting, and marginal results.

Her secretary did everything she could to help Marge out. She spent almost half her time serving as liaison between the team members, carrying work back and forth, and soothing ruffled egos. She gently pushed the laggers who were behind schedule, and she passed along other people's praise to the achievers. She did, essentially, the job Marge should have been doing. With some data processing background, this secretary would have been a far better project manager than her boss was.

Both George and Marge, who were already managers, lacked the skills necessary to be truly successful. As a secretary, you may not have (at least, not yet) the knowledge and experience to do the technical aspects of jobs like theirs, but you may very well have the innate management skills you need.

ANYBODY CAN LEARN TO DO IT

Getting the specific knowledge to do the job is not the hard part. You can go to college and take computer science courses like Marge did. Or you can get purely on-the-job training like George did (he started out as a delivery boy at a large advertising agency just after he graduated from high school).

Learning to be a good manager is the hard part. Dealing with people, maximizing their productivity, motivating them, getting them to work together is much tougher than learning how to fix a bug in a computer program or get the best price from a printer. There are plenty of managers who have little or no *management* skills, and that's where you can get an edge. Secretaries are used to working with people, being cooperative and getting cooperation, sharing information and following projects through to completion. These are skills you can use in your climb up the ladder.

When I first broke the secretary barrier myself, I was assigned, as an assistant/secretary in the marketing research department, to write an economic forecast for the Consumer Products Division of the Borden, Inc.'s Chemical Division—a project my boss had done in previous years. The purpose of the report was to show upcoming trends in purchasing patterns, customer groups, competitive activity and raw materials to help the brand managers make sales and profit projections. I'd had a few courses in economics, but my college major had been English literature. I didn't know anything about economic forecasts but I knew I could find out. And I knew *this* was my chance to show what I could do.

The project took over 3 months to complete. I started by getting the economic forecast reports from the last 3 years. I read them over and over again, and tried to evaluate how well they had accomplished their purpose. Then I interviewed people who would be using the report and asked what improvements they'd like to see, how it could be revised to better fit their needs.

I asked my boss where he had gotten his information for the previous reports and asked for suggestions on additional sources. I met several times with the corporate financial analysis department. I read the past 6 months' issues of all the business magazines, as well as all the trade publications that applied to the division's activities—everything from *Chain Store Age* to *Modern Paint & Coatings* to *Packaging Digest*. When I was finished, I had the information I needed to predict what each of our customer groups would look like over the next 5 years, how material costs and changes in the economy would affect pricing, sales, the size of the customer base, and so on.

I managed to enlist the aid of one of the data processing coordinators. He critiqued everything I did, making recommendations and providing invaluable advice. My English background helped me to clarify the writing in the report. And by asking the product managers how *they* would improve the report, I was able to refine the content and format.

I had no experience in economic forecasting, and some of the economic articles I read were so complex that I had to read them four or five times to understand them. But I handled it. I begged, borrowed and stole all the information and help I could get, and it paid off. I made my mark at Borden with that economic forecast—it was read by everyone from the division president on down. Within 2 months, a secretary was hired, and I was promoted to a full assistant in the marketing research department.

You, too, can learn to do jobs you've never done before. Just like I didn't need 5 years' experience in economics to write an economic forecast, you don't have to have a labor relations background to get a management job in the personnel department. You don't need to have taught seminars to manage a company's training function. You learn and you do any way you can.

A boss once said to me, "Business is just common sense." And that's a fundamental truth. There are basic techniques and principles to follow, but conducting business is primarily a matter of doing what makes sense. There are no magic formulas to make you a success— just your ability to recognize what needs to be done, and your persistence in finding a way to do it.

So don't worry about not having the specific job knowledge to do a management job. You can get it from schools; you can pick it up as you go along; you can copy the good things other people have previously done in the job; you can get help from anybody and everybody you work with. If you're thorough and determined, you'll get the job done, and you'll get it done right.

5. Stop looking like a secretary

Almost all secretaries go to work looking nice, or at least respectable. But very few secretaries go to work looking managerial. And that's a serious mistake, because *to become a manager, you must look like a manager.*

If your appearance says, "You can ignore me, I'm nobody important here," you can bet your bottom dollar that's exactly what will happen. Because if you wear denim skirts, sleeveless dresses, worn-out shoes, or that same old sweater, you don't look like management material. Your appearance says—even louder than job performance—who you are and how committed you are to the company and your future with it. When your appearance isn't right on track, you are sending a message that says: "I'm not interested in or qualified for a better job." A poor appearance says you don't understand the importance of looking good in the business world. And that can be professionally fatal, because in business, image is everything. You are a viable part of the business you work for, and you are a representative of that business—does your appearance reflect that?

The key is visualization. If management can picture you in a higher level job, you can get a higher level job. But if your boss has trouble picturing you meeting clients or directing a staff meeting, you haven't got a chance.

The bottom line is: dress for the position you want, so you can get the position you want. If you want to be a sales representative, start dressing like a sales representative. If you want to be the director of personnel, start dressing like a director of personnel. Dressing like a manager not only makes you look promotable, but it makes you feel better, it improves your confidence, and it makes people take you more seriously.

Wait a minute, you say, my boss is the financial director, and you should see how he dresses. He obviously didn't have to overhaul his appearance to get a good job.

That's true. You'll probably find a lot of managers who don't pay much attention to their appearance. But they've got one thing going for them—*they are already managers*. You're not. The prejudice against women executives, though still with us, is gradually eroding, but the bias against secretaries is showing no signs of abating. You're starting with two strikes against you—one, you're a woman, and two, you're a secretary. Don't let your appearance be the third strike.

AVOIDING THE SECRETARIAL LOOK

Many secretaries dress in a way that makes it easy to tell they're not managers—and are probably never going to be managers. Described below are several of the more common secretarial "looks"—all of them bad, all of them self-defeating. You'll recognize some of these people in your own office—but look closely, do you recognize yourself?

Daddy's Little Girl. She is either young or trying desperately hard to stay that way. She's cute, bubbly, and doesn't appear to have a brain in her head. She can always be found chatting with the other secretaries and scurrying back to her desk when the boss walks in. She's sweet, likable, and very popular.

But she tries hard to hide whatever talent she may have, so she won't be saddled with any responsibility. It's safer that way. If she's not in charge of anything, she can't make a mistake.

She dresses like a high school student, and no one would allow a high school student to manage a department. She's going nowhere.

Plain Jane. The most frequent of the secretary looks, Plain Jane is the invisible woman. She's pleasant, but quiet. She's very punctual and rarely calls in sick, but who besides her boss would notice if she did? She wears little or no make-up, hasn't had her hair styled in years, and she always seems to be wearing the same clothes. You wonder if she wore that dress yesterday, but you can't remember what she wore yesterday, or any other day, for that matter.

Plain Jane may be very efficient and a good secretary, but management has no idea that she's even alive.

The Sergeant-Major. She is always in a position of importance—just ask her. She is the *executive* secretary to the vice president or the senior partner or someone equally as important. She believes her boss is the top dog among the executives, and herself the top dog among the secretaries.

Her appearance is as severe as it is outdated. Her hair is cropped short or pulled tightly back in a bun, and there's never a hair out of place (no hair would dare). Her clothes are austere—nothing fancy or feminine, and her jewelry is minimal and serviceable. She has tight little lines around her lips from pursing them in disapproval—which is frequently directed at the other secretaries.

Her boss thinks she's great, because she is fiercely loyal to him. She has to be—he is her only source of power, without him she is just another secretary. What she doesn't realize is that's all she will ever be.

Mom. Almost every office has a Mom. That older woman whose glasses are either hung around her neck on a rope, or perched on the end of her nose while she peers dimly over them. She always wears some kind of shapeless dress, and no matter what time of year it is, has an old cardigan sweater draped around her shoulders. She fusses cheerfully over everyone in the office, and like most mothers with their children, she never quite seems to be listening to what you're saying.

She is the first person you'd call for a bake sale, and the last person you'd think of for a management position.

The Hot Date. This woman may be almost any age, but she always appears to be on the make. She comes to the office ready for action: 2 pounds of make-up, a quart of perfume, and a low-cut dress. She looks like she's heading to the nearest sleazy bar as soon as work is over. She's constantly chewing gum and talking to the crowd of men standing around her desk.

The only place these guys want to promote her to is the Holiday Inn.

All these women have one thing in common: they don't look like managers. You can't imagine them supervising people, running a department, managing a budget, or working with a team of department heads. Their bosses and other executives in the company can't imagine it either. They are doomed to remain secretaries, because they don't look and act like they could be anything else.

THE FUTURE MANAGER LOOK

So what does the woman on her way up look like? Let's meet one:

The Future Manager. She looks like she's ready to walk into the board room if the call should come. She's wearing a lightweight worsted wool jacket, with subtle gray and white stripes and slightly padded shoulders, and a matching straight skirt. Her white blouse has a stand-up collar and narrow rows of vertical pintucking.

Her accessories include a large gold cameo pinned at the throat. She wears round gold earrings with an antique design, an expensive-looking (if not actually expensive) gold watch, gray pumps, and lightly tinted gray hose.

Her hair is smoothly styled in a collar-length pageboy, and her make-up is expertly applied. She's wearing subtle pink polish on her medium-length nails, and her perfume is light and almost undetectable.

This is a woman who won't be a secretary for long. While this look may be too formal for your particular working environment, it gives you an idea of the impression you need to convey at work.

To decide whether *you* are dressing like a future manager, take this test. Given what you wore to work today, or plan to wear tomorrow, answer the following questions:

	Yes	No
If you were suddenly asked to make a presentation to the department heads of division about your new word processing system, would you be appropriately dressed?	_____	_____
If a major customer had arrived unexpectedly at your office today, were you appropriately dressed to give a company tour?	_____	_____
Are you dressed as well as, or better than, any of the women managers in your company (yes, even the ones at the top)?	_____	_____
If you had a meeting with the vice president of your company tomorrow, would you still wear what you had originally planned to wear tomorrow?	_____	_____
If your boss called tonight and said you'd been promoted to assistant advertising manager, effective tomorrow, would you continue to wear the same clothes you wear now?	_____	_____
Could you have passed for an executive today at work?	_____	_____

If the answer to any of these questions is "no," *you are not dressing right.* Consider a managerial appearance as much a part of your job as typing or filing. You are dressed right only if you dress like a manager every day—because you're being noticed every day. And the day you try to get by with an old skirt and blouse may be the day the research and development manager decides to interview you for a job in his department.

WHAT IMAGE IS RIGHT?

The right image for you depends on who you work for, what industry you're in, how large your company is, and where it's located. What's right for a progressive San Diego publicity agency may be all wrong for a small pipe-fitting manufacturer in Des Moines. What's appropriate for a music publishing company in Nashville won't work for a brokerage house on Wall Street.

Evaluate these factors in deciding what image is the best one for you:

The tone of your company. Is it very conservative, middle-of-the-road, or very liberal? The "glamour" industries like advertising, cosmetics, or film-making allow a more flamboyant appearance. More color, more style, more individuality. Professions like accounting, law, or financial planning dictate a more conservative and serious appearance.

What part of the country you live in. In Cleveland, style is much more subdued than it is in Los Angeles. The more conservative the city, the more conservative your appearance should be. (The reverse, however, is not necessarily true. You don't have to have an avant-garde appearance just because you work in Los Angeles.) You can determine geographic tone just by walking around downtown at lunch hour. How are the businesswomen dressed? Watch them, study them, learn from them. They look like you should look. Forget about the men. There is so little variation in men's clothing that it's not much help in determining the tone of your city. An expensive man's three-piece suit is an expensive three-piece suit all over the country.

How big the city is you work in. Small cities, unless they are trendy spots like Aspen or Santa Barbara, are more conservative than big cities. Fashion trends hit later, sometimes years later, than they do in big cities, and they hit with less impact. What is a major fad in New York City may only be a minor influence sometime later in Fort Wayne.

How large your budget is. How closely you follow the fashion trends depends, too, on how much money you have to spend. If your budget is limited, you can't afford to buy clothes that are out-of-date in 6 months. Wide shoulders and short skirts might be great this year, but next year they may be out of fashion and mark you as passé. Cutting-edge fashion tends to look dated in less than a year and, in 2 years, often looks ridiculous. The less money you have, the more conservative you should dress. Conservative doesn't mean boring, it just means less faddish. Build yourself a conservative, middle-of-the-road wardrobe that, with just a minor change in hemline or lapel width or accessories, will wear for years.

DRESSING LIKE A MANAGER ON A SECRETARY'S SALARY

Looking like a manager is a project that requires the same research, analysis, and planning that any business project requires. It means a total overhaul from head to foot, with a persistent attention to detail. It means learning to manage your money so that you have the resources to change your image.

Okay, you're thinking, I'll just go out and spend $1,000 on new clothes, $200 on make-up, and $150 on accessories. Just as soon as I win the state lottery. The secretary's lament is: if I made $40,000 a year, I could afford to look like I made $40,000 a year. On $1,500 a month, I can barely afford to eat.

You don't have to spend a lot of money to look good, but you do have to spend some. The old principle of "it takes money to make money" is true. You can't take advantage of high interest rates if you have no money to put into certificates of deposit. You can't take advantage of appreciating real estate values if you have no cash to buy property. And you can't become a manager if you don't have the money to "package" yourself attractively.

So where do you get the money? In business when you need to increase your profit margin, you can do two things, and two things only:

1. Increase revenue.

2. Cut costs.

INCREASE REVENUE?

Companies increase revenue by increasing sales. You can increase revenue by getting a raise or working a second job (or marrying a millionaire). It's probably a safe bet that you won't get a raise tomorrow. And unless you are some kind of superwoman, you probably can't handle a second job. You shouldn't even try. A second job can be very draining—emotionally as well as physically—and you'll need all the energy you can get to embark on this self-promotion and self-improvement project. You can't afford to ruin your new image by dragging into work exhausted. So for now, forget the generate-additional-revenue approach. (Those of you who want to look for that millionaire, more power to you.)

MAKING EVERY PENNY COUNT

That leaves the other approach—cutting expenses. Everybody wastes money somewhere. Do you ever get the sinking feeling that you've spent $100 in the last week and don't know where it went? That's a signal you're wasting money. Force yourself to record all of your expenses for at least a month, until you get a handle on your spending patterns. Carry a notebook with you and write down every penny you spend. Figure out where and how much you can cut.

No matter how tight you think your budget is and how little you spend on "extras," you've got room to cut. Sit down with a pencil and paper and analyze every nonessential expenditure you make. What are your weaknesses? Can you cut $5 or $10 off those expenses? Are there cheaper alternatives if you don't want to give them up? Even though you may only save a dollar here and a dollar there, those few dollars add up. Here are some areas where you can probably cut expenses:

A quick drink after work with the gang from the office. Unless you are drinking after work for business reasons, such as to work yourself into the managerial social circle, that quick drink is a quick way to spend $10 or $15. Every time you *don't* have a drink, you save a couple of dollars. Have one and nurse it. Or go home.

You've spent all day with these people, why do you want to spend several more hours in a bar with them?

Long-distance phone calls. Are you spending hours on the phone to Alaska, Florida, or Maine? Even calls to people only 60 or 70 miles away add up if you talk for 45 minutes. Start writing letters, limit your calls (use an egg timer), or sign up for a discount long-distance service. Have those far-away friends call *you* for a change—work out a system where you alternate who makes and pays for the call.

Finance charges. It's so easy to reach for plastic instead of cash (particularly if you're out of cash), and that's one big reason people overspend. Then the bill arrives, you can't pay it, and you're stuck with interest charges. Or worse, you don't make the payment on time and are assessed late charges. If you don't have enough cash, don't buy it, and if you must charge, watch those due dates.

Your kids. Put them on a budget, too. When their allowance runs out, they should wait (barring extraordinary circumstances) until next "pay day" for more money—just like you do. You don't teach your kids money management by being a bottomless financial well.

Cosmetics. Do you have 17 shades of lipstick you never wear? Don't sample cosmetics by buying them—shop where you can try them on first, then only buy what you're *sure* you will wear.

Eating out. It is not cheaper to run out for a fast-food hamburger than to cook at home. More convenient and less strenuous, yes, but not cheaper. Expensive lunches downtown during the work week can really add up, too. One secretary estimated she spent $140 a month just on lunches.

Magazines. One friend I know buys three or four magazines a week. She says it keeps her up on the latest information. Of course, buying all those magazines leaves her broke, but she's certainly in the know.

Movies. Don't go in prime time. You can save several dollars by going to the bargain matinee, or staying home. And you can save lots of money by not ordering the super giant size of popcorn and an extra large soda.

Candy, cigarettes, and other expensive habits. Exercising a little self-control can save a surprising amount of money.

THE PERSONAL DEVELOPMENT FUND

The amount you cut from what you're spending now is the money you will allocate to developing your managerial look. Don't cut $50 a month from your expenses then put it toward fancier dinners for your family. Put it in your personal development fund.

Go to an office supply store, and buy some change envelopes with clasps. When you resist the temptation to buy that fashion magazine, take $2.50 (or whatever the magazine would have cost) out of your wallet and put it in that envelope. When you write a letter instead of phoning long-distance, estimate the cost of the call, and put that money in your envelope. Keep a record on the outside of the envelope of exactly how much money is in it, and where it came from, like this:

PERSONAL DEVELOPMENT FUND
September
Money saved from:

9/3	Cigarettes		$ 1.15
9/5	Magazine		$ 3.18 (don't forget tax)
		TOTAL	$ 4.33
9/6	Writing instead of calling Mom		$10.00
		TOTAL	$14.33
9/9	Brown-bagging lunch		$ 4.50
		TOTAL	$18.83

Short of a life-threatening emergency, don't use that money for anything but the improvement of your professional image. At the end of the month, spend what you have on a small item that will improve your appearance, or move money into another envelope to save for a larger purchase. Don't give in to the temptation to spend this money on anything else.

Sylvia lived less than 2 miles from her office, yet every day at noon she jumped in her car and drove to a restaurant and had lunch. Not expensive lunches, they only averaged about $4 a day, but by the end of the month, she had spent almost $100 on lunches. She could have gone home instead, had a sandwich and a bowl of soup for about 75 cents, and at the end of one year, would have had an extra $900 to put toward a managerial wardrobe—just from cutting her lunch expenses.

Sylvia said she knew she was wasting money, but she felt like she owed herself something because she worked so hard. She said it gave her a lift to go out for lunch—made her feel more important. More important, that is, until she went back to her typewriter and started slaving away again. More important, that is, until she went to her closet in the morning and hated everything she saw hanging there. More important, that is, until she got her tiny paycheck every 2 weeks.

Resist the temptation to reward yourself, if you're bored or depressed with your personal or professional life, by using up precious finances. Reward yourself by not doing the dishes tonight. Reward yourself by taking a 45-minute bubble bath. But don't reward yourself by buying something frivolous. Don't spend money to make yourself feel better. Spend your money on working toward a promotion, and you'll not only feel better, you'll have more money permanently.

Don't derail your long-term career plans with short-term spending sprees.

THE REWARDS

Financial management is an important part of any executive job. When you get into management, you will have to deal with budgetary constraints, you will be responsible for financial planning for your department, you will be accountable for profit or loss. Learning to manage your personal finances is a skill you can't do without. It's the first step to understanding financial management in business.

It's going to cost you at least $100 a month to package yourself properly. Find it. Dig out all that old stuff in the basement and sell it at a flea market. Get the kids a paper route and eliminate their allowance. Get it any way you can, because this is an investment with a high return.

You have to make sacrifices to get what you want—nothing comes easily. Nobody will walk up to your desk someday and say, "Do we have an exciting management job for you!"

That's the Cinderella fantasy. The knight in shining armor who sweeps the little scullery maid away to a life of luxury doesn't exist. Never did, never will. You make your own breaks. You build your own life. If life isn't the way you want it to be, you have only yourself to change it.

The $100 a month you spend for the next year could mean an extra $1,000 a month every year after that. Getting into management means financial rewards—big ones. The money you invest now will bring in returns many, many times over.

Five years ago, Valerie worked as a secretary in a public television station, making so little that she could barely pay the rent on her tiny one-bedroom cottage. She loved her job and the people she worked with, but she got tired of not having enough money to buy clothes or furniture or vacations. So she took a second job, as a part-time book-keeper, to pay for a more professional wardrobe. Thanks to her new look, she landed a secretarial job at a prestigious law firm at twice her previous salary. She worked as much overtime as she could, and made an extra $400 a month. She put every cent into improving her image. She bought expensive clothes, jewelry, coats, and shoes. Her hard work and her outstanding appearance caught the attention of one of the law firm's clients. He offered her a girl-Friday job with his small real estate development firm.

Valerie began building her job and the company's business in any and every way she possibly could. The company grew rapidly and so did her responsibilities. Now she's a vice president, managing several million dollars worth of real estate. She has five people working for her, and makes almost $40,000 a year, plus bonuses. Although she wasn't sure where she'd end up, Valerie spent considerable time, money, and effort creating a very professional image. Combined with hard work, it really paid off.

LETS TAKE IT FROM THE TOP

Your image should be total—hair, make-up, and clothes should all work together to give you the right, promotable appearance. You can't ignore any detail. Just redoing your make-up doesn't give you a new image, and neither does a new hair style. You need to cover every base, and scrutinize every detail.

Starting at the top, the first thing to evaluate is your hair. Whoever said a woman's hair was her crowning glory wasn't kidding. Your hair says as much about you as your clothes, and how it looks can make or break your total appearance. A $500 outfit doesn't improve your image if your hair is dirty, bedraggled or unkempt.

HOW MUCH TIME AND EFFORT CAN YOU INVEST?

The most important factor in deciding which hairstyle is right for you is how much time and effort you want to devote to it. If you have a large family, a quick wash in the shower and a blow-dry may be all you can manage. If you're single with no commitments, or if you like to work with your hair, you may be willing to spend extra time on it. *You* have to decide how much time you can spare and how much effort you want to put into making your hair look good. Just be realistic when you make that decision.

Don't try for a long glamorous hairstyle, with waves and curls, if you have thin, straight hair. Don't attempt a flat, sleek look if your hair is thick and wavy. You'll be fighting a losing battle—and if you don't give your hairstyle the attention it requires, the result will be a lot of awful-looking hair: intricate layered cuts that don't get enough attention, so they hang and droop; thin, straight hair permed into a pile of frizz; hair that makes its owner look like a street urchin.

Be realistic about how much time you're going to spend on your

hair, and what style works best with your particular type of hair, then
get it cut accordingly.

HOW TO AVOID THE HAIR HACKS

Now the hard part comes—finding a stylist who can give you a
good cut. Like any service business, quality and professionalism vary
widely. Some stylists take pride in their work, and they are sincerely
interested in how you look. Others regard cutting hair as just a way to
pay the bills.

How do you find the good ones? Don't use the trial and error
method, where you call any beauty shop in the phone book, ask for
any hairdresser they have available, then let an unknown stranger
work your hair over. This technique has driven many otherwise sen-
sible women to simply give up on their hair. They get it cut only
when they can't stand it any more, they do absolutely nothing with it
in the meantime, and they hate every cut they get. They're the first
ones to say that hairdressers aren't worth a damn.

Don't do this. As a manager, you'll be responsible for purchasing
goods and services for your department. If you can't find a decent
hairstylist for yourself, how will you be able to find decent suppliers
for your department's needs?

Finding a hairdresser is a purchasing project, just like hiring a data
processing consultant for your department would be. How would
you find a qualified data processing consultant? One way is to ask
around until you found someone who had similar needs to yours,
who had gotten good results from a DP consultant, and ask that
person for a recommendation. You'd visit the consultant, talk to him
or her, decide if you thought he could do a good job, then you'd hire
him on a trial basis. Right?

Now do the same with finding a hairdresser. Keep your eyes open
for someone whose hairstyle you like, then approach her, even if it's
a total stranger, and ask her who cuts her hair. She'll be flattered you
asked.

Really look at your prospective reference before you ask. Her hair
may look terrific, but if she has short, straight, baby-fine hair, and
you have long, coarse, wavy hair, her stylist may not be right for you.
Choose someone whose hair *type* is similar to yours. Get the name of

the salon, but more importantly, get the name of the person who does the cutting, because even a shop with a good reputation will have a wide range of quality in its stylists. Get the shop's location and write down all this information before you forget it.

YOU GET WHAT YOU PAY FOR

Good haircuts cost money. You don't have to go to the poshest salon in town, but if you get a $5.95 styling at Fred's Family Haircutting Barn, chances are you won't get a good cut. You want styling and advice, and it's not cheap. As I keep mentioning, you're making an investment in your future. Expect to pay $20 and up for a good cut (the larger the city you live in, the more you can expect to pay). And do it every 2 months, maybe more often if your hair is short or grows quickly. The investment is worth every single penny.

Once you have a recommendation, call the salon and make an appointment. Tell them what you want—probably a shampoo, cut, and a blow-dry for the first time out—and ask how much it will cost. You wouldn't hire your DP consultant without asking the rates first, would you? That way, no surprises. I can remember sitting through an hour's worth of styling thinking of nothing but how much the bill would be because the salon was so fancy.

Just ask. If it's way out of line, cancel the appointment and go elsewhere. Getting your hair done should be fun; it should make you feel pampered. Knowing up front how much it will cost takes some of the worry out of it.

YOU AND YOUR STYLIST—WORKING TOGETHER

A good relationship doesn't come easy—it has to be developed. Assume the responsibility of establishing a good rapport; don't sit passively hoping your stylist will do what you want. Nobody is a mindreader, so don't treat your stylist like one.

Remember that your hairdresser works *for you*. Getting hairdressers, lawyers, accountants, or car mechanics to do a good job for you is excellent practice in managing people—a task you will be doing more and more of as your career progresses.

These eight steps can insure you'll be happy with the styling you get:

1. *Take control of the appointment.* Don't let the stylist race you back to the shampoo basin as soon as you walk in the door. No one can tell what condition your hair is in, or what special problems you have with it, if your hair is wet. Politely, but firmly, tell the stylist, "Before you shampoo, I would like to discuss my hair and how I want it done. Let's go over to your chair."

   If the stylist is not willing to take the time to do this, don't stay for the rest of the appointment. You want an individualized styling that is suited to your particular needs—not a production-line haircut. Be brave enough to say, "You seem rushed for time. Why don't I come back another day?" Then leave and don't go back.

2. *Give your stylist as much information as possible.* While you're sitting in front of the mirror, point out what you like and don't like about your hair. Tell your stylist what problems you have with your hair, how you normally do it, and what amount of time and effort you are willing to put into it.

3. *Describe the hairstyle you want.* Tell the stylist, in as much detail as possible, what hairstyle you want, or what you're working toward if your hair is "in transition." Ask what the best way is to accomplish that goal, and get a detailed explanation of what the stylist intends to do, and what kind of care will be required for your new look.

   Never but never tell your stylist, "I'll leave it up to you. Do whatever you think looks best." That is asking for a disaster. What *you* think looks good and what *somebody else* thinks looks good is strictly a matter of personal taste, and everybody's personal taste is different. Know what you want *before* you go to the salon, and give your stylist very definite boundaries to work within.

4. *Watch carefully what the stylist does.* Don't doze off or read a magazine. Pay close attention to what your hairdresser is do-

ing, particularly during the styling stage, because you'll have to repeat the procedure at home. If your hair is set on hot rollers, be sure to get a look at the back, so you can see the pattern and direction of the rollers. Find out as much as you can about the cut you receive, so that if you like it, you can remind your stylist how it was done on the previous visit.

5. *Help your stylist remember you.* Two months is a long time to remember someone when you're seeing eight or ten customers a day. Try to find an area of common interest between you and your stylist so you'll be remembered the next time you go in.

6. *Give your stylist a chance.* If your hair hasn't been styled for a long time, and you only want a trim, you're not going to get the world's greatest haircut. It may take two or three appointments to get your hair where it should be. There's nothing wrong with a cautious approach—just don't expect miracles. If the style comes at all close to what you want, give the stylist a second chance. The more one person works with your hair, the better that person comes to know you and your hair's idiosyncrasies.

7. *Never accept a substitute hairdresser.* Never let anyone but your regular stylist cut your hair. If you arrive at the shop, and your stylist has gone home ill, reschedule the appointment and come back later—no matter how desperate you are to have your hair cut. The worst haircut I ever got was from a substitute who was filling in because my regular stylist had left suddenly on a family emergency.

8. *Keep track of your stylist.* If you call for an appointment and your stylist has quit (they move around a lot), don't be shy. Ask where he or she went, and if the receptionist doesn't know, ask to talk to someone else who might. Most reputable shops will tell you— unless the stylist left under less than friendly circumstances. Always give your stylist your name, address, and phone number, and ask to be notified if he or she moves on. For some reason, hairdressers seldom ask for this information—you have to volunteer it. Do it! Good hairstylists are too hard to find.

FLATTERING BUT NOT EXTREME

Your actual hairstyle isn't really important—as long as it flatters you, and you don't carry it to extremes. Very short hair can be too masculine, unless you are petite and have incredible bone structure. Very long hair doesn't look good either. If it's left hanging, it makes you look like a college student or Alice in Wonderland—neither of which is appropriate for business. Avoid anything that could be considered a "dramatic" cut. The office is no place for drama.

Once you have a good cut, the rest is up to you. Keep your hair clean and take care of it. If you go to the office with your hair looking bad—everyone, believe me, will notice. If mornings are too hectic, wash your hair at night, then use hot rollers in the morning. Or dampen your hair, and do a quick styling with a blow-dryer and a round brush. Making time to look good says you are not the type of person who takes shortcuts.

MAKING-UP FOR SUCCESS

Make-up is an area of great failing for many women. As teenagers, we spent hours experimenting with make-up. We read all the magazines, studied the latest looks, bought the hottest new colors of lipstick and eye shadow. Then we got older, got busier, and stopped paying attention. Many women still do their make-up like they did when they were 18, or they take the easy way out and just throw on some eye shadow and lipstick.

Well, it's time to start paying attention again.

We all get used to seeing ourselves a certain way, and it's difficult to be objective about your own make-up. To yourself, you look just fine in that luminescent green eye shadow that was "in" in 1973. You've been looking at it for over 10 years, and you're so used to it that you look peculiar to yourself *without* it. Major make-up changes always look strange at first. But it's time to get in step with the current trends. If you think you don't need this advice because you don't wear make-up, you need this advice more than anyone else. I've never met anyone who doesn't look more attractive with the right make-up.

HOW DO YOU DECIDE WHAT LOOKS GOOD ON YOU?

It's time to put those purchasing principles back into action:

Do some research. Go to the library and review the make-up articles in the last 4 months' issues of *Glamour, Mademoiselle, Cosmopolitan, Harper's Bazaar, Vogue,* and other fashion/beauty magazines. (Don't run out and buy all these magazines—save your money for buying make-up.) Though make-up articles aren't as frequent in the women's business magazines like *Savvy* or *Working Woman,* review them as well. Their advice is more oriented to make-up you should be wearing *in the office.* Read these articles very critically. Look for advice that is common to all or most of the articles. Just because one magazine advocates black eyeliner one month doesn't mean that's the trend. If you see it in several magazines, think about using it.

Compare their advice to what you're doing now. Are they suggesting muted, dusky tones for eye shadow, and you're wearing bright blue? Are they showing pale pinks for lipstick, and you're wearing blood red?

In reading these magazines, skip the make-up advertisements. In an attempt to emphasize their products, companies often have their models wearing garish and overdone make-up. Bright purple eye shadow has never been and never will be in style. Ignore the ads, and stick to the "how to" articles.

Get some advice. Many stores, like Merle Norman, or the make-up departments of good department stores, can be excellent sources of advice. Many give you the opportunity to sample products before you buy, and many offer no-obligation make-overs.

Never get advice from the man in your life. Men are the worst— they want you to look just as you have always looked, or they want you to look sexier, which is the *wrong* look for the office. Or to some of them, all make-up looks alike. And because they are with you much of the time, they may be no more objective than you are. Also be careful about taking advice from your teenage daughters, if you have any. They are usually into the latest fads, and their taste is geared for teenagers, not professional women.

Get advice from someone you know and trust, someone whose make-up you think looks good. Just say, "I'm thinking about changing my make-up. Would you give me some advice?" Be aggressive; people hate to tell friends that they don't look right. Ask specific questions based on your magazine research. Say, "Do you think I would look better with a lighter shade of lipstick?" "Do you think my eyebrows are too heavy?" Again, people are flattered to be asked for their opinion—provided they know you are seriously asking for advice and not just fishing for compliments.

Try it on before you buy it. Don't go to the nearest discount store or drugstore and buy make-up off a rack. What looks good under several layers of plastic in the store may look terrible when you get it home. Go somewhere where you can try it on, think about it, get an opinion from a friend, then come back later if you decide you want it.

And don't let a sales clerk pressure you into buying. Cosmetics sales clerks are great for insisting that you must have all fourteen items in their skin care line or else the treatment won't really be effective—don't let them snow you. And before submitting to a make-over, ask if there is an obligation to buy. If there is, go somewhere else.

Those purchasing principles boil down to three easy steps:

1. Decide what you want.
2. Buy only what you need.
3. Buy it at the best possible price.

EXPENSIVE, BUT WORTH IT

Good make-up, like a good haircut, is expensive. You may spend over $75 for a set of cosmetics. But it should last you a year, and that amounts to only $4 or $5 a month to look terrific.

Once you have your make-up in order, keep it looking good. Your lipstick needs to be reapplied during the day, particularly after lunch. By noon, your nose and forehead may be shiny and need powdering. Stay on top of your make-up, so that you look as good at 4:30 as you did at 9:00.

TO SEE OR NOT TO SEE

Glasses and contact lenses also have a tremendous impact on your appearance. Stylish, contemporary glasses can give you a professional, serious look. The mayor of Houston wears glasses during the week to give her an authoritative appearance, but she wears contacts on the weekend.

You don't need to go that far, but do be sure your glasses aren't *detracting* from your appearance. Like your make-up, this is an area where your judgment may fail you, because you can't be objective about your own face. Take an honest, outspoken friend with good taste along when you pick out your glasses. Frames that are too heavy or too small or the wrong color can ruin all the work you've done on your make-up. Don't rely on the sales clerk in the optical store—her taste may be radically different from yours.

Even contact lenses can detract from your appearance. People with hard lenses sometimes develop the habit of tilting their heads back and blinking frequently, which gives them a mousey, clerkish appearance. Ask that honest, outspoken friend if you do this. If so, work on correcting it.

Contact lens wearers can get tinted lenses to enhance their eye color, but the result is often more negative than positive. The wearer ends up with abnormally blue eyes, startling dark eyes, or eyes a color never before seen on a human being. One secretary I worked with had very pale skin and brown eyes. She wore no make-up and had dark brown tinted contact lenses. The effect was like two black bugs had landed on her face. I worked with her for over a year and never got used to it.

THE CLOTHES MAKE THE WOMAN

Now the big expense—your wardrobe. Having an executive's wardrobe doesn't mean you have twenty different outfits each costing $750. It means that what you have is executive *looking*.

What you need, and maybe all you can afford at this point, is a basic executive wardrobe. Classic dresses, skirts, blazers, blouses, and accessories that can work together for a number of different looks. You need at least five different outfits, one for each day of the week. (One secretary said, "If I'm wearing my beige wool dress, it must be Tuesday.") Each outfit should be attractive and totally accessorized. If you're starting from scratch, you can create a one-week executive wardrobe with the following pieces:

- Two suits in basic colors like gray or blue.

- One dress, that coordinates with the suits so you can wear one or both suit jackets with it.

- Four blouses, in a wide variety of colors and styles.

- Two pairs of shoes, one to coordinate with each suit.

- A small collection of accessories—scarves, jewelry, belts and hosiery.

Carefully mixed and matched, this limited wardrobe can yield up to eleven different outfits. A little planning can make it go a long way.

BUILDING A WARDROBE

Because of the expense involved, a wardrobe should be carefully thought out. You can't afford to waste money on mistakes that hang in the closet and never get worn—either because they don't fit right, they don't look right, or they don't go with anything else you own.

Pull your wardrobe together by taking these steps:

More library research. Go back to the library and start researching the fashion trends—just like you did for make-up. The women's business magazines are again a good reference, and there are several good books available on how to achieve a professional image. (See the Recommended Readings section for references.) Read them to find out what clothes are right for you and your industry. Where should your skirt lengths be? Is a layered look in? What colors predominate? What materials give the richest look?

In-store research. Take your research "into the field" by surveying the stores in your area and studying what looks they're showing. Start at the very best store in town and work your way down— you'll see what top-of-the-line clothing looks and feels like (and costs!), and as you move down to department stores and less expensive specialty stores, you'll find the stores that offer the quality you need at the price you can afford.

Take inventory. Look through your closet and pick out what fits those trends, or what, with minor alterations, will work. For a fraction of the cost of a new blazer, you can have the lapels narrowed or the waist taken in on one that's gone out of style.

Remove temptation. Everything that isn't workable should be thrown out, given to charity, or hung in another room where you won't be tempted to wear it. Don't be lured into wearing a blouse that looks terrible, just because it's the only clean one in your closet.

Develop a needs list. Decide what pieces you need to expand your wardrobe. Would a gray wool skirt add two or more "outfits" to your wardrobe? Where would a blouse or a sweater make a big difference? Would the right necklace really dress up an otherwise plain dress? Think in terms of minimums—what's the least you can add and still bring your wardrobe up to managerial level? Think!

Make a purchasing plan. Given your finances, and a basic allocation of at least $50 to $100 a month, develop a plan of what you will buy and when. You may not be able to change your wardrobe overnight, but you can gradually bring it up to snuff.

Learn what to avoid. Knowing what *not* to buy is just as important as knowing what *to* buy. Avoid all of these:

- *The latest fashion trends*. The closer you stay to the main-stream of fashion, the longer your clothes can be worn and still be in style.

- *Cheap clothing*. You're better off with a handful of quality clothes than a closet full of cheap ones. Inexpensive clothing doesn't wear well—after a few cleanings it looks shapeless and worn.

- *The corporate uniform*. In the 1970s, it was de rigueur to wear a man-cut blazer, a matching A-line skirt, and a man-tailored shirt—otherwise known as the corporate uniform. That was assimilation strategy—if we look like men, we'll be accepted like men—and it's no longer necessary. Women aren't a rarity anymore in the executive suites of America. We can go back to dressing like women (professional women, of course), because being female is no longer something we have to hide.

- *Dressing like a man*. You're a woman—dress like one. A professional look is a polished, more formal look, and for that reason, except in *very* casual companies, I object to women wearing slacks in the office. Female executives should wear dresses or skirts, heels, and hose.

THOSE LITTLE EXTRAS

Accessories make a huge difference in an outfit—the difference between nice and noticed. They count because they show that you have the capacity to plan down to the last detail. A black skirt and a black-beige print blouse look nice. But add tinted hose, black shoes, black and gold earrings with a matching black and gold bracelet, and you have a tight, attractive, professional look.

Jewelry. Earrings are the most important piece of jewelry you can wear. Not little gold balls that you wear every day, but earrings that are especially chosen to coordinate with the outfit you're wearing. Coordinate them with the rest of your jewelry—necklaces, bracelets, pins, and your watch. Avoid anything that looks cheap.

Shoes. The professional look requires pumps. You can get away with an open toe or a slingback, but not with sandals, clogs, flats, shoes with short chunky heels, party shoes, or any shoe that is dirty, scuffed, or noticeably worn.

Perfume. A light, delicate scent is fine for the office, but be careful of overdoing it. If people frequently comment on how nice you smell, you're wearing too much.

THE FINISHING "TOUCH"

Nothing ruins an image faster than pointing to a particularly important statistic in the report you compiled and doing so with a finger that has a bitten nail and ragged cuticles. Your hands are noticed more often than you imagine, and how they look says a lot about your attention to detail.

Turn your hand palm up, and measure how much of your nail shows above the tip of your finger. If it is less than 1/16", your nails are too short. If it is more than 1/4", your nails are too long. They should be nicely rounded, not pointed, and not squared off in the corners.

Use nail polish, if you have the time and energy to keep it looking nice. If you can't maintain it, don't wear it. Nothing looks tackier than chipped and peeling nail polish.

Have an on-going maintenance program for your nails. Don't work on them once every 2 weeks—work on them whenever they need it. Trim loose ends on your cuticles before they become nasty tears. Use an emery board every time you snag a nail. If you are a nail biter, or your nails are weak, get acrylic nails. But don't make the mistake of getting them bright red and two inches long. The Dragon Lady look has been out for some time.

THE CONSEQUENCES OF A POOR APPEARANCE

Constant awareness of what's happening in the fashion and beauty world is crucial. Using your appearance to show that you know what's appropriate is the foundation for everything else you do—because not doing it can hold you back.

It's holding back a lady named Julie, and she doesn't even know it. Julie has fine straight hair that's cut very short. Instead of getting a permanent or using hot rollers or a curling iron, she does nothing. She just lets her hair air dry, and it hangs limply in little uneven wisps. She wears a slight amount of blue eye shadow, but no other make-up. The last time I saw her, she was wearing a short-sleeve madras shirt and a corduroy wrap-around skirt.

Julie works for a client of mine, a small college that is planning to expand their admissions department. She is bright and talented, and she would be a great admissions representative, but she's not going to get the job. Her boss feels her appearance doesn't reflect the progressive image of the college—many of their students are professional people enrolled in graduate night programs—but he doesn't have the nerve to tell her. So she's staying a secretary. Good product, sloppy packaging.

6. The total managerial image

Dressing like a manager is only half the battle. Everything around you should add to your managerial image—your work area, your professional accessories, your name, even what time you go to lunch. Good image-building requires thoroughness, and every detail should contribute to your executive appearance.

CREATE A MINI-OFFICE

At work, your furniture and accessories should announce that you're a woman who's moving ahead. Of course, that's easier said than done, if you're stuck with an old tin desk and a rusty filing cabinet. But even that old stuff can make you look more important, if you arrange it properly.

Companies are fond of the "bullpen" arrangement for secretaries, leaving them all out in a big open area. Or they put the secretaries out in the hall next to their bosses' offices. Either way, secretaries are definitely in the cheap seats. Having your own private space is an indication of managerial status—even the most humble supervisor has some sort of an office or cubicle. You may not have an office, or be able to get one right away, but you can create the impression of one by careful arrangement of the furniture you've got:

- Move your desk so that it's not lined up like all the other secretary desks, with everybody facing the same direction. Turn it away from the secretarial crowd, preferably facing the wall. Sitting with your back to the room creates a psychological barrier around you, and makes you look more like an assistant and less like a receptionist.

- Arrange your filing cabinets so they create a physical barrier around your desk and establish a divider between you and the other secretaries.

- Complain to your boss about the noise level, and ask to have partitions put around your work area to block off the sound of people talking and equipment running.

Tell your boss these are productivity-improving moves—to remove you from the general office noise, to get you out of the traffic pattern, to reduce the number of people who stop at your desk. (You don't need to say that you're really trying to improve your image.) Convince him that physical arrangements can help increase the amount of work you get done. Say, "I've really got a lot of work to do, and the noise level out by my desk is getting worse by the day. Would you have any objections if I put the green filing cabinet between my desk and Judy's as sort of a partition? I think it would be a big help in reducing interruptions and increasing the amount of work I get done."

Who could refuse?

WHAT YOUR DESK SAYS ABOUT YOU

Take a look at the top of your desk. It makes a statement about you, so be sure it's making the *right* statement.

TOO MESSY OR TOO CLEAN?

Is your desk piled 3 feet deep with papers, file folders, and print-outs? If so, it tells people you can't handle your job—not that you have an abundance of work to do. You may know exactly where everything is, but nobody will believe it, because people think a disorganized desk reflects a disorganized mind.

Is your desk agonizingly neat? An exquisitely tidy desk, with every pencil and paperclip perfectly aligned, is worse than a sloppy desk, because it's the sign of a narrow or underworked mind. Obsessive neatness suggests that you think cleanliness is more important than productivity. Or worse: if you have enough time to dust your type-writer and polish your stapler every day, you must have very few responsibilities and certainly no important ones. Unless you want the reputation of being compulsive or just taking up space on the payroll, you'd better clutter up your desk a little.

The ideal is somewhere in between. Your desk should look like you work there, that in fact you do a great deal of work there, but that you have it all under control. Before you leave each night, straighten up your desk and work area, but leave ample evidence that you have important responsibilities to come back to the next morning.

TOO PERSONAL?

Check the personal items on your desk. Do you have pictures of hubbie and the kids—or worse, you and your boyfriend at the beach? Have you brought in souvenirs of your trip to the World's Fair, or a kitten made out of seashells that your aunt in Florida sent you?

Personal items like that send out signals that you are not serious about your job, that other things in life are more important to you. Of course they are, but you've got to disguise that fact if you want to get ahead. As a secretary, you are already suspect—management be-lieves you secretly want to be home baking brownies instead of working in the office. Anything on your desk that shows an interest in the outside world confirms the suspicion that you're not career-ori-ented, that you really don't want to be there. Men can get away with personal mementos in their offices, but women still can't. A family portrait on a man's desk shows that under his tough, all-business exterior is a warm human being. A family portrait on a woman's desk makes people think she doesn't know what being tough and all-business is all about.

Take the pictures and souvenirs home, and tell the family you love them anyway.

THE BABY-BLUE BRIEFCASE SYNDROME

Your professional accessories—business stationery, briefcase, calendar, letter opener, etc.—are just that, are business tools that help you do your job, but they also provide an indication of your status and upward mobility. They don't have to be masculine, in fact they shouldn't be, but they do need to look like they belong to a woman on a fast career track. Don't sabotage your image with accessories that are silly, inappropriate, or overly feminine:

At one company I visited, the secretaries were allowed to order personalized memo paper. One secretary, Cindy, picked out a tasteful beige paper with green and brown pinstripes down the left-hand side. She had her full name, Cynthia Garfield, spelled out at the top of the paper. Cindy had a good grasp on what was appropriate for a woman who wanted to get ahead in this firm. Her memo pads were tasteful and fit perfectly into the corporate environment.

At the desk next to her, Vicki (actually Victoria) ordered pink memo paper. At the top was a little poodle wearing a flowerpot hat, along with the words "A Note from Vicki!". She used this note paper to write memos to her boss and other executives in the department, yet constantly complained that nobody took her seriously. She just couldn't figure it out.

A former secretary I talked to had just been promoted to assistant buyer in her company's purchasing department. We sat in her office at the end of one day discussing her good fortune and how hard she'd worked to get the promotion. As we got ready to leave, she reached behind her desk for the new briefcase she'd bought, and pulled out a huge, four-inch deep briefcase that was, I swear, bright baby blue.

During our conversation, I had suspected she might be in a little over her head. When I saw the briefcase, I was sure.

WHAT'S IN A NAME?

Your name and your signature are also professional accessories. How you handle them can make you more managerial—or less.

ESTABLISHING YOUR BUSINESS NAME

Decide what your official business name is, the one you will use to sign formal letters, memos, and other documents, the name typed in below your signature, the name that will be on your business cards.

Your primary consideration in selecting an official business name is the image it conveys to people who don't know you. "Cathi Thomas" creates a much different mental picture than "Catherine M. Thomas." "Cathi" has some desirable connotations—it's more open and personable—but it has considerably less authority, which can be a drawback for a secretary. Secretaries need all the authority trappings they can get.

What your official business name should be depends in part on what name you use now on a day-to-day basis, and what name you want to use in the future.

The standard business name. If you don't use a nickname of any kind, your official business name will be your first name, middle initial, and last name. Although not mandatory, your middle initial adds a greater feeling of authority to your name.

If you are married and want to retain your maiden name, you can use both, such as Janice Siegel Ferguson.

If your first name lacks authority. If your real name is Tami Susan Murray, you may want to use your full middle name to increase the authority level. Although more cumbersome, Tami Susan Murray is more authoritative than Tami Murray or Tami S. Murray.

If you're stuck with a really awful first name, and you're willing to go through a name change, use your first initial and your full middle name. That way Muffy McCafferty can become M. Madeline McCafferty, and you go from being a preppy to being a businesswoman. If you're already using your middle name, this treatment is a must—don't confuse people by signing a first name you don't use.

If you have an authoritative nickname. Some nicknames are as authoritative as the names they are derived from, such as Liz from Elizabeth, or Kate from Katherine. If you regularly use an authoritative nickname, and want to use it officially, drop your middle initial. A less formal business name is acceptable (if you're in a less formal industry), but a middle initial is out of place with it. Use Kate Moskin or Katherine C. Moskin, but not Kate C. Moskin.

If your regular nickname has no power. Your real name is Margaret Kathleen Lanham, but you always go by Peggi? Your official business name is still your first *real* name, middle initial or maiden name, and last name. But to establish that you want to be called Peggi, add your nickname in parentheses to your official business signature:

Sincerely,

Margaret (Peggi) K. Lanham
Communications Department

This is especially helpful to people you write to if your real name could be reduced to a variety of nicknames. Nicknames for Elizabeth could be Liz, Beth, Liza, Betty, Bess, Lisa, or Betsy. Putting the one you use in parentheses keeps the reader from having to guess. (Exception: never include your nickname when signing legal documents like contracts.)

If you have a genderless name or nickname. Names like Pat or Chris, or initial-names like KC or BG, create problems for people who don't know you. Are you male or female? Don't leave them guessing. If your official business name doesn't clear up the gender problem, type *Ms.* in parentheses in front of your name:

Sincerely,

(Ms.) Chris Miller
Housewares Division

Don't put *Miss* or *Mrs.*; it puts too much emphasis on your marital status. And when you sign, just write *Chris Miller*, not the *Ms.*

If you are regularly called by your initials, such as BG, you have a choice:

Beverly (BG) N. Grant

or

(Ms.) BG Grant

DON'T HIDE BEHIND YOUR INITIALS

If you aren't referred to by your initials, don't use them for your official business name, such as S. L. Watkins, to disguise the fact that you are a woman. That ploy was effective 10 or 15 years ago when being female meant immediate discrimination from suppliers, hotels, banks, and other executives. Back then it was advantageous to have them find out later rather than sooner that they were dealing with a woman. But today it's pretentious; and it creates the same gender identification problems as people with names like Pat or KC.

HOW TO CHANGE YOUR NAME

If you want to begin using a more authoritative name or drop your nickname, don't simply announce that starting tomorrow you are

Barbara instead of Bunny, and correct everyone who slips and calls you by your old name. Make the transition as painless as possible for the people you work with:

1. *Don't mention a minimal change.* If you're going from Patti to Patricia, or from Deb to Deborah, no announcement is necessary. Nobody's going to get confused if mail arrives addressed to "Patricia" instead of "Patti," or if people ask for "Deborah" instead of "Deb" on the phone.

   Only correct someone if you are introduced by your nickname. When the person introducing you says, "This is Patti McCormick," smile, and as you extend your hand for a handshake (yes, shake hands with *everybody* you are introduced to), mildly correct the introduction by simply saying, "Patricia."

   Once you stop using your nickname, people in the office will gradually catch on and stop using it, too.

2. *Inform the people you work with if you make a major change.* When making a radical change, like going from Betsy to Liz, or from your first name to your middle name (say, from Bertha to Evelyn), you have to advise those you work with. Otherwise, they'll respond to callers by saying "Who? We don't have an Evelyn working here."

   A brief memo to people in your immediate department should handle it. If anyone asks, be up front about your reasons—tell them you want a more adult name or a more attractive name. They'll understand. But don't lean on them if they forget. Old habits die hard.

3. *Start using your "new" name right away.* Begin signing your letters and memos immediately with your new name, and answer the phone with it. If callers are confused because the change is drastic, explain briefly that you're using Evelyn now and not Bertha, and move quickly into the conversation.

4. *Be patient, but don't give up.* Some people, out of habit, stubbornness, or spite, will never call you by another name. Be patient, but don't let them wear you down—don't give up and

go back to your nickname. As you progress in management, you will develop a new circle of friends and associates who won't have any problem at all calling you by the name of your choice.

The higher you go in the organization, the less you should use an unauthoritative nickname, even in day-to-day interaction in the office. If your nickname is cutesy and could be easily expanded to your full name, such as Susi into Susan, or Ellie into Eleanor, start using your full name immediately—both verbally and in writing.

WHAT YOUR SIGNATURE SAYS ABOUT YOU

Take a look at your signature. It provides subtle clues about your status in the company. Managers are always looking for ways to do things faster, quicker, and more efficiently, and that philosophy carries over to their handwriting. They take shortcuts to get it done and over with. The more they write and the more they sign, the more illegible their writing gets and the more stylized their signature becomes. Because most secretaries don't write much and rarely sign their names, they still have nicely rounded, well-spaced penmanship—and it gives away their status in the company.

Your signature is your trademark; it makes a statement about you. It can say you are assertive and on the move, or it can say that you are timid and content to stay where you are.

Look at these signatures:

Karen K. Robinson
Vice President

(signature)

Charlotte Thorne
Personnel Manager

(signature)

Sherri Few
Secretary

(signature)

Denise Faulkenbury
Secretary

The difference between the executive signatures and the secretary signatures is obvious. The secretary signatures are weak; they don't make their owners look bold and professional. The executive signatures are strong, and they make a very positive statement.

Your signature is especially important when you use something ambiguous like "Purchasing Department" instead of a title to avoid identification as a secretary. A strong signature over "Purchasing Department" might belong to an executive whose company eschews the vanity of titles. A weak signature says: "I don't have a title, because I don't have any authority around here."

Make sure *your* signature sends the right message about you. It should say, "I'm important, I'm successful, and I'm proud of it. I'm not intimidated by the business world."

9 TO 5 AND BEYOND

Time is another area secretaries let work against them, because they underestimate what long hours (or the *appearance* of long hours) can do for their image. Secretaries may work hard, but they seldom work long. When forced to work overtime, the wailing can be heard all the way to the Federal Bureau of Unfair Labor Practices.

Managers, at least successful ones, have a different attitude toward time. Managers feel time is a resource—like money or employees or raw materials—that has to be managed. They don't regard time as something they give to the company in exchange for a paycheck, that they owe the company the hours from 8:30 to noon, and from 1:00 to 5:00. They have a commitment to get the job done, and if it takes from 8:30 until midnight, so be it.

STOP PUNCHING THAT TIME CLOCK

Most secretaries, on the other hand, have a factory-worker mentality about time. The company only pays them for 8 hours a day, so that's all the company gets—unless of course, the company wants to start paying overtime.

In large companies, you can practically set your watch by the secretaries. Herds of them enter the building at 8:30 sharp, leave precisely at high noon, re-enter the building on the stroke of 1:00, and stream out again before the clock has stopped striking 5:00. It's as if a silent whistle blows four times a day, telling them exactly when to start and stop work.

One of the most pathetic sights I've ever seen was a secretary with stacks of work on her desk who shut off her typewriter at 12:00, opened up a brown paper bag, ate her lunch, then read a magazine for an hour. Promptly at 1:00, she turned her typewriter back on and continued working. The company owed her a lunch hour, and by God, she was going to take it—no matter how much work there was to be done.

WORKING OVERTIME—FOR YOU

Until you get rid of this time-clock attitude, you can forget about becoming a manager. I'm not advocating 60-hour weeks—you're not getting paid enough to do that—but you should be willing to work 3 to 5 extra hours a week (up to an hour a day) without complaining or asking for overtime pay.

Put in those 3 to 5 hours, not just for the company, but for *yourself*. When you work overtime, you aren't giving away hours of your precious personal time to the company. Instead, you are improving your image, making yourself look more dedicated, accomplishing more, and earning points for being more productive. You are making yourself look more professional and more committed to the company and to your career.

The company is not your adversary. It's not you versus the company. Everything you do at work you actually do for yourself. When you work extra hours, it makes *you* look good. When you run an errand for your boss on your lunch hour, *you* look more dedicated. When you get coffee for your boss's visitors, *you* appear more cordial and company-oriented. When you make that extra effort, the company is not getting one over on you—quite the contrary, you are making an investment in your future. Show your boss and other executives that you have a managerial outlook on your workload, that you are willing to give the extra time it takes to get your job done and done well. You may not get paid today for the extra hours you work, but you'll get paid tomorrow—with a better job and a higher salary.

COORDINATE YOUR HOURS WITH YOUR BOSS'S

Adjust the overtime hours you work to your boss's schedule. Everybody has a different time they prefer to work—some bosses come in late and stay late, others come in early and leave relatively early. By matching your extra hours to your boss's, your overtime will get more attention and gratitude.

I once worked for a man who came in very early, sometimes as early as 5:30 in the morning, and always left promptly at 5:00 p.m. I could never get to work early, in fact, being a "night person," I just barely made it in on time. But I worked a lot of hours and usually stayed until 7:00 or 8:00 p.m. My 10-hour days meant little to my boss, though, because he wasn't around while I was putting them in.

If your boss gets in early like mine did, it's especially important that you be on time or slightly early. Once the workday begins and the phone starts ringing, your absence hinders your boss's productivity, and he won't be happy about it. Conversely, if your boss comes in late, he may not notice the extra effort you make to arrive a half hour early. He will notice, though, that at 5:00 when he's really busy, you're on your way out the door.

Of course, there are the super-achievers who come in early and leave late, but don't drive yourself crazy trying to keep up with them. Any more than 5 hours of overtime is uselessly sacrificing your personal life for the company, and it buys you nothing except a feeling of being used. The more you work overtime, the less it is regarded as a favor, and the more it becomes accepted and expected behavior. Be cooperative and flexible, but don't run yourself into the ground.

AFTER-HOURS: EXECUTIVES ONLY

My ex-boss notwithstanding, most executives work after 5:00. Putting in overtime at the end of the day can give you an entrée into the management world, and start you on the road to becoming a legitimate member of it, because after-hours is almost exclusively the province of executives. The secretaries, clerks, first-line supervisors, and those in the managerial slow lane have gone home, and only the real movers and shakers stay on.

When I first started working as a secretary, I made it a point to never leave for the day before my boss left. (Fortunately for me, he was always gone by 5:30 or 6:00.) I'd always stay at least 15 minutes longer than he did, which drove him crazy, because I appeared to be more dedicated than he was. But that appearance gave me an edge. Frequently, other executives in the department would come by to see my boss after hours, and since he wasn't there, they gradually began talking to me. Because I was there in the twilight "executive hours," I seemed to be more than a secretary. I gained respect and credibility, and I began to be included in the managerial circles.

It also wasn't long before I knew almost as much about what was happening in our division as my boss did. After-hours conversations tend to be more informal, more leisurely, and definitely more open than daytime conversations. On a busy Thursday afternoon with everyone in the office, news of the impending reorganization is considered confidential. Later that evening when most everyone's gone home, that news gets passed around fairly easily. When you're there too, it gives you a chance to tap into the executive grapevine for information that may be useful in advancing your career—like new jobs opening up or problems that you can help solve.

To strengthen your executive appearance, do what appears to be nonsecretarial work after hours. Don't spend from 5:00 to 7:00 p.m. typing letters or filing. If you have reports to do, information to collect, trade publications to read, anything that doesn't look like routine secretarial work, do it during the twilight hours. You look more managerial, and when executives stroll by and ask what you're doing, you can say something like, "Just trying to put these sales reports together for tomorrow." They can relate to that, and it may lead to longer conversations with them—business conversations that can help you work your way up. If you have a report or memo that needs to be distributed, after 5:00 is a great time to hand-deliver the copies. It gets you into the executives' offices and makes your overtime visible and noticeable.

YOU'RE ONLY MINUTES AWAY FROM A MANAGERIAL IMAGE

Business is still a game of images, and the appearance of long hours can often be as effective as longer hours themselves. With a few time tricks, you can score points for being a go-getter without spending every waking minute in the office. Use them to make it *appear* that you work longer hours than you really do, that you put in much more time than the average secretary.

Lunch is a perfect opportunity to use time tricks. Don't sacrifice your lunch hours, and work from noon until 1:00. If you're working hard, you need the break. You need the mental relief of getting out of the building and away from your desk for awhile. But more than that—working through lunch is a wasted gesture, *because no one notices you were there.* Everyone else goes out for lunch, and they don't realize you stayed in.

Do, however, make it *appear* that you don't take lunch. Don't charge out the door at precisely 12:00 with the rest of the secretaries; instead, leave at 10 minutes after 12:00, after they and most of the executives have left the building. Then return to your desk at 12:55, instead of 1:00. (You can cut your return a little closer, because people rarely come back early from lunch.)

Those who took a regular lunch hour will think you never left your desk. Many of them will ask, "Did you eat lunch?"—which gives you an opportunity to say with a weary, hard-working smile, "Oh, I just ran out and got a quick bite to eat." That quick bite was only 15 minutes quicker than the one they got, but they'll never know.

In the morning and at the end of the day, be at your desk when the other secretaries are coming and going en masse. Come in 5 minutes early in the morning and leave at least 10 minutes late at night.

Enhance your nose-to-the-grindstone image by *working*—don't spend those extra minutes chit-chatting or washing coffee cups. In the morning, be busily typing letters, making phone calls, or filling out reports by the time everyone else arrives. Don't be coerced into making coffee every morning just because you arrive before the other secretaries. Do your share, but make them take their turn—it's not your fault they aren't as motivated as you are. At the end of the day, when the other secretaries wind down at 4:45 and kill those last 15 minutes by staring at the clock or cleaning off their desks, *keep working*. And work until at least 10 minutes after they're gone.

When the secretary herd stampedes out of the building at 5:00 on the dot, and you're not with them, you can be sure the right people will notice.

ABSENCE DOES NOT MAKE THE HEART GROW FONDER

Unless it's absolutely necessary, don't be gone for personal reasons during the regular part of the working day. Your absence forces other people into doing more jobs—answering phones, looking for files, typing last minute letters—not an activity designed to win friends and influence people.

Schedule any personal appointments as close as possible to the lunch hour, then skip lunch or bring your lunch back with you to the office.

Minimize your absences from the office even when they are business-related. Don't dawdle when you have an errand in the middle of the morning or afternoon. Do it as quickly as possible and get back to the office. Or do it at lunch time *without* extending your lunch hour to cover the time you "lost." Cut your lunch hour short, and get back to the office on time.

> I recently had an 11:45 appointment with a client, arrived early, and was sitting in the lobby waiting for her, when her secretary Sally stormed in. Not realizing I was there, she snapped to the other secretary, "My boss wants me to take this package to the downtown office on my lunch hour. Can you believe that?" She was really indignant. "I'm not doing anything for this company on *my* lunch hour! Tell her I'll be a half hour late getting back." She stomped out.
>
> Good attitude, Sally. Go directly to your desk, do not pass GO, do not collect a better job.

Instead of exhibiting an "I can't wait to get out and stay out of this office" attitude, make them think that you can't bear to be away from it.

THE MAKE-IT-UP PHILOSOPHY

While some secretaries feel abused if they work an hour of unpaid overtime, they feel no obligation whatsoever to the company if they take 3 hours off to go to the dentist. Because many secretaries are underpaid, they don't mind shorting the company an hour here, an afternoon there. They figure any time they can squeeze out of the workday for themselves is a bonus. But they're wrong. You may not be convinced you should put in more than 8 hours a day, but you certainly don't owe the company any less.

Many bosses keep a mental account of how many hours you spend in the office each week—and naturally, absences loom larger than overtime. If your boss feels that you're working less than you should be, he feels cheated, and your image goes down the drain. Regardless of your salary, you accepted the responsibility of delivering 40 hours of work every week. If you only deliver 35, you've broken that agreement, and you're headed for trouble.

Develop a "make it up" philosophy. If you have a doctor appointment or car trouble, tell your boss that you'll stay late to make up the time you missed. He may tell you that's not necessary, but make the time up anyway. Show that you understand the bargain you've made with the company and that you intend to keep it.

Always inform your boss that you are making up time. It does you no good to make up missed hours if nobody knows you're doing it. Don't announce self-righteously to your boss, "I'm staying late tonight because I owe you a half-hour from coming in late yesterday, and I don't want you to think I'm taking advantage of you." Just casually say, "If you need anything done this evening, I'll be here until 6:00 or so. That flat tire this morning really set my schedule back, and I want to get caught up."

Make up the time you miss (illnesses excepted), but always get credit for it. Give a little more than you need to, and build up an account that you can use in negotiating a raise or a better job.

Cheryl, secretary to a small company, had a real shortcoming—she was always late to work. Not a few minutes late, but a half-hour or 45 minutes late. She was always running behind, and always in a race to catch up with the workload, which was extremely heavy. But no one in the office had any sympathy for her, because she was cutting her work week short by about 3 hours—at their expense. She was very good at her job, could handle all kinds of responsibility, and was interested in getting promoted to a better position, but instead of discussing career plans with her, her boss finally told her to either arrive on time or get another job.

If Cheryl had stayed late or worked weekends to make up the time, it might have been different. But she didn't. She didn't have a make-it-up philosophy.

BABYSITTERS AND OTHER CHILD-RELATED PROBLEMS

Children can represent a real problem when you're trying not to miss work. They get sick and have to be picked up from school, or wake up sick and never go to school in the first place. They have to go to the doctor, they forget to return their report card, or any number of things that can call you away from the office—if you let them.

Obviously you can't send your children to school when they are ill, but long or frequent absences from the office because of your children is poor form. Being a businesswoman means keeping your personal responsibilities covered during the day while you're at work. Managers don't stay home all day because their children are ill, and neither should you.

Shop around your neighborhood for someone who is home during the day who can babysit if your children get sick. If you must leave to pick your children up from school, take them directly to the babysitter and get back to the office.

And don't allow your children to harass you with phone calls all day. Make it clear that your job is important and that it is *not* all right for them to call you whenever they get the urge. One secretary I knew allowed her daughter to call at any time for any reason. Her daughter would call at 3:00 when she got home from school and ask if she could go to a friend's house. At 4:00 she would call to ask what they were having for dinner. At 4:45 she would call and ask if Susan was going to leave the office on time.

Until they are teenagers, children need babysitters or somewhere to go after school so they are not left alone. You can't raise children over the phone, and children get lonely and scared when left by themselves. The increasingly common situation of "latch-key" children, kids who have no babysitter after school but themselves, is not a healthy one for your children or for you. You get no points for being a professional if your boss wants to talk to you and you're on the phone arguing with your son about whether he can ride his bike to K-mart.

As cruel as it may sound, you have to reduce the amount of personal and social activities you do during your workday. When you take the afternoon off to supervise the third grade Valentine's Day party, you are not sending a career-oriented message to your boss.

NO COOKIES OR COSMETICS

In addition to foregoing elementary school get-togethers, don't sell cosmetics, cookies, magazines, or anything else in the office. Not if you want to become a manager. People .dedicated to their careers don't use office time to sell products to their office associates. Nothing lowers your status more than having a stack of cosmetics or cookies on your desk that have to be handed out to your office "customers."

IF IT'S FOR SECRETARIES, POLITELY DECLINE

Future managers don't participate in activities specifically designed for secretaries.

Wait, you're saying. I went to a secretarial seminar last year, and it was great. I got out of the office for the day, had lunch in a posh hotel downtown (or better yet, out of town), and I had the opportunity to meet other secretaries and exchange ideas.

Close, but not quite. The real story is that you got a day or two off, spent some of the company's money, learned absolutely nothing you didn't already know, and probably had an all-day bitch session about how awful bosses are and how terrible it is to be a secretary. You got a break from the office, but you wasted your time at a seminar that did nothing but reinforce your status as a secretary.

If you want to become a manager, don't go to secretarial seminars. Going to a secretarial seminar says that either you *want* to be a secretary, or you aren't totally comfortable with your secretarial skills and you need some additional training. It doesn't convey the impression that you could do your job with your eyes closed and that you're ready to move up.

Seminars, particularly out-of-town and particularly in resort locations, have long been rewards and mini-vacations for managers.

Your boss may offer to send you to a seminar as a perk, his way of giving you a bonus, which is great, but avoid the stigma of going to a *secretarial* seminar. Tell your boss, "I'm not sure I'd get anything out of this. Most of the topics seem rather basic. *However*, I think I could really benefit from a seminar on data processing (or accounting or whatever skill area you need to work on)—it would have a greater impact on my job performance. Why don't I see if I can find a seminar like that?"

Of course, you should make sure you aren't being sent to a secretarial seminar because the boss feels you need improvement in some area. Find out if he has any concerns about your current job performance, because you'll have to get those corrected before you can move on. If he says you seem to have trouble managing your workload, ask to go to a time management program. If he thinks you could handle customers better, suggest a communications seminar. Just make sure they are seminars for *managers*, not secretaries.

Future managers also don't start secretarial support groups or unionize. Spend your time, money, and energy on advancing your position in the company. For the foreseeable future, that's the best use of your resources.

7. Sound like a manager

A managerial image tells the people you work with that you're on the move. But how do you spread that message to people outside the company, or to people in other departments? By communicating like a manager. When people outside your company or department receive a call from you, let them know they're hearing from someone who's on the way up. When they find out that you are a secretary, let them be surprised: "She's a secretary? I thought she was a manager or supervisor. Well, if she isn't one, she ought to be!"

Don't reduce your chances for success by sounding like a secretary.

WHY SOUND LIKE A MANAGER?

The more managerial you appear to be, the more managerial you can become. Sounding like a manager adds another dimension to your managerial image. It helps the powers-that-be to visualize you as a manager. And as I've said before, when they can visualize you as a manager, they will make you one. So make sure you are obviously out of place behind the typewriter, instead of quite comfortable there.

MANAGERS DON'T WANT TO TALK TO SECRETARIES

Another important reason for sounding like a manager is that executives don't want to deal with secretaries. They don't mind leaving messages with them or setting up appointments through them, but they don't want to *work* with them. The higher a person is in an organization, the more true this is, and the less likely he or she is to give a secretary anything but his name, rank, and telephone number.

Secretaries who insist on being nothing but message-takers add fuel to this fire with responses like:

"I don't know anything about that. You'll have to talk to someone else. Can you hold while I try to find somebody?"

"Mr. Smith isn't here right now, and I have no idea where he is or when he's coming back."

"There's no one in the office right now who can help you."

"All I can do is take a message."

"Could you spell your last name for me just one more time?"

The anti-secretary attitude is also compounded by managers who use their secretaries as pawns in little ego games. Do these sound familiar?

The Game: You Can Wait Because You're Less Important

A secretary calls and says, "I have a call for Mr. Brown from Mr. Smith. Is he in?"

Mr. Brown gets on the line and hears, "One minute, Mr. Brown, Mr. Smith will be right with you." Then Mr. Brown gets to hold and listen to elevator music while the secretary gets Mr. Smith on the line.

Mr. Smith is so important (just ask him) that he can't be kept waiting—but Mr. Brown, a much less important person (according to Mr. Smith) can be. Very degrading.

The Game: It's Too Trivial for Me to Handle

"Mr. Brown? This is Mr. Smith's secretary. He asked me to call you back about your request for information on our new contract policy. I'll be glad to explain it to you."

Mr. Smith is too important (just ask him) to deal with matters so mundane, and Mr. Brown is not worthy (according to Mr. Smith) of the time it would take Mr. Smith to personally return the call.

People don't want to talk to secretaries, because useless secretaries and arrogant managers have made them feel put-off and put-down when they do.

So the best thing to do is make them think you're *not* a secretary.

DON'T LET THE TELEPHONE WORK AGAINST YOU

It's not hard to tell when you've reached a secretary on the phone. The first thing she says almost always gives her away. If it doesn't, her second response will. You know you've reached a secretary, because secretaries talk on the phone in predictable ways—predictable *secretarial* ways.

Let's look in on the firm of Promotions Unlimited, where the phone is ringing in several departments:

"Promotions Unlimited, this is Nicki." Is Nicki (actually Nicole) a secretary? Probably. A manager would have added her last name.

"Good morning, Promotions Unlimited." Is this a secretary? No doubt. She doesn't even use her *first* name.

"Mr. Brogan's office. May I help you?" This isn't a person, it's an office. One secretary so unfailingly answered the phone "Mr. Klein's office," even on internal calls, that the other managers began calling her "Mr. Klein's office." "After a few weeks of that," she said, "I started using my own name on the phone. People said they were glad to find out that I had one."

Even in this more enlightened era, people still assume that if a woman answers the phone, she's a secretary. A man could answer the phone using any of the above responses and not be taken for a secretary. But secretaries and receptionists are an organization's first line of contact for the outside world, and according to the Bureau of Labor Statistics, over 99 percent of the secretaries and receptionists in this country are women. So a female voice answering the phone still spells "secretary" to the caller—unless you make it sound otherwise.

HOW MANAGERS ANSWER THE PHONE

Nicole, Mr. Brogan's secretary, could have answered the phone in any of the following ways and sounded like a manager instead of a secretary:

"Promotions Unlimited, Nicole Perry speaking."

Or: *"Purchasing Department. This is Nicole Perry."*

Or the best, a simple: *"Nicole Perry."*

With responses like this, Nicole could be taken for a vice president whose secretary happened to be away from her desk or a department manager who likes to answer her own phone.

Even if her boss insists on *his* name being used, she can say: *"Mr. Brogan's line, Nicole Perry speaking."* "Line" sounds less secretarial than "office."

THE SECOND-RESPONSE GIVEAWAY

If Nicole doesn't sound like a secretary, the caller may plunge ahead, thinking he's reached someone who can help him: "I need some clarification on a purchase order your company placed last week for 12,000 widgets. You didn't specify whether you wanted the 3-inch or the 4-inch size." The caller is hopeful Nicole will know something about this—maybe she's the buyer who issued the unsigned purchase order.

"I'm sorry," Nicole says, "there's no one here who can help you. They're all out to lunch. Would you like to call back in an hour, or shall I take a message?"

So much for thinking Nicole is a buyer.

At best, Nicole is a secretary. Maybe one who just started working there this morning. She knows nothing about what's going on in her department; she doesn't tell the caller who to talk to, she doesn't even really want to take a message ("Would you like to call back . . .?").

Or maybe she's a passing stranger who wandered in off the street, answered the phone, and was bright enough to notice there was nobody around. That's the impression she gives.

SUCCESS MAY BE JUST A PHONE CALL AWAY

An astute secretary assumes every contact she makes may be helpful in her drive for success. The supplier who calls your purchasing department may need to hire a salesperson next year. The vice president of acquisitions who calls your financial department may need an assistant next month.

Nicole should have answered the phone with: "This is Nicole Perry." Then said, "I believe Mary Kenyon issued that purchase order, but she has left for lunch and isn't expected back this afternoon. I'll see what I can find out and try to call you back later today. If I can't locate the information, I'll have Mary call you first thing tomorrow morning."

The caller still doesn't know Nicole is a secretary. She could be a manager in the purchasing department, another purchasing agent, maybe even Mary's boss. She certainly sounds more efficient than Mary, who forgot to sign the purchase order and specify the part size. If Nicole follows through, chances are the caller will ask to speak to *her* the next time he calls.

BE MORE THAN A CALL ROUTER

Don't be a mere conduit, passing calls and requests on to someone else. Everybody's looking for a quick and easy way to get things done, a fast way to get information, a shortcut to getting results, and that gives you a chance to insert yourself into the action. By giving people the help they want, you can start taking on management responsibilities.

Chris, just out of college with a journalism degree, took a secretary's job in the research department of a large corporation. She quickly realized she was in an opportune place for getting to know people—executives from all over the company called in with requests, reports, and project proposals. "I regarded everyone who called," she said, "as a potential boost to my career. Everyone I talked to might, somewhere down the line, help me move up in the company. So I never let anyone off the phone without asking them the all-important question: 'Is there anything *I* can do for you?' You'd be surprised how often people said 'yes' to the neophyte 22-year-old on my end of the line.

"I always tried to be pleasant and helpful, and I followed through on every request—even if it meant calling back to say I couldn't locate the information and I'd have to pass the request along to my boss. I gained a reputation for being easy to deal with and eager to help."

Today, 15 years later, Chris is the national accounts manager for one of the corporation's prime profit centers, with a compensation package (salary plus commissions) totaling nearly $80,000 a year.

MAKE GOOD ON YOUR OFFER TO HELP

Follow-through is essential. Don't ask if you can help, then drop the ball because you aren't sure how to respond to the caller's request. Here are two different ways a call might go—one in your favor, one not:

The caller: "Richard Zimmerman, please?"

You: "I'm sorry, he's in a meeting. This is Maggie Stein, is there anything I can help you with?"

The caller: "This is Alan in the long-range planning department. I wanted to know when Richard's industrial development proposal would be finished. I could really use his estimates for the project I'm working on."

You, with the wrong answer: "Oh, I don't know anything about that. You'll have to talk to Mr. Zimmerman—I'll have him call you."

And you fade out of sight. You asked if you could help, but you didn't follow through. You might as well not have asked in the first place.

Here's how to stay *in* the picture:

You, with the right answer: "I know Richard has been working on that report, but I don't know what his completion date is. If it's going to be a while before the proposal is finished, maybe we can get you some preliminary numbers that will work for your project. Which part of the proposal were you specifically interested in? I'll check with Richard and get back to you. Will tomorrow morning be soon enough?"

You introduced yourself, you offered to help, you promised to get the information the caller needed, and you even provided a suggestion to help him out.

STAY INVOLVED

When Richard gets out of his meeting don't just turn Alan's request over to him. Instead, take over responsibility for it. Inform him of the situation, *and ask if you can continue to handle communications with Alan.* Ask your boss:

"Are you close enough to completion on your report that we can give Alan final numbers? Or can we send him some preliminary figures?" And most importantly: "I told him I would try to get back to him by tomorrow morning." Not that Richard would call him back, but that *you* would.

In most cases, your boss will let you take care of it, because you're making life easier for him. You're handling routine business for him.

Staying involved means continual follow-through. Stay with it until the end. No loose ends. Your goal is for people to ask for you, rather than your boss, whenever possible. They'll do that only if they know they can count on you for results.

I recently called my insurance agent, and an unfamiliar voice answered the phone. "Who's this?" I asked.

"This is Phyllis. Ray's with a client right now. Is there something I can do for you?"

Ray must have hired an assistant, I thought. I explained the information I needed, and Phyllis said, "I'll look that up and call you right back." Great, I thought, Ray's always been hard to get in touch with; an efficient assistant will make dealing with him so much easier.

A day went by, two days went by—finally on the following Monday, I called back. Ray's regular secretary, Beth, answered the phone.

"Hi, Beth," I said. "Phyllis was going to call me back with some information last week but I haven't heard from her."

Sounding disgusted, Beth said, "That doesn't surprise me. She was just a temporary we hired to help out while I was gone last week. Apparently she promised everybody she'd do everything for them, then did absolutely nothing."

So much for follow-through. When Ray finally does get around to hiring an assistant, Phyllis won't have to worry about him hounding her to take the job.

FIVE EASY STEPS INTO MANAGEMENT ACTIVITIES

To sum up, five simple steps can put you into the flow of management business in your office:

1. Always introduce yourself on the telephone—first *and* last name.

2. If the person the caller wants to talk to is not around, always ask if *you* can be of help.

3. Commit to helping the caller—even if it's only to find out when your boss can call him back.

4. Follow through, and actually help the caller. Don't throw messages on your boss's desk and expect him to follow up on your

promises. When you make a commitment, live up to it—it's *your* reputation that's on the line.

5. Establish yourself as the contact point for future calls.

KEEP THE BOSS ON YOUR SIDE

Some of you have paranoid bosses who may see this behavior as impudent or threatening. If you're working for someone this short-sighted, you need to exercise a little political savvy and some good old-fashioned psychology.

Bosses who are insecure and afraid of talented subordinates fear that those subordinates will outshine them or usurp their authority or steal their jobs. But their insecurity makes them easy to manipulate if you're careful. Constant praise is your best bet—light and continual ego-building—along with constant assurance that your sole motivation in life is to lighten the staggering workload they, as important members of the business community, have to bear. They'll buy it every time.

TALK LIKE A MANAGER

Once you insert yourself into management projects, beef up your image by talking about yourself and your work like a manager would:

1. *Refer to yourself by name.* Don't call yourself "Mr. Zimmerman's secretary." A manager would never say "This is Mr. Zimmerman's director of marketing," would she? You have a name—use it.

2. *Refer to your department, not your boss's office.* Don't say, "This is Maggie in Mr. Zimmerman's office." To people inside the company, say, "This is Maggie Stein in the purchasing department." To people outside the company, say, "This is Maggie Stein with Promotions Unlimited."

3. *Refer to your department, instead of your position.* Don't advertise your current secretarial status by saying "This is Maggie Stein, the secretary in the purchasing department." A simple "This is Maggie Stein in purchasing" is sufficient.

4. *Make projects sound like your work, not your boss's.* When your boss assigns a project, or a portion of a project, to you, don't dilute that authority by referring to it as your boss's work. That project (or portion thereof) is now *your* project. Talk about it that way. Don't say "I'm doing a report for my boss," when you can say "*I'm* working on a cost-benefit analysis." Don't preface requests with "My boss asked me to get some numbers for him for a report he's working on," when you can say "*We* need some numbers for a report *we're* working on."

5. *Sound as if you have authority.* Don't hedge every commitment with "I'll have to ask my boss." If you feel you should ask your boss, tell the caller, "I think we can help you out with that, but let me check into it a little further and call you back to confirm it." No need to say you have to get permission.

6. *Learn business-ese.* Every organization has its own language, its own buzzwords, its own way of talking about things. Learn that language and don't be embarrassed to use it. If the executives in the computer firm you work for are fond of talking about "downloading" information from headquarters to the regional offices, "downloading" should become a regular part of your corporate vocabulary.

   The language spoken by business executives around the country has a cadence, a ring, a sound all its own. It has a certain formality not found in ordinary conversations. Take this simple question: "Have you made up your mind yet?" In business-ese, it sounds like:

   > "I just wanted to touch base with you and see if you had had an opportunity to review that proposal I sent to you last week, and come to any decision yet. Perhaps there are some questions I can answer for you? Or if you need more time, I'll be glad to call you back at a time that might be more convenient for you."

It's formal, polite, diplomatic, and usually full of industry-specific buzzwords. The larger the organization, the more formal, polite, diplomatic, and buzzwordy it gets. Listen to the executives in your office, and no matter how stiff or phony it sounds to you, start talking like them. You need to learn the language—you'll be using it constantly as a manager.

7. *Get on a first-name basis as quickly as possible.* The first time you talk to someone, it is only good manners to address them as *Mr.* or *Ms.* The fourth time you talk to someone (assuming you're working with them and not just routing calls), it's subservient. You don't need to ask for permission to call them by their first name, just start doing it. As a rule, as soon as someone calls *you* by your first name, you should feel free to call *them* by their first name—except, of course, for callers who are quite a bit older or at a much higher level in the organization than you are. The 80-year-old chairman of the board won't appreciate it if you address him as "Milt" the second time he calls.

8. *Sound confident.* Speak up, be relaxed and informal, and don't hem-and-haw. Sound like you have a right to be there. Sound like you know what you're doing, and that you can handle whatever comes up. Sound convinced of that, and the caller will be, too.

YOUR VOICE'S APPEARANCE

Your voice has an "appearance," and that appearance leaves a critical impression. Do you sound like a dynamic, confident person on the threshold of a brilliant management career, or do you sound like someone with no potential?

Don't assume that because you are an excellent secretary you convey an excellent impression on the phone. One secretary I know, though only in her thirties, sounds like an old lady on the phone—her voice is thin and creaky. Another secretary, whose voice is just fine, is so busy that she keeps working while on the phone, and she sounds distracted, uncertain, and unprofessional.

Here are some do's and don'ts to give your voice an authoritative quality and an executive appearance:

DO speak up. Don't yell, but speak in a full, well-modulated tone.

DO smile into the phone—it makes you sound pleasant. On days when you're less than cheerful, make it a point to take a deep breath and smile *before* you answer the phone.

DO lower your voice if it is squeaky or high-pitched.

DO give the caller your complete, undivided attention.

DO sound confident. Remember that you're an equal member of the team. Sound like it!

DON'T grovel. Be genuinely interested in helping, but don't fawn all over the caller, grateful for the privilege of serving.

DON'T be overly formal. Extreme formality is an admission of inferiority. Don't refer to your boss as *Mr.* or *Ms.*, as in "Mr. Zimmerman asked me to tell you . . . "—again, unless your boss's age or position dictate this extra formality. And don't address the caller as *sir* or *ma'am*. Managers don't talk like that, English butlers do.

DON'T wedge the phone into your shoulder or use a shoulder rest. It makes you mutter.

DON'T use phrases that indicate mental vacancy. If you find yourself saying "uh," "um," "gee, I don't know," or "I have no idea," put the caller on hold and think for a minute.

DON'T try to finish your filing or tune into the conversation at the next desk. And never let other people talk to you while you're on the phone—it's rude to the caller, and it indicates how low you are on the totem pole. People don't interrupt vice presidents while they're on the phone—why let them interrupt you?

DON'T be afraid to clarify what the caller has told you. There's nothing wrong with saying, "Just to make sure I understand what you need, let me go over this one more time." In fact, some callers (I'm one of them) appreciate any attempt to reduce miscommunication.

MAINTAINING EMOTIONAL CONTROL

Another trait essential for a managerial image is emotional control. You'll notice I didn't say emotional control is a *characteristic* of managers—I've worked with more managers than I care to remember who yelled, screamed, snarled, whined, sulked, pouted, cried (really!) and generally acted like anything *but* managers.

But like anybody else who's trying to get in, your behavior has to be one step better than those who are already there. It should not only be better, it should be exemplary.

THE THREE MANAGERIAL DISPOSITIONS

There are three, and only three, emotional attitudes you can display in the office and still be considered a management candidate:

1. *Genuine, but reserved, friendliness.* Don't be all business all the time. An important element of being promotable is being likable. People rarely promote people they don't like, especially if they'll be working closely with that person.

   Tell jokes, laugh when you're told one, relax and have a cup of coffee with the gang once in a while.

   But be reserved enough that co-workers don't mistake your friendliness for a shoulder to cry on, an offer to goof off together, or a sexual come-on. Take the time to ask, "how was your weekend," or "have you had any luck finding an apartment yet?" But don't say, "I heard your marriage is in trouble. Do you want to talk about it?"

   Save that level of concern for your family and closest friends. It's nice to be needed, but people with problems who find a sympathetic ear often don't know when to quit. They can't work because they're upset, and you can't work because they won't stop telling you about it.

Overly personal concern can also get misconstrued as a sexual advance—which means serious problems. A reputation as a flirt or a tease will ruin your career. Keep in mind that people are always watching for signs of an office affair—it usually doesn't take much to get the rumors started.

2. *Nose to the grindstone.* When there's work to be done (which should be most of the time, if you want to get ahead), do more than your share. Show them you regard hard work, deadlines, and pressure as a challenge, and that you enjoy rising to the occasion. Get serious, get tough, and get things done.

3. *Controlled displeasure.* Things invariably go wrong, and when they do, you don't have to hide your feelings. But you do have to control them. You can be annoyed, disappointed, concerned, bothered, chagrined, or impatient. But you *cannot* be defensive, hysterical, furious, grouchy, rude, loud, weepy, huffy, bitter, or sullen—at least not on the outside. Problems in the office are *business* problems. Handle them in a professional manner.

These three dispositions are not only acceptable, they are all *necessary* if you want to appear to be a well-rounded human being.

AVOID TYPICALLY "FEMALE" EMOTIONS

Because of the long-standing complaint that women are too emotional for the big bad business world, it's especially important to avoid emotions considered typically "female:"

Crying. Short of a death in the office, there is no excuse for public crying. No excuse whatsoever. If you have a personal crisis that causes you to cry, leave the office and go home—you won't get any work done anyway. If it's a business problem that brings on the tears, control yourself or remove yourself from the scene, but never, *ever* cry in front of a business associate over a business matter.

One secretary was denied admission to her company's management training program on the grounds that she was emotionally unstable—she had been seen crying in the office several times over her impending divorce.

Pouting. No matter how often pouting got you your way as a child, you're not a child now, and pouting is a totally inappropriate response to *anything* in the office. When you don't get your way, take it like a man (if you'll excuse the expression), put the best possible face on it, and go on. There will be other days when things *will* go your way.

Throwing temper tantrums. In a business context, throwing a temper tantrum constitutes anything from stomping off in a huff to telling someone off. A temper tantrum is the epitome of emotional immaturity. Business problems aren't solved by angry shouting; they're solved by taking corrective action—fixing the mistake, reprimanding or even firing the perpetrator, or setting up guidelines to prevent it from happening again.

Business people don't have fights in the sense that a husband and wife, or a parent and child, fight. They don't yell, slam doors, throw things, or not speak to each other. Business people fight more subtly—by backstabbing, in-fighting, spreading rumor and innuendo, and making power plays designed to reduce the opponent's status or position. All of which are techniques you need to know—not to use yourself, but so you can recognize when someone's using them on you.

THE ART OF EMOTIONAL CONTROL

Since most women were raised to freely express their emotions, getting control of them in the office can be difficult. When faced with highly charged emotional situations, keep the following in mind:

Diffuse the situation before it gets out of hand. When things go awry, address the problem as soon as possible. It benefits no one to pretend that problems or bad feelings don't bother you and hope they will go away. It lets resentment build until you blow up, or until somebody blows up at you.

Don't succumb to the End-of-the-World Syndrome. If you end up in an emotional confrontation anyway, keep in mind that business is business. On the world scale of importance, it ranks well below death, war, and personal bankruptcy. The world will not come to an end if you make a mistake or if your boss gets mad at you. Mistakes can be corrected, ruffled feathers can be smoothed, and relationships can be mended.

Your reaction can determine the outcome. The more professionally you react to an emotionally charged situation, the sooner it will be favorably (or at least tolerably) resolved. The more emotionally you react, the worse you make the problem, and the more prolonged its resolution will be.

Remember your career goals. Think about what an emotional outburst will do to your career plans. Two minutes of screaming and crying can undo the months of careful preparation you've done to put yourself in line for a management job.

Keep a stiff upper lip. If you're really in a losing position—you've been reprimanded, passed over for a promotion, or handed an awful assignment—that's the time to reach deep down and show them what you're made of. Hold your head up, smile, and be just as cordial and courteous as you would be on the best of days. Show them that you can handle whatever they throw at you, that there is nothing they can do to make you fold.

When all else fails, leave the room. If you really feel you're about to lose control, leave the room. Say, "I'm sorry, but I don't seem to be able to discuss this calmly right now. Let's continue this discussion later this afternoon." And walk out. Go to the restroom and cry, or go out and walk around the block, but remove yourself from the scene until you've regained your composure. Before you go back, develop a reasonable, rational approach to the situation, and tackle it one more time. *Don't* use the time to plot the demise of the person that's giving you trouble, and go back even more upset than when you left.

Leaving is also an acceptable approach if the person you're talking to comes unraveled. You do not have to take verbal abuse from *anybody*, not the mail room clerk, not the president of the company, not even a customer. When someone starts yelling, say as politely as possible, "I don't think shouting is going to resolve it. If we can discuss it calmly, I'd like to continue this meeting. If not, I suggest we wait until later." If that doesn't slow them down, excuse yourself and leave, saying "I'll come back in about a half-hour when we can both be a little more rational." Don't say "when *you* calm down" or "when *you* can be more rational," say "*we*" to help the other person save face.

If the person yelling threatens to fire you if you leave, you can do one of two things—stay put, and listen to the tirade (then start looking for another job—you don't need to work for someone like this); or get gutsy and say, "I'm sure you don't mean that—you're just upset. We've had an excellent working relationship up until this particular problem developed, and I'm sure we will again when it's resolved. I'll be back in a half-hour." And head for the door.

That's the way a manager sounds. You can sound that way too—it just takes a little effort and a little guts.

8. And write like a manager

Everything you write, from casual memos to new policy proposals, should show you have executive potential.

What policy proposals, you say—you rarely write anything more complicated than phone messages? Well, sharpen your pencil—you're about to break into print.

WRITING FOR SELF-PROMOTION

Because writing is such an integral part of business, it's a golden opportunity to get the real message across: that you are ready for a management job. It can open doors for you by:

Increasing your visibility. Memos, and copies of memos, can go where secretaries are not normally allowed to tread.

Improving your image. Carefully written, well-thought-out memos impress people.

Increasing the credit you get. Your ideas are tougher to steal when you put them in writing.

ANYONE CAN WRITE LIKE AN EXECUTIVE

When writing original memos and proposals, do you feel like you don't know what to say or how to say it? Do you conclude that you have no writing ability?

Nonsense. You don't need a lot of writing ability. You only need a copy machine.

DEVELOP A "PROTOTYPES" FILE

Read all the memos, letters, and proposals that cross your desk, and select the ones that are well written. Make copies of them and put them in a file called "Prototypes."

Copy anything that is the type of memo/letter/proposal you might need to write yourself—even if you already have five prototypes of that particular document. There's no such thing as too many examples to work from. Then when you have to write, say, a letter to a customer about a new product, pull out the customer letters you've copied and work from them.

Use other people's writing as a model—copy their style, their format, their tone. It saves you time (no point in reinventing the business communications wheel), and it insures that your writing will have the right business "feel." You have an unlimited supply of samples, examples, and prototypes of good, solid business writing right at your fingertips—everything that arrives in the mail and everything you type can be appropriated for your own use.

Your writing needs to be coherent, succinct, readable, and professional, but it doesn't have to compete for the Nobel Prize for Literature. You don't need to create new and unusual phraseology to become a first-rate business communicator—you only need to know how to follow someone else's lead.

If you have trouble deciding which correspondence qualifies as well written, look for these attributes (which, by the way, you should incorporate into your own writing):

Directness. What is the point of the memo? The easier the point is to find, the better the memo is. If the purpose of the memo or letter isn't immediately and completely clear, don't add it to your "Prototypes" file.

Brevity. Is the point made in as few words as possible? If so, add his work to your file. In business, time is money—don't waste it for other people by forcing them to wade through paragraphs of irrelevant information.

Thoroughness. While succinctness is important, don't be brief at the expense of thoroughness. Give the reader all the information needed to respond to your correspondence. "Please forward a copy of the report you mentioned in our meeting two weeks ago," may go unanswered because the recipient of the memo doesn't remember which report you're talking about and doesn't have time to look it up.

Readability. Writers who use big words to impress or intimidate their readers should be thrashed with their own thesauruses. The words you use in writing should be the same ones you use in conversation. Don't write about the vice president's "propitious promulgation," when you can call it a timely announcement.

Structure. Formats such as lists, graphs, charts, tables, schedules, numbered paragraphs, and frequent headings make documents easier to read. Use them as often as possible.

The information in the table below is instantly understandable:

INSURANCE CLAIMS SUBMITTED BY DEPARTMENT

Department	November 1984	November 1985	% Change
Sales	$33,821	$45,086	33.3%
Financial	$26,472	$28,363	7.1%

The comparison of the insurance claims by the sales and financial departments is quite clear in this format—much more so than it is in running text. Nobody wants to read paragraphs like this:

The Sales Department showed a 33.3 percent increase in insurance claims from $33,821 in November, 1984, to $45,086 in November, 1985. The Financial Department showed a smaller increase of 7.1 percent for the same time period, with claims only rising from $26,472 to $28,363.

WHOSE LEAD TO FOLLOW

In choosing examples for your "Prototypes" file, look at the quality of the writing, not the title of the writer. Successful people don't always necessarily have good writing skills, so don't just blindly copy the style of the head honchos and fast-trackers in your office.

I once worked for a man, head of a division and very talented, who was the world's worst writer. He would sit in his office at night and dictate long, rambling, almost incoherent memos. His secretary typed them, apparently without reading them (who could blame her?), and passed them out to us—memos up to twelve pages long, single-spaced, broken only occasionally into paragraphs. No summary. No numbered key points. No relief.

Because he was the division head, we all did our best to plow through these tomes. We applauded his business decisions, but we groaned every time we saw his secretary coming with a stack of papers in her hand.

PICK UP ON YOUR ORGANIZATION'S STANDARDS

To blend in with the executive crowd as much as possible, pay close attention to the format and style they use:

Use the accepted format. Every organization has a standard format for their written communications, especially their internal correspondence. Do the executives sign interoffice memos or just initial them? Do they initial them at the top or the bottom of the memo? Are the names on the copy list arranged alphabetically or by their position in the company? Is everybody in the world copied, or is distribution restricted to a minimal, need-to-know list?

Learn your organization's format, down to the last semicolon, and follow it religiously.

Use the accepted style. Do you work for an accounting firm where memos are formal and staid—or a teenage fashion magazine where all sentences end with exclamation points?

Study your organization's correspondence for style clues. Is "In reference to your letter of June 4, . . ." a more common opening than "Thanks so much for getting back to me right away . . ."? Are memos long and thorough, or brief and to the point? Does your organization practice the CYA (Cover Your Ass) philosophy by putting everything in writing, or are formal memos reserved for important issues only?

Write so that your memos are indistinguishable from that of any other executive in the organization—even if you disagree with the accepted format and style. When *you* become a manager in the accounting firm, you can write in a more personable manner. When *you* are an editor at the fashion magazine, you can get rid of the exclamation points. In the meantime, show them that you understand the company's communications standards and that you're eager to conform to them.

ESPECIALLY WATCH YOUR BOSS'S STYLE

Taking over some of your boss's writing chores is an important move in getting ahead. When you first start writing for your boss, mimic his tone as closely as possible—he will be more likely to approve letters that sound like his own writing (or what he perceives his own writing to sound like) than ones that don't. Your boss believes (as does everyone about their own writing) that the way he writes letters is the way letters should be written. If you do it differently, he'll think you did it wrong.

If your boss asks you to write to a customer, write the letter exactly as he would (you should have hundreds of examples to choose from). Don't launch some off-the-wall creative effort, or you may find yourself back to square one—typing instead of writing.

Dana, regional franchise manager for a fast food company, hired a secretary who had 10 years experience in the legal field. Pleased with

her secretary's performance, Dana decided to let her handle routine
inquiries from the franchisees. She gave her secretary the next request
that came in and said, "Send our promotion calendar to this franchisee, with a cover letter saying thanks for the interest and to let us
know if he needs more information."

Dana had written dozens of these letters—which her secretary had
typed—and she expected her secretary would draft a letter that read
something like:

> Thanks for your interest in the upcoming promo-
> tional schedule. We've got several new programs that I
> think you'll be very excited about—they should be real
> business-builders. They're explained on the enclosed
> promotional calendar. If you need more information,
> please don't hesitate to give me a call.

Instead, her secretary wrote the following:

> Per your request of August 24, we are hereby enclos-
> ing one copy of the calendar describing promotional
> activities for the fourth quarter of 1984. All the infor-
> mation you require is covered therein. Should you re-
> quire additional copies or further information on this
> matter, please contact this office at your earliest con-
> venience.

Dana couldn't believe it—this letter was about as friendly as a sub-
poena. Why was her secretary still writing for lawyers when a friendly,
customer-oriented tone was called for?

"After months of typing my letters, I just assumed," Dana said, "that
she would know my style—casual, as personal as possible—but she
didn't. She hadn't been paying attention. And when I gave her the
assignment, she didn't think about it. She didn't take the time to pull
two or three of my letters out of the correspondence file and copy
them. She just wrote what she'd always written—legal-ese. If I'd let
the letter go out that way, the franchisee would have thought we were
a bunch of stuffed shirts.

"It was the last writing assignment I ever gave her."

Dana may have been a little hasty in cutting her secretary off from future writing assignments, but her disappointment is understandable. Her secretary didn't realize that she'd been given a chance to display her communication skills, and that she'd failed miserably. Most importantly, she'd failed to capitalize on an opportunity to increase the management content of her job.

If you're not sure what the tone should be when your boss asks you to write a letter, ask for some direction: "How formal do you want this to be?"

On your first few letters, take them to your boss in rough draft form, and get his opinion. Say, "Since this is the first time I've handled this for you, would you look this letter over and tell me if any changes should be made?" Your boss will be more comfortable making changes on a rough draft than on the finished copy, and he'll appreciate your desire to deliver a top quality letter.

Take his comments seriously, even if you're not in total agreement with them. Once you've established yourself as a quality letter writer, and your boss is no longer looking over your shoulder, you can start using your own style and including your own ideas. In the meantime, make the boss happy by incorporating his changes, and your writing assignments will multiply.

HOW A POORLY WRITTEN LETTER CAN HURT YOU

Like Dana's secretary, you may not get a second chance if you botch your first assignment. A low quality letter says one or more of the following about you:

1. *Your writing skills are hopelessly inadequate.* A poorly written letter may lead your boss to conclude that you just can't communicate—which can bring your promotional possibilities to a halt if you're aiming for a job that requires frequent written communication, as most management jobs do.

   Poor language skills are not a good excuse for poor writing. If your skills are that bad, recognize it and deal with it. Get someone to help you. Take a business writing course at a local college or business school. Ask a secretary with a flair for words to write memos for you in exchange for doing some of her typing. (Keep this little arrangement quiet, of course—there's no need for anybody but you and her to know you can't write.)

2. *You don't understand what's appropriate.* The tone and style of a letter must be adjusted to the *audience* it's directed at. Letters to customers shouldn't sound like they were written by a Supreme Court Justice, and letters complaining of poor service shouldn't end with "Have a nice day." A secretary who does this is not paying attention. Not an attractive quality for a future manager.

3. *You're lazy.* Some people don't take the time to do the job right—it's too much trouble or too much work. If you give this impression, your boss won't waste his time giving you a chance to get ahead.

Your boss may have no idea which of these factors caused your letter to be unacceptable—and he may not bother to find out. If he assumes you're just lazy, you're finished. You'll be cut off from a very significant avenue of advancement—direct involvement in the information flow.

PRACTICE MAKES PERFECT

Good business writers aren't born, they're made—and you can make yourself into one by working at it. The advantage of written communication is that you can do it over and over again until it's right. So what if it takes you 2 hours to write a perfect three-paragraph letter?

When you have to write a memo or a letter or a report, pull an appropriate example from your "Prototypes" file, then work on your memo until it sounds just like an executive had written it.

It takes time and effort, but your practice will pay off. Soon memos that used to take six drafts can be done in two drafts, maybe even one. After all these years, I can write a marketing research report in just a few hours—one draft with revisions. When I first started, a report like that took me 3 days and a dozen drafts.

FIND A REASON TO WRITE

Use any excuse you can to write. Write to everyone you can, and copy as many people as possible.

Even though we all have self-promotion as an ulterior motive, nobody ever admits that they actually write to make themselves look good. The *real* reason we write is to facilitate business communications. Writing isn't always the best approach, but it does offer certain advantages. Read the following list with your own particular workload in mind—which of those tasks could provide a legitimate excuse for a memo, letter, or proposal?

Better documentation. Six months after the fact, your recollection of what was decided at a meeting may be quite different from someone else's recollection. A written record is indisputable.

Increased accuracy. Estimates from three different suppliers on fourteen different items can't be conveyed verbally—at least not so everybody can understand or remember them. The printed word is the only way to get that information across comprehensibly and accurately.

Increased authority. Written information carries more weight and is more believable than spoken information. The authority level is also influenced by the *form* the writing takes. The results of a customer opinion survey are more credible when presented in a formal report instead of rough, handwritten notes.

Increased formality. Written communication is generally more formal than verbal communication, such as sending a letter offering congratulations on a promotion instead of phoning to say, "Glad you got the new job."

More flexible message reception. One of the nice things about written information is that you can read it whenever your schedule permits. When people call or visit, you're stuck receiving the message at *their* convenience.

More flexible message delivery. Although it takes longer to write something down than to say it, writing eliminates the problem of what to do with the information if the intended receiver isn't around. You can relieve the mental burden of carrying the message around ("I've got to remember to tell Jim when he gets in . . ."), and possibly forgetting it, by writing it down and putting it on Jim's desk.

More distance. Writing lets you deliver a proposal at arm's length—giving the recipient a chance to review it before you meet to discuss it. It's an especially effective way to deal with people who never give you a chance to fully explain your ideas.

PUT YOUR WORK ON PAPER

Examine your responsibilities, and make a list of all the written communication you could generate. Here are some examples to get you started:

- Status reports on your overall workload—projects, major assignments, priority activities, etc. (if you don't do status reports now, start immediately!)
- Documentation of major problems (within your span of control or influence) and possible solutions
- Replies/requests to customers, suppliers or people within your organization
- Results of research projects assigned to you
- Proposals for new policies or procedures

Although business observers complain about the current memo blizzard raging through American corporations, you can't afford to be a member of the "Stop the Memos" movement. *You've got to get noticed.* Don't write inane or superfluous memos, but write whenever you can find a legitimate reason to do so.

WHAT NOT TO PUT IN WRITING

Putting everything on paper has some limitations. Some things, put in writing, can damage your image and adversely affect your advancement:

Threats. Threats are ill-advised in any event, but threatening people in writing is an especially bad idea, because it can backfire on you.

After numerous discussions with the mail-room manager about delays in receiving mail, Connie wrote him a memo saying, "If we continue to experience delays of this sort, it will be necessary to inform the vice president of administration."

The mail-room manager made the next move by taking the memo to Connie's boss and saying innocently, "Gee, this woman is a hot-head. I hadn't realized the problem was so bad, but I'm sure if she had discussed it with me in more detail we could have worked something out."

Connie's boss called her in and gave her a long lecture about working with people and resolving problems. What she really needed was a lecture about what *not* to put in writing.

Don't hesitate to document problems in writing if talking isn't getting results, but make sure it's documentation, not a threat. Send a memo that says:

> As I mentioned to you on the phone two weeks ago, we are experiencing delays in mail being delivered to our department. Since these delays are continuing, could we meet to discuss the problem? My schedule is open all next week. Please let me know what time would be convenient for you.

A series of memos like this—outlining the problem, calling for meetings, summarizing agreed-upon solutions—gives you the ammunition, if you need it after all this, to go to a higher authority without looking like a tattle-tale.

Attempts to corner people. Never try to pressure, in writing, someone who's at a higher level in the organization than you are. Managers can *sometimes* get away with this; secretaries never can. Like threats, memos designed to back someone into a corner can come back to haunt you.

Despite numerous requests, Alice couldn't get her boss to commit to giving her a raise. During her performance review, the most she could get him to say was that the company had no money for a raise right now, but that he would probably be able to give her one in 6 months. "I knew he was putting me off again, so I decided to force his hand. I figured if I documented his promise of a raise, I could hold him to it."

Alice wrote a formal memo summarizing her review and emphasizing the fact that she had been promised a raise in 6 months if the company's financial picture improved. Feeling like she had finally pinned him down, she put the memo on his desk while he was at lunch.

"My boss never mentioned the memo, but it seemed to me that our relationship got more and more strained. Then at my next 6 months' review, I found out why. He handed me a certified financial statement showing the company's profit picture—which was even worse than at my last review. Then he gave me a formal letter stating that the company's financial difficulties made it impossible for him to give me a raise for at least the next year—and the real kicker, he sent a copy of the letter to the corporate attorney. In fact, that letter sounded like it had been *written* by the corporate attorney."

Alice's boss apparently thought she was setting him up for a lawsuit if he didn't give her a raise, so he carefully documented the company's financial situation and his rationale for not giving her a raise, in case he ended up in court.

Of course, by then, he had no intention of ever giving her more money. Alice took the hint and started looking for another job.

Personal problems. Never deal with a personal problem via memo. Problems between you and any other employee should be handled face-to-face behind closed doors.

During a meeting, Joyce, an assistant vice president in a bank, pulled a memo out of her in-basket and handed it to me to read. The memo was from a loan officer. It was addressed to Joyce, with a copy to her boss, a full vice president.

I couldn't believe what I read. It was a two-page, single-spaced tirade about Joyce's and the VP's conduct. The loan officer described in detail five instances where she felt these two had undercut her authority, had reversed policies she had established, and had publicly questioned her decisions. The loan officer demanded something be done about it immediately.

Joyce shook her head sadly, "This is the first I'd heard there was a problem. She was a little inexperienced, but she seemed to be growing into the job. Lou (the VP) is so mad, he wants me to fire her, or at the very least, demote her."

Criticism in any form. If you've got something critical to say, and you're sure *you* are the person to address it, do it in person. No one likes to be criticized, and they certainly don't want it written down and lying around in a file somewhere.

There are two exceptions to this. First, if you need to build a case for dismissal, you can and should document substandard performance to prevent future legal problems. Just make sure it's objective, depersonalized documentation—no veiled insults or sarcastic comments.

The second exception is suppliers. If you purchase a product or service for your organization, and what you receive is unacceptable, you have the right, and the obligation, to complain. If a phone call doesn't solve the problem, put it in writing. Don't turn it into hate mail, but do thoroughly explain the problem and their failure to resolve it.

Then copy other people in the company who also use this supplier—that applies pressure to the supplier, and shows those on the copy list that you can solve problems in a businesslike fashion. If you don't want to embarrass the supplier, send blind copies of the memo to the other people in the company with a handwritten note that says, "FYI (For Your Information)—I thought you might like to know the problems we're having with this supplier since you use them, too."

GIVE IT THE 24-HOUR TEST

If you *must* write a memo or letter containing any of these negatives, give it the 24-Hour Test. What sounds like righteous indignation today may sound vindictive and self-serving tomorrow. Giving it at least an overnight rest will let you look at it objectively.

Also use the 24-Hour Test on documents that need to be letter-perfect. Once it's sent, there's no way to get it back, so take the time to make it right in the first place.

WHO TO WRITE TO

Do you write for your boss—drafting up letters or memos, then sending them out over his name?

If you do, you're giving up one of your best opportunities to start adding management responsibilities to your job. Here's how you can write letters and memos that go out over *your* signature—and have your boss approve:

Remember that telephone technique? If you've been conscientious about introducing yourself on the phone and interjecting yourself into the day-to-day management business in your office, you already have reasons to write your own correspondence. Those callers are now working with you, not your boss.

Take over the small stuff. Ask your boss for permission to respond to some of his routine correspondence. Say something like, "I noticed there's a letter from a college in Nebraska wanting information on our training programs. Would you like me to handle that for you?" Unless your boss specifically tells you to send it out over his name, send the response out over *yours*.

Let them know who sent it. When you send anything like a brochure, a catalog, a computer report, or a copy of a contract outside your department, always send along a brief cover letter. Use these opportunities to get noticed and to establish contact—don't waste them by jotting down a handwritten note or enclosing the requested information with no note at all. Make it known that *you* are the person who responded so quickly and efficiently to their request, and that *you* are the person to contact in the future.

Let them know somebody well-informed sent it. Don't write just a "here's the information you requested" cover letter. Add some additional information to show that you are an integral part of your department's business—and not just someone who stuffs envelopes.

If you take a request from the advertising department for a copy of last month's profit-and-loss statement (and your boss okays sending it), include an informative cover letter—signed by you, of course:

To: Denise Brenton, Manager
Advertising Department

From: Marjory Price, Industrial Products Group

Re: January Profit-and-Loss Statement

Date: February 23, 1986

Enclosed is the preliminary profit-and-loss statement for January you requested. Although January returned-goods have not been figured in yet (that information won't be available until the end of this month), we don't expect significant changes in the numbers shown here.

If you need any additional information, or a copy of the finalized statement, please let me know.

Notice that although you listed Denise's title, you discreetly left yours off. There's no point in emphasizing the fact that you are still a secretary, and there's no point in taking a chance that Denise may be sensitive about dealing with secretaries. The more people think you already have some type of a management position (even an entry-level assistantship), the better your chances are of getting involved and staying involved in management activities.

ESTABLISHING CONTACT WITH EXECUTIVES

Writing to executives, other than your boss, in your organization, is a self-promotion bonanza, because these people can have a direct impact on your advancement. Other departments may have management positions open up, and executives in those departments may recommend you if they know who you are and what you can do.

Claudia, secretary to the director of advertising in a large corporation, reviewed magazines, collected ads run by the company's competitors, and wrote a monthly analysis of the competitors' advertising schedules. The information went to her boss and then into the file. She knew there had to be a way to get more mileage out of the work she was doing.

She casually approached her boss: "I'm sure the manager of the coffee product line (which Claudia reviewed in her report) would be interested in what I'm doing—why don't I send her a copy of my report every month? Just to let her know we're doing something down here." Her boss, not paying much attention, said sure, fine, go ahead.

The next month Claudia wrote her report much more formally. She spent an extra two days making sure it was top quality. She addressed it to her boss, and copied the coffee product manager.

Using the same technique, she developed a direct line of communication with several of the other product managers—and at last report, she was being interviewed for an assistant position with one of them.

Anyone in the organization who might be even vaguely interested in what you are writing should be copied. Once you establish the habit of formalizing your reports to your boss, it's a short jump from there to copying other people in your department, and then to copying other people in the company.

A LITTLE MANEUVERING

If you have trouble getting permission from your boss to copy people outside your department, involve the person you want to copy *before* you write the memo. Mention to the coffee product manager, while you and she are waiting for an elevator together, that you do a monthly analysis of competitive advertising and that perhaps she might be interested in seeing it. You can ease into a conversation like this by saying:

"I research magazines for competitive coffee ads, and I noticed the new ads our competitor Ace Coffee started running this month. They seemed to have really stepped up their advertising, don't they? By the way, have you seen the competitive advertising analysis I do every month?"

If she isn't aware of it, she will probably ask for a copy on the spot. If she doesn't, offer to send her one if she'd be interested. She will be.

When and if your boss asks why you sent a copy of the competitive analysis report to the product manager, you can say, in all honesty, that she expressed interest in receiving it.

FYI MEANS FMA (FOR MY ADVANCEMENT)

Even if you're not in a position where you regularly talk with executives from other departments, you can still let them know, via interoffice mail, that you exist.

You and your boss are deluged everyday with information—magazines, seminar brochures, industry reports—much of which may be of interest to other departments. That article in *Computer Dealer* about future trends in financial software can be sent to the controller. That seminar brochure about *Improving Relations Between the Customer Service Department and the Sales Force* can be forwarded to the customer service manager. The report in this month's *Purchasing Digest* which shows how new legislation will affect raw materials imports can be sent to the head of research and development.

Anything you run across that might be valuable to an executive should be sent to him with a note that says: "FYI—thought this might interest you. Marjory Price." FYI, for those unfamiliar with it, means For Your Information. Write your note on the front of the article or brochure, so your name will be around as long as the article is.

When you do this, be sure to send only information that the executive would not have otherwise seen. Chances are the head of production doesn't read *Marketing Communications*—if you find an article in there relating to production, copy it and send it off. On the other hand, he does read *Production Techniques Quarterly*. Don't insult him by sending an article he probably read before you did.

WHO NOT TO WRITE TO

Never write to, or copy anyone who's at a higher level in the organization than your boss. At least not without your boss's permission. You may make him nervous if you start dealing with people he reports to. Even if you are contacted directly by someone higher up, don't respond without telling your boss. Keep him on your side by keeping him informed.

Never send a formal memo to a receptionist, a clerk, or another secretary. Managers never write to these people, because as we've discussed before, they don't consider them real team members. (Snobbery runs rampant in the corporate world.) You don't have to share that unenlightened attitude, but you do have to play by the rules if you want to get ahead.

THWARTING WORK AND IDEA THEFT

The more proficient you are, the more likely you are to find your work and ideas being stolen—usually by your boss. Putting your work in writing, and getting copies of it to other people, is the best way to prevent your boss, or anyone else, from taking the credit *you* deserve.

As a secretary in the corporate meetings department, Kay surveyed hotels for costs and accommodations, she made arrangements for meetings, and she performed cost analyses on past meetings. Because she was so involved, she was frequently able to suggest improved procedures or locate more cost-effective meeting sites.

She enjoyed her job, but nobody realized how much she was doing, because her boss repeatedly took her work and passed it off as his own. When Kay gave a handwritten or rough-typed memo to her boss, he'd rewrite it and send it out over his name—with no mention of Kay.

"As far as the rest of the company was concerned," she said, "I didn't exist. I was doing a lot of work and getting absolutely no credit for it." To protect her work, she decided to write her memos to her boss formally, on interdepartmental stationery, so he wouldn't rewrite them over his own name. To: Mike McNally. From: Kay Osborne. Re: Proposed Sites for Regional Sales Meetings. Carefully typed, copy to the project file. Kay said, "I thought that would stop him. I thought he surely wouldn't have me retype my own memo and put his name on it.''

Wrong. The next day her boss gave her a handwritten memo to type. To: Steven McGillis, Vice President of Sales. From: Mike McNally, Director of Corporate Meetings. Topic? Proposed Sites for Regional Sales Meetings. It was Kay's memo, only slightly reworded—again with no mention of Kay.

"Now I was really steaming," she said, "but I didn't know what to do about it. I was afraid to confront him." So she decided to start addressing her memos to people outside the department.

Her next assignment was to cost out a 5-day conference for the company's numerous research and development departments. She called the manager in charge of the conference, got more specifics from him, and promised she would get the numbers to him just as quickly as possible. When she got them, she wrote up the results and addressed them, not to her boss, but to the manager who needed them. She copied her boss.

"Then I sat back and waited for the explosion. I figured my boss would be furious. I had my explanation all ready—that the memo had simply relayed information the manager had requested, and that he was in a hurry for it. To my surprise, my boss never said a word about it! Probably because his only real objection could have been that he didn't want me signing my name to my own work."

Once Kay had broken that barrier, she began working directly with many of the executives in the company, and in less than 4 months, her boss's boss recommended that she be promoted to assistant meeting planner.

You may have a suspicious boss who insists on seeing any correspondence before it leaves your department. If you're afraid he'll steal your work, type your memos and letters in finished form, ready to send off, then give them to your boss for "final approval." A small note paperclipped to the memo, which says "Please review this before I send it out," will help keep an unscrupulous boss in line.

9. Stop acting like a secretary

The difference between a secretary's attitude and a manager's attitude can be summed up in one word: control. Managers and executives control their work, their resources, and their careers. Secretaries don't. They let themselves be pushed around; they feel helpless; they think there's no way to take charge.

But they're wrong. To become a manager, you *have* to take control. You have to:

- Stop being timid and allowing yourself to be intimidated.

- Accept the responsibility of solving your own problems—don't wait for someone else to solve them.

- Control events instead of letting them control you.

- Work with your boss to establish goals and priorities, instead of accepting direction from him blindly and without question.

- Be calm and confident—even in crisis situations.

By taking these steps, you can structure your job in a way that is more satisfying both to you and to the people you work for. You can manage the pressures and problems of your job, and set the stage for promotion.

THE INTIMIDATION FACTOR

If you're like most secretaries, you have been conditioned to be timid. You've been intimidated by executives who treated you like a personal servant or their office wife, who never had the courtesy to inform you of their schedules when they were going out of town, to provide advance notice when they needed you to stay late, or even to introduce you to their visitors. You were expected to stay in the background—seen but not heard.

Maybe you don't view yourself as timid, but what would you do in these situations?

- You're in the middle of compiling the monthly accounts receivable report when your boss asks you to order flowers for his wife's birthday. "Shop around and see if you can save me a few bucks," he says.

  Do you grit your teeth and start calling the seventy-three florists listed in the Yellow Pages?

- Your boss dumps a six-page product specification sheet on top of your overflowing in-basket and says it needs to be typed by noon.

  Do you silently wonder how you're going to get it done in time and start typing faster?

- Your boss asks for a copy of the memo he sent to the production department last month, and you haven't had a chance to do your filing for 6 weeks.

  Do you tell him "no problem" and frantically search through the stack of papers on your desk until you find it?

That's how intimidated people act. They don't take control, they just react, running faster and faster to keep up, letting events, situations, and other people be the driving force in their lives.

IT'S ALL DOWNHILL FROM HERE

Intimidation is a degenerative disease that is, at best, debilitating, and at worst, professionally terminal. Responding with silent submission to excessive workloads, personal pressure, or unreasonable standards can start you on a downhill slide that's characterized by these four stages:

Stage 1—Scrambling. You try to combat an overwhelming workload by working faster. The quality of your work steadily declines as you attempt to cram a growing number of projects and assignments into an 8-hour day. The goal is no longer to do the job well, it's just to get it done any way possible.

When the boss accepts nothing less than perfection, the exact opposite may happen. You spend all your time trying to get one task absolutely right, and have no time to complete the others. You can't get anything finished, because nothing is ever done to your boss's satisfaction.

Stage 2—Despair. When the workload or the pressure becomes intolerable, you plop into a chair in your boss's office, distraught and upset, and say, "Please help me. I've got too much work to do. I can't keep up. I don't know what to do."

This "woe is me" approach doesn't work. By presenting problems instead of solutions, you appear to be just another woman who can't take the pressure of the business world. Your boss thinks you don't know how to handle your job, so he brushes you off with something like, "Well, do your best," and ignores your problem.

Stage 3—Disgust. Not getting any help, you develop a bad attitude toward your job, your boss, your company, or all three—and you start letting things go. Quality has already gone by the wayside, and now completing tasks no longer seems so important. You spend more time complaining than working.

Stage 4—Failure. This pattern of professional decay results in your being miserable at work, and you end up leaving the company and finding another job (where the pattern may repeat itself), or getting fired.

WHOSE FAULT IS IT?

Most secretaries don't realize that this pattern *is their own fault*. It comes from a lack of self-assertion. Instead of informing the boss that the workload is unmanageable or that his standards are counter-productive, they just move into the Scrambling Stage. They set themselves up for the Despair Stage by hoping that someone else will solve their problems. When that doesn't happen—the boss refuses to play Big Daddy—they slide into the Disgust Stage. And the Failure Stage inevitably follows.

When the boss is unreasonable, rude, or overdemanding, don't sit back and take it. Don't meekly accept whatever is dished out, then go home and slam doors or kick the dog or yell at your kids. That's taking it out on the wrong party. Your doors, dogs, and kids aren't the cause of your on-the-job frustration. It's not even your boss's fault. It's *yours*—because you allow the situation to exist. You are intimidated because you *let* people intimidate you.

It's time to start standing up for yourself.

ACCEPT YOURSELF AS SIGNIFICANT

The first step toward overcoming intimidation is to accept yourself as an important part of the "team." No one will treat you as an equal team member until you first see yourself as one. You must recognize that you play a significant role in both the short- and long-term operation of your organization. You are the focal point of the office communications, and without you, they quickly come to a halt.

Have you noticed that when the boss is gone for the day everything just keeps rolling along? In the short run, he isn't really missed. But when you're gone, chaos quickly ensues. Your boss can't get that important proposal typed or find the sales figures to finish the monthly report, the phone rings off the hook, and appointments are missed because you aren't there to remind him. He can't wait for you to get back.

You, as a secretary, are the glue that binds the layers of an organization together. You facilitate contact with the outside world. You are critical to the smooth operation of the business.

You can't get respect from other people until you start respecting yourself.

TAKE THE INITIATIVE

Respecting yourself means not hiding behind your typewriter. Take an active hand in controlling your professional destiny, and show that you're a member of the team by taking the initiative. Speak up. Make suggestions. Object now and then.

Start asserting yourself with your boss. Conversations between bosses and secretaries are usually nothing more than order-giving and order-taking sessions, while conversations between executives are dialogues—two-way conversations in which information is exchanged and discussed, and goals are set. One party may be in fact giving orders, but the other is questioning, suggesting, and working toward some mutually acceptable way of accomplishing assignments.

As an equal member of the team, you have the right, in fact *the obligation*, to turn your boss's monologues into dialogues. Make contributions; offer ideas, suggestions, and recommendations. Don't wait for him to tell you what to do and how to do it. Suggest what *you* think should be done and how it should be accomplished. Most bosses won't involve you in the process of making decisions, developing goals, and establishing priorities, unless you make an effort to be included. *You* have to make the first move.

YOUR RIGHT TO KNOW

Secretaries often have trouble getting involved in the decision-making/goal-setting process, because they lack information. Many bosses are notoriously reluctant to share "management" information with their secretaries. They spend hours with other executives discussing an inventory shortage, and never think to tell their secretaries—who then have no idea what to say when the sales people call in complaining about lack of deliveries. Secretaries aren't given equal access to information.

REFUSE TO KEEP YOUR HEAD IN THE SAND

No manager would tolerate being left in this uninformed state. A sales manager who wasn't given information about inventory shortages would storm into the production manager's office and demand an explanation. And he'd get one. Secretaries for some reason don't believe they have a right to information like this. They rarely ask for it, let alone demand it, and so they never get it.

Not asking for information is relinquishing control of your working environment. The meek may inherit the earth, but the uninformed will inherit only typing and filing.

Getting information is simple—all you have to do is ask. I don't mean you corral your boss immediately following a meeting and demand to know what went on. But you *can* stop in his office and say, "How did your meeting go? Is there anything I should know about?" The first few times you ask, your boss may reflexively say no, nothing he can think of. But don't give up. Every time he attends a meeting, or is involved in any situation that might generate information you need, ask if there's anything you should be aware of. Keep asking—politely and cordially—but keep asking. Eventually he'll start passing along information.

Arrange brief, 5-minute scheduling meetings each morning, just between the two of you, to discuss priorities, projects, upcoming events, and whatever else might need your time and attention. Assume responsibility for making that meeting happen. Round him up every morning—don't wait until he comes to you. And don't let him put you off. These meetings are for your benefit, not his. They allow you to gain control over what happens the rest of the day.

One secretary said, "I'd be afraid to ask my boss what's coming up for the day. Every time I ask what he needs done, he comes up with about thirty new projects. I'm already drowning in work."

Whoa! These meetings are not order-giving sessions—they are scheduling sessions. Their primary purpose is to keep you from being buried with work. If your boss dumps thirty assignments on you, you work *with him* to establish priorities and develop a timetable for completing those assignments. Don't say, "thank you very much," and develop a migraine headache.

LEARN TO BE ASSERTIVE

A boss once said to me, "There's nothing wrong with being aggressive as long as you're polite about it." That's some of the best advice I ever got. Although *aggressive* has given way to *assertive* as the proper terminology (advertising campaigns can be aggressive, women aren't allowed to be), the advice holds:

- You can ask for anything if you ask in a way that doesn't offend.
- You can question anything if you phrase your objection properly.
- You can refuse anything if you do it in a logical, businesslike way.

You don't have to sit back and let someone else control your life and your profession.

THE ASSERTIVE-BUT-POLITE APPROACH

How often do you tell your boss that he's made a wrong decision, given you inadequate direction, or hasn't thought his priorities through? How often do you suggest a better way to do an assignment? How often do you tell someone in the office, particularly your boss, that you can't do something, that you *won't* do something?

Probably never. But you're going to start. You are going to use tact, logic, and some good old-fashioned manipulation to (1) make your life easier, and (2) prove that you have management potential.

There are three ways to deal with problems in the office—whether they're work problems, people problems, or just a need to get someone to change direction:

1. *The Standard Secretarial Approach*—if your boss makes an unreasonable demand, cower and scurry off to do his bidding.

2. *The Aggressive Approach*—tell the boss, in the most colorful terms possible, what he can do with his unreasonable demand.

3. *The Assertive-but-Polite Approach*—face the problem squarely, take steps to solve it or manage it, and maintain a cooperative and helpful attitude.

The Standard Secretarial Approach and the Aggressive Approach don't work, because they create more problems than they solve. With the Standard Secretarial Approach, you accept the total burden and resign yourself to an ulcer. With the Aggressive Approach, you don't try to solve the problem, you just refuse to deal with it—and earn yourself the reputation of being uncooperative and belligerent.

Only the Assertive-but-Polite Approach works, because you're in control—acting professional and solving problems.

Let's take an example:

THE SITUATION: The office just held a going-away party for Linda, the secretary who sat at the desk next to yours. She's off to greener pastures. The next morning your boss calls you in and tells you that, because of budget cuts, you are taking over Linda's workload, effective immediately, in addition to keeping all your current responsibilities.

Stunned, because you are already overworked, you ask: "Is this temporary or permanent?"

"Well," the boss clears his throat nervously, "the company has had to cut back, production costs are up, sales are down, times are tight—we've got to cut back."

Oh. "Is there a raise to go along with the increased workload?"

"Well, the company has had to cut back, production costs are up, sales are down, etc., etc."

Oh. "I've got too much to do now—how will I handle it all?"

"Well," the boss looks at his watch, stands up, and heads for the door, "I'm sure you'll manage."

You have three choices:

The Standard Secretarial Approach: Stagger back to your desk in a daze, swallow a handful of Tums, and try to figure out if you can learn to type 300 words per minute.

The Aggressive Approach: Tell your boss, "Not only is this more work than I could possibly handle in an *80-*hour work week, it's more work than I intend to *try* to handle. You guys can save your nickels and dimes somewhere else. You're not going to break my back with work—I won't do it!"

The Assertive-but-Polite Approach: Calmly say to your boss, "That's going to be quite a challenge, but I'm sure we can work it out. I'll make a list of everything I'm doing for you, then I'll interview my new boss and outline everything I'll need to do for her. After that, the three of us can get together and review those lists to establish priorities. Of course since there's more work than one person could possibly do, we'll need to decide which tasks we can eliminate or postpone. I know it will be tough on all three of us, but I'm sure we can work out a compromise that will make everyone happy."

DON'T FORGET TO FOLLOW THROUGH

The company attempted to overload you with work, but:

1. You refused to be intimidated.
2. You refused to get angry.

You used the professional approach, asserted yourself, and addressed the problem facing you. That's good, but it's not enough. A key part of the Assertive-but-Polite Approach is follow-through. You have to take steps to solve the problem. Follow through by making up those tasks lists and having that meeting. Being assertive doesn't mean just speaking up about what's bothering you. It means *doing* something about it.

LEARN TO SAY "NO"

Sometimes simply refusing is the best response to an unreasonable or inconsiderate demand. Though cooperation should be your watchword, there are limits. If your boss regularly goes too far, here are two techniques that can help you say "no" gracefully:

1. *The "Consider the Consequences" Technique* uses simple logic—in order to do Activity B right now, you will have to stop doing Activity A, and that will have some less-than-desirable consequences.

2. *The "I'd Love to But I Can't" Technique* relies on the development of a fairly inflexible reason why you can't do what's being requested or ordered. You say you'd like to help out, but there's just no way you can. Then you suggest several helpful alternatives—none of which includes your giving in.

THE "CONSIDER THE CONSEQUENCES" TECHNIQUE

This is a good method for dealing with a boss who has trouble establishing priorities:

THE SITUATION: You are working hard on a financial report that your boss said was top priority, when he suddenly rushes out of his office with a handful of scribbled yellow paper, and says, "Type this memo and get it over to the sales department right now!"

The Standard Secretarial Approach: Stop working on the financial report, hurriedly type the memo, and race it over to the sales department. Rush back to finish the financial report, only to find your boss standing there saying, "Where's the financial report? Why isn't it done? My meeting with the VP of finance starts in 5 minutes!"

The Aggressive Approach: Turn to your boss and snarl, "Didn't they teach you anything about organization, delegation or prioritizing when you went to business school? Any fool can see that I can't do the sales memo and the financial report at the same time!"

The "Consider the Consequences" Technique: Say to your boss, before he dashes back into his office after handing you the sales memo, "You also said you needed this financial report done right away. If I do the sales memo, I won't have time to get the financial report done for your 3:30 meeting. Which do you want me to do first?"

Don't let yourself be trapped into deciding which is more important and which should be done first—you don't have enough information to make that decision. Only your boss knows what his
needs are; make him establish the priorities.

This technique works particularly well for eliminating trivial requests: "Sure, I'd be happy to go down to the corner drugstore and
get you a pack of cigarettes, but I'll have to stop working on the
production schedule you said was a rush job. Is that what you want
me to do?"

That's a nice way of reminding your boss that you have *real* work
to do. If he wants his cigarettes bad enough to send you anyway, go
and don't worry about it. He's established the priorities. And when
things don't get done on time, he'll know why.

THE "I'D LOVE TO BUT I CAN'T" TECHNIQUE

For truly unreasonable requests, you may have to take more serious action:

THE SITUATION: For the third time this week, your boss has
rushed out of his office at 4:45 p.m., waving a ten-page proposal
and saying, "I've *got* to have this typed for the meeting tomorrow
morning at 8:30!" What do you do?

The Standard Secretarial Approach: Type the proposal, and go
home at 7:15. The next day, tell the other secretaries and anybody
else that will listen to you that your boss is an inconsiderate creep
who's incapable of planning ahead.

The Aggressive Approach: Tell your boss that this is the last time
he's going to pull this stunt on you, that you can't stay in the office
until 7:00 or 8:00 p.m. several nights a week, that you have a
family and a personal life, and they come first. Then go home.

The "I'd Love to, But I Can't" Technique: Say to your boss, "I'm
really sorry, but I've got guests coming for dinner tonight, and I
can stay only until 5:30. Had I known you needed this done
tonight, I would have changed my plans, but at this hour, there's

nothing I can do about it. Perhaps one of the other secretaries can stay—I'll be glad to ask around. Can I say that we'll pay them overtime for staying late? Or maybe you could write a brief, one-page summary of your proposal? I'll type it first thing in the morning, and you can make a verbal presentation on the background material. Which would be best for you?"

Smile pleasantly and wait for this to sink in. What you really just said to him is: "You screwed up. You waited until the last minute to do what you should have done last week, and now you're in a mess. If you had given me some advance notice, I would have been able to help you. As it stands now, you're up the creek without a paddle. But here are a few alternatives to help you out."

Involve your boss in the consequences of his actions instead of carrying the burden yourself or lashing out at him. Show him that his lack of planning has unpleasant ramifications for both of you—someone less familiar with his work will have to type the proposal, he'll be paying overtime, or he'll have to go to the meeting not fully prepared.

However it works out, follow through. Plant yourself in his office the next day and discuss scheduling. Say, "I really feel bad about having to leave last night. Is there a way we can work together to plan ahead and make sure I have enough time to prepare materials for your meetings?"

COPING WITH THE OFFICE CRISIS

Sometimes a boss who can't plan or set priorities throws the department into crisis. And sometimes crises come from other causes: your company shipped out 10,000 defective widgets, half the production department comes down with the flu, or the hotel where your national sales meeting is being held burns down. Don't let them overwhelm you. There will always be crises—it's how you handle them that counts.

You can gain control of any crisis situation, and make yourself look like a hero, by following these four steps:

1. *Assume responsibility for calming everybody else down.* You can't function if the people around you are hysterical. If your boss panics—yelling and screaming and digging through the pile of paper on your desk, searching for that request from the president he'd forgotten about—resist the temptation to panic with him. Help solve the problem, don't add to it. Calm him down by telling him that you'll look for the missing memo and bring it to his office as soon as you find it.

2. *Lay out a plan of action.* Ask yourself: what is the best way to handle this situation? Most office crises don't involve the building being on fire or someone having a heart attack, so a couple of minutes won't put anyone's life in danger. Take that time to decide what the most appropriate course of action is. Where should you look for that memo? Are you sure your boss received it? Should you call the secretary who typed it and ask her to discreetly run you off another copy?

3. *Follow through on that plan.* Don't switch back and forth from one course of action to another. Don't dig furiously through your desk for a couple of minutes, then pick up the phone and start to call the other secretary, then hang up before she answers, and start looking in the filing cabinet. Go slowly and be thorough. If you make the wrong decision about which line of attack to take, you'll survive, and so will the company. If one approach doesn't work after you've followed through on it, try the next best course of action, and so on, until the problem is solved.

4. *Learn from the experience.* After the "crisis" is over, get a cup of coffee and take a few minutes to do a postmortem on it. What really was the problem? Could you have prevented it? Can you keep it from happening again? How did you behave in trying to solve it? What should you do differently next time? Make notes, because crises have a way of repeating themselves. Next time, you'll be better prepared.

BE CALM AND CONFIDENT

Reacting calmly and confidently to any situation is the hallmark of a person who's in control. Confidence is highly valued in any employee, because it indicates a belief in your ability to do your job well. Confident people are level-headed. They stay calm and collected—physically, emotionally, and intellectually. Regardless of what happens in the office, they seem to be able to cope with it.

If you don't have self-confidence, don't worry—you can develop it. Confidence comes with practice, and by acting confident, you become confident. Start by developing the *appearance* of confidence. Here are some guidelines to help you do that:

Don't ramble. When you talk to your boss, be brief, but thorough. Don't tell him everything he never wanted to know about the filing system or the Federal Express delivery man. Make your point, and let him (and you) get back to work.

If there's a problem, and your boss puts you on the spot with questions, don't start stammering and stuttering. Stop and think, then answer as succinctly as possible. If you can't think of an answer, say so: "I really don't know how to respond to that right now. Let me think about it, and I'll get back to you this afternoon." That's what your boss says when *his* boss puts him on the spot. He doesn't say the first thing that comes into his head. You are better off saying nothing than saying something stupid or untrue.

In confrontations, silence is often the best response unless you are asked a direct question. When your boss is ranting and raving about something, don't interrupt him and start explaining. Just listen carefully to what he is saying, and let him wind down. He may talk himself into an answer or an explanation while he's carrying on, or he may realize that the situation isn't as bad as he thought. By listening instead of talking, you also buy yourself time to formulate an appropriate answer.

Don't fidget. When your boss calls you into his office, do you sit on the edge of the chair chewing your lip, tugging at your hair, tapping your foot? Do you look and act uneasy?

Stop these nervous habits and your appearance of confidence will go up dramatically. Concentrate on sitting as motionless as possible, so you look relaxed instead of apprehensive. Sit against the backrest of the chair as if you were settled in for a friendly chat. Smile, and look interested in what your boss has to say—even if you suspect it might be critical.

Sit in your boss's office like an equal, not like a student in the principal's office.

Don't get emotional. Confidence shows itself when, no matter how big (or small) the problem is and no matter how angry, frightened, or unhappy you are, you appear restrained, relaxed, and in control. You may be having heart palpitations, weak knees, and an adrenalin rush, but outwardly you should appear unruffled. There's only one way to do that: think before you act or speak. When you feel yourself about to run wildly around the office, or start shouting at someone, stop. Take 10 seconds and think: how would a calm and confident person react in this situation?

Don't be obnoxious. Confidence doesn't mean you act as if you know everything. Confidence quickly becomes arrogance when it's misused. If you're privy to inside information, don't say, "I'd love to tell you, but it's strictly confidential information. Will you be surprised when you find out!" This is grade-school stuff. Don't insult other people by implying that you're on the inside track and they aren't.

Don't be afraid to say "I don't know." Pretending to know something you don't will always get you into trouble. If you don't understand what someone is saying, say so. Don't be afraid to ask questions like, "What do you mean by a disk operating system?" Or "I'm afraid you're losing me. Could you go over that one more time?" And keep asking until you're sure you understand it.

10. No risk, no reward

Being a secretary can be a safe job—you don't have to make major decisions and you don't have major responsibilities. You don't have to worry about how to make more sales, how to cut production costs, which stock to invest in, what business should be the next acquisition, or whether to hire that hot-shot from San Francisco. When you go home at night, you can put the job behind you. You may worry about how to accomplish everything that needs to be done tomorrow, but you don't have to carry the success of your company on your shoulders.

And that's why your salary is so low.

IT'S NOT WHAT YOU DO, IT'S WHAT YOU KNOW

People get paid to *think*, not to do. Brains, not brawn, generate big salaries and generous perks like travel, expense accounts, fancy offices, company cars, bonuses, and stock options. Vice presidents do very little "work"—they don't make sales calls, fill out reports, verify purchase orders, or issue checks. They spend their days in meetings, reviewing what other people are doing, studying trade publications and financial reports, and most importantly, making decisions. Their salaries are high because they make judgment calls—they guide the organization, set goals, and decide on the right course of action.

The more risk you assume and the more often you are right, the more you will get paid. You may work twice as hard as your boss, but he gets *paid* twice as much because he makes the decisions. As you become more successful, the physical workload decreases, but the mental workload and the pressure to be right increases. When a manager is right more often than he's wrong, he gets to keep his job. But when he's wrong more often, or wrong on the big ones, he may get fired.

Decision-making and problem-solving are the yardsticks used to determine salaries, promotions, and success, and management's perception of *your* decision-making ability will determine your future.

PROBLEM-SOLVING IS MANDATORY FOR SUCCESS

To reach a management job (with a management salary and management perks), you must solve more problems, make more decisions, and take more risks. As a secretary, you're not likely to have responsibility thrust upon you, so you have to actively pursue it:

- Tackle each and every problem that comes your way.

- Take responsibility for problems that involve you directly, and go after the authority to solve problems that concern you peripherally.

No other trait is as indicative of your management potential as problem-solving, because the basis of management is judgment—being ready to use it, and being right when you do.

Remember the old adage that "there are no problems, only opportunities?" A friend of mine responds to that by saying, "To hell with opportunities, if this building catches on fire, we've got a problem!" He's right, problems are not always opportunities for organizations, but they can always be opportunities for *you*. Whenever a problem arises that you can solve, you have an opportunity to demonstrate your management ability.

OVERCOMING FEAR OF RESPONSIBILITY

Despite the need for more problem solving, it seems to be what secretaries fear most. If you are asked to take more risks, make more decisions, and accept more responsibility, don't react with:

- "That's not in my job description."
- "Oh, no, *I'm* not going to make that kind of decision."
- "I'll let my boss decide."
- "If you want me to take on that kind of responsibility, you'll have to start paying me more money."

And the big one:

- "What if I'm wrong?"

I agree, it's scary. What if you *are* wrong? What if you cost the company a lot of money? What if you make your boss look bad? What if you get fired?

These "what-ifs" can get you down and hold you back from obtaining the management responsibility you want. Letting these what-ifs rule your life will *ruin* your life, because you will never let yourself take the steps you must take, *that you are capable of taking*, to get into management. Instead of asking "what if," ask yourself: "What's the worst that could happen, and if it happens, will I survive?"

THE WHAT-IFS EXAMINED

Let's see how valid those what-ifs really are.

What if you are wrong? Nobody is right all the time. It's a matter of percentages—successful managers are right more often than they

are wrong. *But they are occasionally wrong, and the less experi-*
ence they have, the more often they make mistakes. Neophyte
managers, just like beginners everywhere, make errors. The ones
that don't crumble and give up, that learn from their mistakes and
go on, become experienced managers with good judgment. They
can be relied upon to make the right decision at the right time.

You're not perfect, and your decision-making record will not be
perfect. Failure is not a defeat, it's just nature's way of telling you
to try a different approach.

What if you cost the company a lot of money? It's a matter of
perspective. A secretary who makes a mistake and costs the company $100 is appalled and may worry about it for weeks. A man-
ager with a $750,000 budget who makes the same mistake says no
big deal, because he knows $100 is insignificant.

A frugal attitude toward corporate funds is desirable and com-
mendable, but try to view your mistakes in context. If you work for
a $2.3 billion corporation, don't berate yourself about purchasing
a $150 calculator you could have bought somewhere else for $95.

All managers, at sometime during their careers, make decisions
that cost their companies money. Sometimes substantial amounts
of money. For example, when management at Texas Instruments
cut their computer prices to below cost, they were convinced they
could make up the loss on software and auxiliary sales. They
overestimated the size of the home computer market and counted
on an unrealistically high growth rate. They were wrong. Their
losses in the second quarter of 1983 alone were $100 million.

When the airline industry was deregulated, Braniff Airline's upper management decided to grab up hundreds of new routes. To
service these routes, they had to buy almost $1 billion worth of
new airplanes. Their route system was poorly designed, they
didn't have enough well-trained service and maintenance personnel, and their fuel needs increased so much that they had to buy
fuel on the spot market, where prices are considerably higher than
contract rates. By 1981, their losses were over $160 million, and
their long-term debt had reached $733 million.

In both cases, bad decisions were to blame.

When managers make costly mistakes, they do three things:

1. Minimize the loss as much as possible.

2. Let as few people as possible find out about their mistake (no point in broadcasting your errors).

3. Try not to make the same mistake again.

Do the same. And remember that over the years, you will have the opportunity to make *good* decisions that will save or earn your company much more money than you ever cost them.

What if you make your boss look bad? Making your boss look bad is not a good idea—it's hard on your relationship. And it's unnecessary, because it can be avoided in the simplest of ways—through communication. Discuss decisions of any importance with your boss, and don't make unilateral decisions without consulting him. Let your boss sign off on what you're about to do, so you're covered if your decision doesn't work out well.

On Wednesday, you receive a rush order from a new "distributor," Paint Supply Company. They need fifty cases of paint right away for a special customer, and they're willing to pay extra freight charges to get the shipment immediately. The problem is that they claim they don't have enough time to collect the bank references and customer records needed to establish their status as a distributor. They want you to take their word for it that they are a distributor, rush the order to them, and give them the distributor price discount instead of the smaller dealer discount.

You could hand your boss the request and see what he decides, but to show your capability you make a suggestion on how *you* would handle it. You point out that if the order can be shipped before Friday your department will make sales quota for the month. You suggest taking a chance and trusting their claim that they are a distributor.

Your boss thinks it over, and agrees. You ship the order. A week later four of your dealers call, irate because they heard your company is selling paint at distributor prices to another dealer in their area. That dealer is Paint Supply Company.

Oops. Paint Supply Company wasn't a distributor, and you've aggravated several of your best dealers.

But you discussed it with your boss first, and you and he worked together on the decision. You kept him informed, so you're not to blame. Your boss may be unhappy, but he approved your decision.

Imagine how this little scenario might have gone if you *hadn't* asked your boss to approve your recommendation, if you had gone ahead on your own and given Paint Supply Company distributor status. It could have resulted in your being fired, or at best reprimanded for not following the established company policy of requiring documentation from new distributors. Ultimately, your boss is responsible for everything you do—as are all bosses for the actions of the people working for them. When you screw up, your boss takes the rap for it from his superiors, because he's supposed to know what you're doing. To avoid putting your boss in a vulnerable position, run your decisions by him for approval—at least until you have a management position or are assigned definite areas of responsibility.

What if I get fired? Good secretaries are hard to find, and they're getting scarcer all the time. According to the Bureau of Labor Statistics, "highly qualified secretaries are in great demand," and there is actually a "shortage of qualified secretaries in many parts of the country." Secretaries are third on the Bureau's list of occupations with the largest job growth projected for 1982–1995. If the worst happens, you won't have any trouble finding another job.

But if you keep your boss informed and follow prudent decision-making techniques, you won't get yourself in a position where you *can* be fired.

THE ONLY WHAT-IF THAT MATTERS

The only what-if question you should ask yourself is: "What if I don't start taking some risk and making decisions and solving problems?" You can worry all you want about the consequences of getting in over your head and making a bad decision, but the consequences of *not* taking some risk in the first place are even worse: you never get promoted.

Being a manager means taking responsibility for a major piece of the business, not just making sure a letter gets typed or the filing is caught up. When you refuse to *try* to handle problems, you relegate yourself back to "invisible woman" status.

HOW TO MAKE A GOOD DECISION

The best way to overcome your fear is to learn how to solve problems. Problem-solving requires good decision-making, which is both a science and an art. Decision-making is a science because there are prescribed steps you can take to formulate a good decision. It's an art, because sometimes those steps leave you short of a definitive answer, and the final decision has to rest on what "feels" right.

Whether the decision is a big one or a small one, one that will affect only yourself or one that has company-wide impact, these steps can insure that your decision is a good one:

1. *Find the real problem.* Don't get side-tracked into thinking a symptom is actually the problem. The fact that you're disorganized and can never find anything may be just a symptom of a larger problem—too much work, too little work space, lack of storage facilities, or a reluctance to throw anything away.

   Use the "Because" approach to find the real problem: I can't find last month's accounts receivable report, *because* . . .

- I misfiled it.
- My boss took it off my desk without telling me.
- I don't have room to file anything.
- I don't have *time* to file anything.
- I gave it to the sales manager and she lost it.

List all the reasons you can think of, and when you've decided which of those caused the problem, use the "Because" approach again: My boss took the report off my desk, *because* . . .

- He didn't have his own copy.
- He lost his copy.
- He gave his copy away.

If your boss had a copy, but gave it away, maybe you aren't distributing enough copies of the report, or you are distributing them to the wrong people. Now you've arrived at the *real* problem, not just one of its symptoms.

A word of caution: don't jump to premature conclusions. Your boss may have taken the accounts receivable report off your desk because it's confidential information that he doesn't want left lying around for anyone to see. That's a different problem with a different solution.

2. *Get the authority to investigate the problem.* As a secretary, your decision-making responsibility is limited, and in some cases, may be actively restricted by your boss. If the problem involves other people in your department, if the solution might be time-consuming or expensive, you may need to get your boss's approval to become involved. Explain to your boss how the problem and its solution affect your job, then request permission to explore possible solutions. Make sure your boss understands that you will keep him informed and that you won't make commitments without his approval.

3. *Gather information and advice.* Use every possible source to acquire information about the problem and its possible solutions.

- *Talk to experts in the field.* If your problem concerns word processing, meet with a member of your company's data processing department. Talk to computer dealers and members of word processing associations. Attend computer trade shows and talk to exhibitors.

- *Read trade journals, consumer magazines and any other pertinent printed material.* The experts you talk to can refer you to the right publications if you are not already familiar with them.

- *Discuss the problem with the people who are involved in it.* Get everyone's perspective on the problem and what solutions are possible and palatable. Someone may have the answer you're looking for.

4. *Develop a list of solutions.* Work out all the solutions you can, and no matter how far out they seem at this stage, write them down. Work with the list, adding to it and figuring out the details of each solution. Consider:

- *Cost versus benefit received.* Price—especially value received for that price—is always a consideration. The *ideal* solution may be much too expensive to be the *best* solution.

- *Time needed to implement the solution.* Does the problem need to be solved this week, or is next month soon enough? Is a time-consuming solution feasible, or do you need one you can implement quickly?

- *People needed to implement the solution.* How many people will each solution require? Is a particular person necessary, and if so, will you be able to get them to cooperate? The "perfect" solution won't work if it depends on someone who doesn't want to be involved.

- *Future needs.* How long should the solution last? Solutions shouldn't be outdated tomorrow, but most of them don't need to last for the next decade. Does the solution need to be flexible enough to accommodate future growth?

- *The Big Picture.* How does each solution impact the organization as a whole? Analyze any possible far-reaching effects your decision might have. And don't automatically assume that, as a secretary, you'd never make a decision that would have widespread implications.

5. *Give it the 24-Hour Test.* Let your subconscious work on the problem, at least for a night—longer if the decision is a major one. Solution A (or B or C) may seem like the right one today, but it's smart to wait and see if it still feels right tomorrow.

6. *Make a decision, and commit to it.* Make your decision in a reasonable time period, and once you decide, don't second guess yourself, and don't change your mind a week later (unless conditions change unexpectedly). Even the best solution won't work if you implement it half-heartedly.

7. *Sell it to your boss.* Get approval from your boss (or whoever has the authority to approve it), and be sure you have a commitment for the money, time, and personnel you'll need.

8. *Implement your decision.* Once the decision is made, the real work begins—implementing it. Lay out a plan, step by step, for accomplishing the goals you've set. If other people are working with you, assign responsibilities and deadlines. Then monitor everyone's progress (including your own), and stay on it until the project is completed.

Not every decision requires all these steps, but if you use this decision-making procedure regularly, it will become second nature. You'll go through the steps without realizing it.

AVOID MAKING A BAD DECISION

A run of bad decisions can undermine your chances of success, so steer clear of these traps:

Don't shoot from the hip. Magazines are full of highly successful business mavericks who claim they make decisions solely on "gut feel." They eschew research and advisors and base their decisions on what feels right.

Good for them.

The truth is these people have highly developed instincts about the marketplace, usually from having been in the business for many years. Until *you* become a highly successful business maverick, don't try to imitate them. Make your decisions on sound information, research, and decision-making principles. You don't have to completely ignore your intuition—if you have a nagging feeling that one solution is the way to go, it probably is. But that's what the 24-Hour Test is for—to give your instincts a chance to work.

To rely on your hunches without doing your homework is dangerous.

Don't make decisions in a vacuum. Deciding to redesign the filing system is great, but if you proceed without informing and conferring with the other people who use the system (even if it's only your boss), you're asking for trouble.

People dislike change, and when it is forced on them without notice or consultation, they dislike it intensely. Your decisions and your solutions to problems will be much more readily accepted, and therefore more easily implemented, if the people who are affected by them are kept informed from the beginning.

Don't wait too long to decide. You will never have all the information you need to make a fool-proof decision. You will never have totally reliable research data, and you will never get everyone to agree on one solution. Decisions have to be made on the best information you can gather in a reasonable period of time.

If you wait for the perfect solution to present itself, you will postpone making a decision until long after one was necessary. You will research your decisions to death—the death of your career, probably—because making no decision can be as bad, and sometimes worse, than making the wrong decision.

PASS ALONG SOLUTIONS, NOT PROBLEMS

Active problem solving means that you never bring a problem to your boss without bringing him a solution. Never dump a problem on your boss's desk and say, "I don't know how to handle this. What do you want me to do about it?"

Here's a perfect example of how *not* to handle problems:

> Gail, receptionist, secretary, and girl Friday, works for a lecture bureau I frequently deal with. I was just leaving the president's office one day, when I saw Gail answer the phone. She put her hand over the receiver (not bothering to put the caller on hold), and yelled to the president. "Chuck? Max Howard is on the phone—he says he's lost his records, he's months behind on his billing, and he doesn't remember how much he should invoice us for the work he did earlier this year." She stopped.
>
> "I don't know," Chuck said blankly. He had been in mid-sentence to me about some future projects he was considering, and Gail's question took him by surprise. He turned to me. "You were involved in that, do you remember what Max did for us?"
>
> "Not without going back over the records," I said.
>
> Gail offered no help. She just sat there with the phone in her lap, looking vacantly into space, waiting for somebody to deal with the problem. Chuck's assistant wandered by, and Chuck grabbed him. "Do you remember what Max did for us earlier this year?"
>
> The assistant looked puzzled and said, "I don't know, I think Gail's got the records. No, wait, they might be in my office. I'll go check." He headed for his office.
>
> Meanwhile, good old Max is sitting in Gail's lap, paying $1.15 a minute from San Diego to be ignored. Chuck turned to me and said, "Are you sure you don't know? . . ."
>
> "Wait a minute," I said. I turned to Gail and in my best drill instructor voice barked, "Gail, tell Max that Chuck will look for that information and call him back when he finds it, then *hang up*."
>
> Having finally received an instruction from someone, she hung up.

This is no way to take charge and solve problems, and certainly no way to demonstrate that you have management potential. Instead of immediately telling Max that Chuck was in a meeting, that she would get the information and call him back, Gail decided to act like she'd had a lobotomy.

THE BENEFITS OF DEVELOPING SOLUTIONS

Have at least one possible solution in mind before you ever relate a problem to your boss, and present it for consideration when you present the problem. This is critical for two reasons, both equally important:

1. *You gain practice solving problems.* Stop being frustrated by difficulties in the office, and start devising ways to eliminate them or circumvent them.

2. *You gain respect from your boss.* Show your boss that you want to help, that you're eager to share the load, and that you won't leave every bit of thinking that's done in your department up to him.

You may not always be right, but you will leave the impression that you are *thinking*, that you are making an effort to become a more productive part of the team. As you get better at solving problems, your boss will begin to rely more and more on your help and your judgment.

PRESENT SOLUTIONS DIPLOMATICALLY

Some executives who welcome comments, criticism, and suggestions from their peers don't want to hear it from their secretaries. Not having much respect for secretaries' ability, they take it as an affront when their secretaries have the "audacity" to suggest there's a better way. So it's important to present your solutions in a palatable form.

If you have been the silent partner in your office duo until now, don't send your boss into apoplectic fits by suddenly countermanding every order with: "You *must* be kidding. It would be so much easier, not to mention more logical, if we . . . ." You may find yourself on the unemployment line.

Present your solutions in the form of helpful suggestions. After you've explained the problem, introduce your solution by saying, "Would it be a good idea to . . ." or, "Maybe we could . . ." or,

"What do you think of . . .?" Once your boss begins to accept you as a thinking, contributing member of the team, you can get more forceful.

But don't play dumb, shuffle your feet, and say, "This may be stupid because I don't know anything about it, but I thought maybe we could, uh, do it this way." No attempt to solve a problem is stupid, and if you treat your solution as uninformed or unworthy of consideration, that's exactly how your boss will treat it. Playing dumb puts you in a subservient position—something you're trying to get out of.

I'm not suggesting you offer solutions for anything and everything that happens in the office, or try to one-up your boss on everything he suggests. But do offer a solution if you could in any way be involved in implementing it, and *never* fail to offer a solution if you are the one who calls attention to the problem.

"ENLIGHTEN ME SO I CAN DO A BETTER JOB"

Don't be embarrassed, insulted, or discouraged if your boss doesn't accept your solution, if he turns it down, or wants to do it differently. Your solution may be a good one, but some bosses (some people) want things done their way and their way only. Or your solution may be wrong—your boss has more experience than you do, and he may have a better perspective on the problem. Either way, get his rationale for doing it differently, and learn from what he tells you. Say, "I'll be glad to handle it that way. My solution seems to be somewhat off the mark, but I'm not really sure why. Could you explain to me where I went wrong?"

This is a particularly good question to ask if you suspect your boss is just being stubborn about doing things his way. It puts him, politely, on the spot. But don't offend your boss by acting like he doesn't know what he's talking about (even if he doesn't).

Treat it as a learning experience, with you as the student and your boss as the teacher. Don't hang sweetly on his every word, but let him know that you want to learn and that he, being in a superior position in the company, can help you. Your attitude should be "enlighten me so I can do a better job." He'll be flattered and glad to give you more information on the "whys" of what he's doing.

ON YOUR OWN

Your best bet for reducing the risk of solving problems is getting your boss's approval before you act. But bosses have an unfortunate habit of being gone just when you need them most. At those times, you have three options:

1. Do nothing until you can talk to your boss.

2. Ask someone else to make the decision, such as your boss's boss, or one of the other executives in the office.

3. Take the bull by the horns and make the decision yourself.

Which you choose depends on the magnitude of the problem and how urgent it is. Each option has its advantages and disadvantages.

Do nothing until the boss is available. This is the best choice if the decision is a major one, and if you're sure it can wait until your boss gets back.

Just don't make yourself look bad if you have to postpone handling a problem: "I'm sorry, Mr. Hunter, my boss is out of town, and I don't know anything about it. I really don't know what to tell you. All I can do is take a message. You'll have to wait until he gets back."

Your boss's absence lets you work directly with people who usually by-pass you. Even if you can't solve their problems, handle as much as you can, and tell them when they can expect an answer and what you will do to expedite it. Use these situations to increase your visibility and get your name known.

Turn the problem over to another executive. You may not be able to wait for your boss if he's on a 2-week vacation and not expected to call in. If you have to hand the problem off to someone else in the office, make sure getting the burden off you doesn't backfire. Choosing the wrong person to handle the problem can make the problem worse. Consider:

- Does the person have enough information and background to make a sound decision?

- If you take the problem to your boss's boss, will your boss resent you going over his head?

- Given your boss's alliances in the office, is the person a good choice? Never take a problem to your boss's arch rival.

- Is confidential information involved?

When you involve another manager, use the opportunity to make yourself look good:

- Deliver a suggested solution along with the problem, just like you would with your boss:

"We've had a problem come up that can't wait until Jim gets back. I think handling it in the following way would be appropriate, but I'd like your advice on it."

- Make your presentation calm and polished—you're a professional turning a problem over to someone who has more authority.

- Make your presentation short and to the point—don't waste the executive's time.

Since this is a chance to interact with other executives and show them your stuff, choose someone who's on the fast track. They'll remember you and may be able to help your career later on.

Make the decision yourself. Sometimes your only option is to handle it yourself. As soon as you can, tell your boss about it, so he won't hear it first from someone else, and so he can make corrections as soon as possible if your decision wasn't right on the money.

Jeff and Ron were partners in a firm that produced electronic parts. They were constantly fighting over allocation of the money they made. Jeff wanted certain bills paid, while Ron wanted to spend more money on development. Jeff was able to maintain fairly good control over the books, because Ron had his office in his home, about 45 minutes from the main office. Most of the wrangling went on over the phone. But then Jeff decided to go hunting for a week.

He was no sooner gone than Ron called Jeff's secretary, Trudy, and told her he would be over the next day to review the books and write some checks. Trudy was in a panic. She knew Jeff would be furious if he came back and found Ron had spent the company's money. She knew she couldn't tell Ron not to—he was the co-owner of the company. What to do? She thought about it and decided that the best thing that could happen would be if nothing *could* happen. She put the books in Jeff's filing cabinet and locked it. Since she didn't have a key to the filing cabinet, she couldn't unlock it until Jeff got back. Then she called Ron and told him she had discovered the books were locked up, and that he'd have to wait until Jeff returned on Monday. Ron was annoyed, but there wasn't much he could do about it.

As soon as Jeff got back, Trudy told him what she had done. She explained she wasn't trying to undercut Ron's authority, but she felt she had to protect Jeff's interests because he was her primary boss. Jeff was delighted. Because Trudy had kept the corporate funds intact, he was able to pay some critical bills.

Most situations aren't that tough, but sometimes you just have to jump in and handle it yourself. When you have to go it alone, make an extra effort to make a good decision.

START SMALL

Problem-solving is a skill, and like any skill, it can be learned. Start taking responsibility for solving small problems, ones that involve only yourself, and work your way up to solving departmental problems. Think of problems as being stratified into three levels:

Level I: Just You. These concern only you and don't have much impact on the people around you—your work area is disorganized, or the office goof-off spends all of his time bothering you. You can solve Level I problems without committing time and money resources, and whatever solution you come up with can probably be implemented alone.

This is the place to start practicing problem-solving and decision-making. Your exposure is low, and the consequences of choosing a poor solution are minimal. If you make a mistake, chances are no one will notice.

Level II: Your Problem, but Others Are Involved. This level affects other people, and your solutions for them may require time, money, and manpower.

For example: your old typewriter is constantly breaking down, causing delays for the three managers you work for. The maintenance costs are getting out of hand, and your bosses are getting impatient with the work backup, but replacing that old typewriter with a word processor will take time and money, and there'll be a slowdown in production while you learn the new equipment.

Although you are primarily involved, the solution to this problem will consume resources and will change the way you and the people around you work. If you're responsible for recommending which equipment is right, your choice needs to be a good one—several people are depending on you.

Level III: Someone Else's Problem, but You're Involved. Handling problems at this level means you begin to *assume* management responsibilities. But as a secretary, you will probably never be asked to solve a Level III problem. To get involved, you'll have to volunteer. Nominate yourself as the best person to work on the problem. Convince your boss (or whoever's making the assignment) that you're the person to handle the job.

Solving Level III problems can launch you into management, because it shows your ability to accept responsibility, solve major problems, work with people, and implement new programs and policies.

Jackie was one of three secretaries working in the editorial department of a book publisher. Because of haphazard planning, each secretary had a different computer, and each computer had a different word processing program. To make matters worse, none of the three women was trained to use the other two systems. When one of them was gone, the other two couldn't cover for her, and it was impossible to double up on large projects.

Their bosses didn't know how to solve the problem, so they just ignored the situation and put up with the inconvenience. It never occurred to them to ask one of the secretaries to work on the problem, to let one of the people actually using the systems look into developing a more workable set-up.

Jackie decided to take the initiative. She asked her boss if she could investigate the problem. She offered to do an evaluation of each system, develop a list of options—such as cross-training or purchasing new equipment or new software—and perform a cost-benefit analysis on each option. She emphasized her qualifications: word processing experience and an ability to work with people. Her boss, relieved that someone was finally willing to tackle the problem, gave her free rein to study possible solutions.

After talking to the other secretaries, interviewing computer dealers, and reading the latest office management and computer magazines, she made this recommendation:

1. A new software program—one that had more features than any of the three programs the secretaries were now using—should become the office standard.
2. To save money, separate versions of the program would be bought for each machine (software is configured differently for each computer on the market), instead of replacing two of the computers.
3. After learning the new program, the secretaries would be trained to use each other's computers.
4. Over a period of 5 years, the computers would be replaced and standardized.
5. She would be put in charge of purchasing and training for the new software, and later, the hardware conversion.

On the strength of that proposal, Jackie was offered a job as an assistant in the personnel department, with special responsibility for word processing installation throughout the rest of the company. Her future looks very good, because she was willing to take on a problem that fell quite a bit outside her immediate realm of responsibility. She took some risk, and it paid off with a promotion.

11. The world beyond the filing cabinet

Imagine yourself walking down Fifth Avenue in New York City, heading for the Empire State Building. Traffic is terrible, you have trouble crossing the street because of the crowds, and right in front of the building, a street vendor is having a shouting match with one of his customers over whether the customer gave him a $20 bill or a $10 bill. The vendor and his customer have the sidewalk blocked, and you edge around them to get into the building. This is New York City all right, and you're right in the middle of the action on the street.

You walk in the door of the Empire State Building and get on the elevator. Every few floors, you stop, get off and check the view. The higher you go, the more you can see. Finally, standing on the Observation Deck at the top of the building, you have a view of the whole island of Manhattan, Central Park to the north, New Jersey to the west, and the Atlantic Ocean to the south.

But from the Observation Deck, you can hardly see the street corner you just fought your way through. You can't tell if the street vendor is fighting with that customer or selling him a hot dog. In fact, you can't see the street vendor at all. Is that a traffic accident below? Hard to tell, and really not all that important anymore. From your vantage point, that fire in another skyscraper nearby, or that ominous weather front coming in from the west, look much more important.

THE ORGANIZATIONAL HIGH-RISE

Companies are like buildings. The people at the top have a completely different view than those at the bottom. As a secretary, you have a street-level view—a very limited perspective. You can see what is going on around you in great detail, but your vision extends only a few blocks.

The president of the company, on the other hand, is standing on the top of the building, and he can see what's going on for miles. He has a much larger perspective, but he makes a sacrifice for it—he can't tell what's going on at street level. Because there are so many other things to look at and be concerned about, he doesn't know what's happening down on the street corner, and he really doesn't care. As long as they don't affect the well-being of his building, problems at the bottom don't worry him.

THE POINT-OF-VIEW PROBLEM

Being at the bottom causes secretaries considerable frustration, because it distorts their perspective. I've heard secretaries say:

- "They have no idea what's going on down here, or they never would have instituted that policy."

- "I can't understand why someone doesn't fire my boss—he's arrogant, obnoxious, and I'm doing all his work for him."

- "Nobody around here cares."

They (meaning upper management) don't care, because they don't have time to care. They've got other things to worry about—that profits are down by 20 percent this quarter, that research and development is 6 months behind on a critical project, or that the company's strongest competitor has just launched an aggressive new advertising campaign.

As long as your department meets its objectives, they don't care about what goes on day-to-day in your office.

It's a tough realization for secretaries to make, but problems at the "bottom of the building" office don't matter to the boys upstairs as long as the "Big Picture" items like budget, sales, costs, and quality control are properly covered.

WHAT MOTIVATES MANAGEMENT

To see how this all works, let's look at what drives the different levels of management:

The owners of a corporation have only one priority: what's best for the company's financial welfare. What's best for the employees, or anybody else, comes second. Fortunately, in many instances, what's best for the employees and what's best for the company's coffers coincide: it's in the company's best interest to keep union members happy so they don't go out on strike; and it's in the company's best interest to keep its star employees happy so they don't quit and take their talents elsewhere (especially to the competition).

But when those two interests don't coincide, the owners will always do what the bottom line dictates. The most paternalistic company in the world will close or sell a division that continually loses money—even if it means putting hundreds of people out of work.

One international company that had to lay off a large number of executives in the mid-1970s made a special effort to relocate its managers. Programs were set up through the human resources department to research possible employment opportunities; assistance was provided for preparing résumés and making contact with executive search firms. Despite the financial problems that made the lay-offs necessary, the company devoted time, money, and personnel to make the separation as painless as possible. For about a month, that is. Then the people in the human resources department were laid off, and the altruistic relocation activity came to an abrupt end.

Upper management reports to the owners, and their primary concern is to keep the owners happy, so they can hang on to their prestigious jobs and lavish perks. That again means doing what's best for the bottom line. People in upper management are highly motivated and highly competitive, and for most of them, business is an all-consuming passion. Acquisitions, price-to-earnings ratios, and pre-tax profits get their adrenalin going. But being at the "top of the building," their ability to see people extends only to the uppermost layers of middle management. Below that, they see only numbers.

Middle management wants to become upper management, so they do everything they can to make the owners and upper management happy. In other words, the bottom line is still king. A middle manager knows that a screw-up by one of his people may mean *his* head rolls, so he wants team players working for him who understand the corporate goals and know how to reach them. All others are a threat to the middle manager's upward mobility and are treated accordingly.

First-line managers, under the weight of all this scrutiny, are scrambling for results so they can keep their jobs. They are expendable and replaceable, and they know it. Some will be cheerleaders and some will be tyrants, but their goals are the same—to get results from their people anyway they can.

Public-sector managers don't have the profit motive driving them, but they still have to answer to the owners (the taxpayers) and upper management (elected officials), and they need to continually justify the existence of their position, department, or agency. They have the same personal motives as private industry managers—they want more money, more power, and more prestige.

WHAT YOU OWE THE ORGANIZATION—AND VICE VERSA

So what should you expect at work? What do you owe the organization and what does it owe you? It's important that you know.

You owe the organization to:

1. *Take responsibility for all your job duties and accomplish them at the highest possible level of performance.* Not *part* of your

job responsibilities—all of them. If filing is part of your job responsibilities, make sure it gets done—no matter how distasteful it is. Reduce the amount of paperwork generated by your office, simplify the filing system, hire someone else to do it, or whatever is most practical. But *you* take responsibility for it. Give it your best possible effort and try to get the best possible results—on filing and every other assignment you handle.

2. *Work the hours you are assigned.* If office hours are 8:30 to 5:00, *be there* from 8:30 to 5:00. Not 8:40 or 8:50, but *8:30.*

3. *Work a reasonable amount of overtime without complaining or demanding additional pay.* The company expects you to put in a little extra effort when the need arises, and that expectation is not unreasonable.

4. *Appear loyal to the organization and to your supervisors. Appear* is the operative word here. You have an obligation not to bad-mouth the organization, its products and services, or your boss—particularly to people outside the company. In reality, of course, *you,* not the company, are number one on your professional loyalty list. The company is, should be, and expects to be a distant second.

5. *Offer reasonable cooperation in helping the organization meet its goals and objectives.* "But it's not in my job description" just doesn't cut it. You owe it to the company to be part of the team. You owe it to the company to pitch in and make a special trip to the post office because a bid *has* to be in the mail today, or help another secretary collate materials for the national sales meeting that starts tomorrow morning—even though you don't have to, even though it's not in your job description, and even though you're not getting paid extra for it.

WHAT THE ORGANIZATION OWES YOU

A list of what the organization owes you might be developed by simply flip-flopping the list of what you owe the organization. If you owe the organization the best possible performance of all your assigned duties, then the company owes you well-defined job responsibilities and the resources you need to perform them.

The list might be generated that way, but it isn't. The list is much shorter than that:

What the Organization Owes You

1. A paycheck.

That's it. A paycheck. Money for work received. Everything else you can expect to earn the hard way. The company doesn't owe you a job tomorrow, a raise, a promotion, good working conditions, a pleasant supervisor, health insurance, a retirement plan, or an explanation about anything it's doing. If you get any of those from the organization you work for, consider them gifts, bribes, and tools of negotiation.

The organization that provides anything above and beyond a paycheck does so to:

1. Recruit good quality employees who can help the company make a profit.

2. Increase the employees' contentment level, so that productivity will increase and profits will rise.

3. Reduce turnover, so that replacement and retraining expenses don't drain profits.

Anyone who believes an organization provides benefits for any other reason is kidding themselves.

Does that shock you? It shouldn't, because that's the way the business world works. Business is competition—for jobs, for money, for position, for prestige. The players' primary concern is getting the best advantage and the maximum pay-off for themselves.

THE BARTER SYSTEM

Expect the organization to try to get as much out of you as possible. That's part of the game. It is an on-going series of negotiations—you give here, they give there. Upper management provides benefits to its employees to help the organization get what it wants. You, in turn, put in extra effort to help *you* get what *you* want.

That the organization (meaning your boss or some other level of management) wants you to work all weekend does *not* mean that you have to work all weekend. *You* make the decision about whether you will, and you make it on factors like: will it help me get a raise? Is this really an "emergency?" Can I trade this off for that extra vacation day I need?

Just because they ask doesn't mean you are obligated to comply. Naturally, if you decide to say "no," you offer regrets and a good excuse why you can't—you don't say, "I don't want to and I don't have to."

By the same token, the organization expects *you* to make demands. If you come up with a cost-saving innovation that reduces expenditures by $75,000, the organization will expect you to demand reciprocation in some form—a raise, a bonus, a promotion, or a new title. You may not get all you ask for, but the organization will generally abide by the rules of the game and give you something. If you don't ask, they will feel quite free to give you nothing. If you don't ask, you forfeit your turn in the negotiations.

The concept that women have to work harder than men to get the same promotions is true, but many women think they have to work at some superhuman level to get ahead. One legal secretary I knew allowed her bosses (she had two) to call her at any time of the day or night—and because she let them, they took full advantage of it, including having her work one Sunday from midnight to 4:00 a.m. She got overtime pay, but she did it because she felt she had to, because her *bosses* wanted her to.

She didn't understand that her bosses may have *wanted* her to spend half the night in the office, but they didn't really *expect* her to. When these unreasonable requests began, she could have said, "No, I can't, but I'll be glad to come in an hour early in the morning." Her bosses wouldn't have pushed her around, if she hadn't allowed herself to be imposed on. They expected her to say "no." When she said "yes," they took full advantage of it, and she ended up feeling used.

After you've fulfilled the items on the "What You Owe the Organization" list, everything else is optional. Everything else you can say "no" to. Everything else that you do say "yes" to can and *must* be used to negotiate improvements in your salary, your title, or your career.

THAT'S THE WAY IT IS

Some secretaries refuse to accept that the business world works this way, or they accept it, but refuse to deal with it as it really exists. They make comments like:

"That may be the way it is in big corporations, but the company I work for is like a family." That may be true in good times, but what happens when the going gets tough? In hard times, family members sometimes get thrown out on the street.

"That's the way our company is, and I think it's disgusting. All they think about is making money." The only reason corporations exist is to make money. Why else would a company be in business? Complaining about the rules of the business game is like complaining about the rules of tennis. The rules are not up for discussion; they're a given.

Everyone on the managerial level understands that the first rule of business is to make money. You'll never move up if you don't understand and accept that, too.

"Last week they fired the sales manager, who was one of the nicest people I've ever met. I don't want to work for a company that treats people like that." Then you don't want to work for any company at all. Your organization is not a charitable institution that employs and pays people because they're "nice." All companies can and *should* fire people who don't perform. Keeping nonperformers on the payroll drags down the morale of those who do perform, weakens the overall effort of the organization, and may even jeopardize the corporation's existence. The company you work for is not the Sisters of Mercy Home for Wayward Employees. If you don't perform, you're out.

THE RULES OF THE GAME

As all this begins to sink in, your outlook on a number of things should change. As simplistic as it sounds, business is business. It is not home, school, or family. Women, because they are so heavily socialized in that direction, often try to recreate their home/school/family environment in the office. They treat their bosses like parents. They turn other secretaries into close personal friends. They expect to be rewarded for being "good girls."

And they are usually disappointed.

The business world, whether it's public-sector or private industry, operates on a completely different set of rules and standards than the personal world does. The rules that govern your behavior at home, school, or in the family *do not work in business*. The concepts of loyalty, friendship, fairness, and reward change radically when moved from private life to the business arena.

WHAT THE GAME WON'T PROVIDE

Because business is a game and profit is the objective, it's a mistake to try to get out of business what it was never designed to give. Marriage, family, even school are human institutions that give rise to human emotions—love, compassion, friendship—but business is a *non*human institution that provides none of these things:

In business you won't get and shouldn't try to find:

Loyalty. You might put it all on the line for a close friend, but don't be foolish enough to do it for a boss or co-worker. They won't do it for you.

Don't be misled by the benevolent boss who's a joy to work for, who genuinely likes you as a person, and who always goes to bat for his employees. People like that are wonderful to work for, but when the chips are down, and it means his job or yours, look out—you're headed for the unemployment line.

Jennifer, now a financial analyst for an insurance company, said she learned the loyalty lesson very early in her career. "My first job was in a large division where a real power struggle was going on. The vice president didn't like the general manager and wanted to get rid of him, but the general manager had a lot of support from his department managers. The department managers really liked him, they respected his ability, and like good team players, they made a lot of noise about what they'd do if the vice president forced him out. They said they'd quit, they'd "walk right out the door behind him," and they'd never work for his replacement.

"One Monday morning we came to work to find the general manager gone," Jennifer said. "The vice president had fired him late Friday night, after everyone else had left.

"Naive as I was, I expected a full-scale exodus, with department managers throwing their resignations on the new general manager's desk in disgust—and I was ready to go with them. But nothing happened. Nobody left, nobody even complained very loud—at least not so any of the new regime could hear them. Nobody went anywhere. They all had families to support, and they just couldn't afford to make the grand gesture."

Friendship. The office is the wrong place to find personal friends. When you get promoted, you may have to manage, direct, criticize, or even fire those friends. Managers avoid office friendships for that very reason.

Romance. The fact is that office romances happen all the time. But you'd better do everything you can to avoid having one. If you're single, he's single, you work in widely separated divisions of a large corporation, and you do your utmost to keep it secret, it *might* not work against you. Even then, once the news gets out (as it always does) the emphasis shifts from your professional ability to your romantic involvement, and you've lost ground in your promotional drive.

If you have an affair with your married boss, and it ends (as it always does), you and your career, at least with that company, are history.

Automatic reward. At home as a child, you got an allowance just because you were a member of the family. At school, your teachers always noticed extra effort and praised you for it. At home, your husband or boyfriend takes you out to dinner because you've been working so hard. But in business, there are no automatic rewards. Just working hard won't get you anything but that next paycheck and one of those famous Secretary's Week lunches. Working 50-hour weeks doesn't guarantee you anything—it just gives you an extra bargaining point in your on-going negotiations with management.

Personal approval. Everybody wants to be liked, but most successful business people learn to control this desire at work. You can't make everybody happy and have everyone like you—it just isn't possible. And the higher you go in an organization, the more true this is. Some people will dislike you just because you're the boss; others, regardless of how they feel about you, will try to take over your job or usurp your authority; still others will try to prevent you from gaining power in the first place. Nothing personal, you understand, it's just business.

BUT IT'S FUN

All that awful, dehumanizing, profit-oriented stuff notwithstanding, business can be fun, because it *is* a game. Success is a natural high. Getting promotions and raises uplifts your psyche and your lifestyle. Seeing a project pay off that you've worked hard on provides tremendous satisfaction. You get to work with and learn from some exciting, talented people.

The business world is a place to go to compete for riches and rewards—a place where you can put on your best suit and your businesswoman persona and feel good about yourself and what you can accomplish. If you don't succeed today, there's always tomorrow, and if you do succeed, there's more ego gratification than you'll know what to do with.

HOW A BIG PICTURE PERSPECTIVE CAN HELP YOU

Understanding the Big Picture—what's happening in your industry and your organization, how your job and your boss's job fit into that picture, and what the rules of the game are—can get you those rewards. It can make both today more pleasant and tomorrow more profitable, because seeing the Big Picture lets you:

Understand changes in the organization. If you have a Big Picture perspective, you won't get caught off-guard by a major reorganization, the sale of a division, or a series of lay-offs.

Stop taking organizational changes personally. You also understand that those changes are not directed at you personally. Staff reductions and budget cuts are attempts to overcome financial difficulties, they're not attempts to make your life miserable.

Depersonalize criticism. Most bosses don't criticize employees because they enjoy it. They do it because the employee is not meeting the company's standards or goals. Take the long view, and address criticism as an indication of a business problem, not a personal problem.

Determine potential career paths. See the organization as a whole, and you'll see areas where you can make an impact and slots you can move up into—a new management job in your department or opportunities in another department.

Get yourself in step with organizational goals. Understand where top-level management wants to take the organization, so you can gear your efforts around those goals. You don't want to be emphasizing cost control if better customer service is the number-one priority.

Relate better to executives. When you understand the Big Picture, you have something to talk about to the organization's managers and executives. An intelligent conversation about trends in your industry or the condition of your organization shows you've got a managerial outlook.

HOW TO GET A BIG PICTURE PERSPECTIVE

Getting a view of the Big Picture takes more work for secretaries than it does for managers. Managers are naturally exposed to it; in fact, they are inundated with it. They attend planning meetings with other managers and higher level executives. They attend conferences, seminars, and conventions, where they meet with executives from other organizations and industries. They read trade publications, industry newsletters, and general business newspapers and magazines.

Secretaries don't have these advantages, but with a little digging, snooping, and scrounging, you can get the information you need on:

The industry you work in. What market trends are affecting your business today, and what trends will influence it 5 years from now? Is your industry in a growth phase, or on the decline? What impact is international competition having? What are the market leaders in your industry doing that keeps them on top?

Any manager worth her salt knows the answers to those questions off the top of her head, and you should, too.

The general economic climate. Your industry operates in a regional, national, or international marketplace, and you should be aware of the financial, political, and social condition of that marketplace.

The organization you work for. Find out how your organization fits into your industry and the general economic picture. What position does your company hold in the marketplace? What is your company's growth rate compared to the industry as a whole, or compared to your major competitors? If you work for a government agency, how does it compare to similar agencies in other states or other branches of the government? You need to know.

Your boss's job. Find out exactly what your boss does (or what he should be doing), so you can help him do it better, and start assuming some of those responsibilities yourself.

Your own job. You already know your own job? It's typing, filing, answering the phone, and babysitting your boss?

Not at all. Your job is information management—including communications, word processing, and recordkeeping. Your responsibilities are to:

1. Find the most efficient and productive means of doing your job.

2. Coordinate your efforts with the goals of the organization.

3. Assist your boss in maximizing his efficiency and productivity.

The better you manage your own job, the better your chances for getting ahead.

It's time for more homework. Only this isn't just homework. It's on-going research you will do as long as you hold down a job—because this research is a regular part of a manager's job.

START READING THE TRADE PUBLICATIONS

You can't go to trade shows, and you don't get asked to strategy meetings, but you do have access to the trade publications, because your boss reads them.

Industry publications. If you're in insurance, he might read *National Underwriter* or *Best's Review.* If you're in computers, he might get *Datamation* or *Computerworld.*

Ask your boss if you can borrow his copies when he's through reading them. Set up a library system, and keep back issues on file, where you can refer to them. If your boss tears his copies up to save articles and other information, locate another copy coming into the office, or get your own subscription.

If your boss isn't reading any industry publications, talk to the other secretaries and find out what *their* bosses are reading, or consult industry publication directories such as:

- Standard Rate & Data Service's *Business Publication Rates and Data.*

- *The Standard Periodical Directory.*

- The Working Press of the Nation's *Media Encyclopedia, Volume #2, Magazine Directory*.

- Ulrich's *International Periodicals Directory*.

You can find these directories in most libraries. Your company's advertising department or agency has a copy of the Standard Rate & Data Service directory. Call the advertising manager or agency account executive and ask what publications cover your industry. They'll be happy to look them up for you.

When you locate the right publications, suggest to your boss that you get subscriptions to the top two or three for your department. (If you're not sure which are the top publications, use circulation, which is also listed in the directories mentioned above, as a guide.) Companies pay for business magazine subscriptions, and many trade publications provide free subscriptions to qualified applicants (this is called controlled circulation).

General business magazines. It's always tempting, when you decide to become a business success, to start reading *Business Week, The Wall Street Journal*, or one of the other general business publications. You'll need those publications when you get further up the corporate ladder, but at this point in your career, general business publications cover too broad a spectrum. Don't waste your time reading about off-shore drilling problems if what you really need to understand is the airline industry.

Occupation-specific publications. Your boss also probably reads magazines directed at his particular occupation. If he's in purchasing, he might read *Purchasing Magazine* or *Purchasing World*; if he's in advertising, *Marketing & Media Decisions* or *Magazine Age*; if he's in meeting planning, *Meetings & Conventions* or *Successful Meetings*—every occupation has dozens of magazines and newsletters devoted to it. (Of course, many of these publications serve double-duty—if you work in the data processing department of a computer manufacturing firm, *Data Communications* will cover both your industry and your department.)

Again, ask to borrow these magazines from your boss—or find

out which ones he *should* be reading and get subscriptions for him (and yourself).

Office management publications. To get information about improving your job performance and ideas on how to upgrade office efficiency, read at least one office management publication regularly.

Here's a list, by no means exhaustive, of magazines that can help you. If you're not familiar with them, write or call their circulation departments for a sample copy:

Modern Office Technology
111 Chester Avenue
Cleveland, Ohio 44114
(216) 696-7000

The Office
1200 Summer Street
P.O. Box 1231
Stamford, Connecticut 06904
(203) 327-9670

Office Administration and Automation
51 Madison Avenue
New York, New York 10010
(212) 689-4411

Today's Office
645 Stewart Avenue
Garden City, New York 11530
(516) 222-2500

While all this may sound like you'll be carrying a stack of magazines with you wherever you go, you may be able to handle your research by reading only three magazines per month—one for your industry, one for your boss's job, and one for your job. If you are going to be accepted into the managerial ranks, you have to do more than just dress, act, and communicate like a manager. You have to be informed like one, so you can think like one.

Information is power—it gives you the extra edge you need to get ahead.

NATIONAL AND LOCAL NEWS

Read one general news magazine, like *Newsweek* or *Time*, or watch the national news, to get general information on the economic climate. (Trade magazines also regularly publish articles about the general economy and how it affects the industry they cover.) You'll also get information that can help you improve your image. When you interact with executives, you need to talk about different topics than the ones you discuss with the secretaries. Children, clothes, and man trouble need to be replaced with discussions of mortgage rates, the recent lay-offs at a competitor's headquarters, or who's going to win the Series (that's the World Series, for the uninitiated).

A word of caution: following sports is a nice touch, but it's still largely a male purview, so go easy. Be familiar with major events like the Olympics, the Super Bowl and the World Series, but don't rattle off the batting averages of the Cleveland Indians' starting line-up—it makes you look like you're trying too hard.

How much attention you should pay to local news depends on your organization. If you work for an international marketer of gourmet foods, it won't affect your company if the Firefighters Local 415 files a grievance against the fire chief. But if you work for a local real estate developer who gets building plans approved by the fire department, this news may affect the way you deal with fire department officials.

INTERNAL PUBLICATIONS AND REPORTS

If you work for an industry leader, the trade publications will talk about your company—what its financial condition is, what its future plans are, the success or failure of its new product introductions. If you work for a small company, that information is harder to come by, but you can learn a lot from:

Annual reports. Get a copy of your company's annual report from your boss, or check the local libraries—many of them carry annual reports. Read the report thoroughly, and if you can get copies from the past 4 or 5 years, read them as well. The annual report gives you a view of the company from upper management's per-

spective. You may see your company primarily as a perfume manufacturer—because that's the division you work for—but upper
management may view the company as an international conglomerate with interests ranging from lumber production in Oregon to
cattle ranching in Argentina.

Keep in mind, though, that annual reports are given to stock-
holders and potential investors, so they paint as rosy a picture of
the company as possible.

Business, marketing, and operating plans. Here's where you'll find
the real scoop. These plans show what management really expects
to accomplish in the next 1 to 5 years. They analyze the company's past performance, and describe the nuts-and-bolts of how it
expects to reach its future goals.

Financial reports. The various financial reports issued by your organization or department (see Chapter 4 for a description of the
most common ones) tell you how the company is currently doing
compared to the projections in the business, marketing, or operating plan.

ASK YOUR BOSS

Don't overlook your boss as a source of information. Even if he's
not on the fast track or he's out of favor with upper management, he
still understands the industry, the organization, and his own job. He
may know much more than his standing in the organization would
indicate. If he *is* on the fast track and he *is* in the good graces of upper
management, then he's a gold-mine of information—not only about
the business, but how to be successful at it.

Once you're up to speed with your trade publication reading, it's
time to start pumping your boss. Do this in two phases:

Phase One: Request General Information. Explain to your boss
that you want more information *so that you can do your job better*.
Tell him you want to understand the organization and its goals,
how it fits into the industry in general, how your department fits
into the organization, and what the department's goals are.

Ask to see a list of the department's goals. If they aren't written down anywhere, take notes, or write them down when you leave his office, so you'll have them for later use. Don't let him get off the track onto what *your* job goals are; tell him you want to know where the department is headed.

Ask if you can read the annual report, the business plan, and his trade magazines. Then arrange to discuss them with him. If you have a difficult boss, use a little flattery about his level of knowledge and experience, and say how grateful you'd be if he'd share that with you. That's manipulative, but totally justified if your boss is reluctant to give you information.

Phase Two: Give So That Ye May Receive. To get inside information from your boss—the status of the corporate takeover, what's really happening in the new division—you have to offer something in return, something he can't get elsewhere.

What have you got to give? All that dope you get through the secretarial grapevine. Anything circulating through "unofficial" channels is information your boss is interested in and may not be able to get. Go into his office, shut the door, and say, "This is strictly from the rumor mill, but I thought you ought to be aware of it." Keep your sources confidential, to show that you can be discreet.

Over time, your boss will begin confiding in you, if:

1. *He senses that you are bringing him information for his benefit.* If the marketing manager's secretary tells you her boss is considering using an outside agency instead of your department (which is advertising), that's information your boss wants and needs to know. Because if he knows somebody is trying to cut him out, he can begin preparing a defense, and he'll be grateful you clued him in.

2. *He understands that you keep everything he tells you in strictest confidence.* When you ask your boss for inside information—"Is there any truth to these rumors about layoffs?"—assure him that it will go no farther than his office. Then make sure it doesn't. Telling even one person in the company, even someone who's a good friend and someone

whom you trust, may be disastrous. If the information is significant enough, that friend may tell one other person—in the strictest of confidence, of course—and that person may tell only one person, and so on until the whole company knows. Once it gets out, you can be sure it will be the last piece of confidential, semi-confidential, or even vaguely confidential information your boss ever tells you.

THE RELUCTANT BOSS

Some secretaries don't believe they can get inside information from their bosses.

"Are you kidding?" one secretary said. "My boss wouldn't tell me what time of day it is, let alone what's going on in the executive suites. It's just 'do this' and 'do that.' "

It takes time and some serious effort *on your part* to develop a relationship where both parties confide in one another. Don't wait for your boss to make the first move—make it yourself. If he doesn't respond immediately, keep at it; he'll come around eventually.

Other secretaries complain that their bosses are too far out of favor, too incompetent, or too uninformed to have any worthwhile information to pass along. Wrong, wrong, wrong—as this story indicates:

Amy worked for a man she described as permanently on the verge of being fired. "In fact," she said, "a few years after I left the company, someone did finally fire him. But because he was a department manager, he was included in all the staff meetings and the planning stage of most projects. He was ineffective and definitely not one of the prime movers, but he knew what was going on. I maintained a good working relationship with him and talked to him when nobody else wanted to, and I became his confidante. He told me everything he found out in meetings and planning sessions, all the changes coming up, new projects, etc."

Amy was able to use this information to move herself into position for a better job. When her boss complained to her that the training department was being expanded while theirs was being kept at last year's level, Amy did a little self-promotion with the training manager and landed herself an assistant's job.

ASK OTHER MANAGERS IN YOUR DEPARTMENT

If your boss is inaccessible or not interested in the relationship of being a confidant, you may be able to trade information with another member of your department:

Gloria's boss, the sales manager, was out of town 3 to 4 days a week, calling on major accounts or visiting his sales representatives. On the rare occasion he was in town, he was busy trying to catch up on paperwork and meetings with other managers. Gloria could never find a good time, let alone any time at all, to sit down with him and discuss what was happening in the office.

"Because Ross was gone so much," she said, "I started talking to John, the assistant sales manager, who filled in for Ross when he was gone and picked up the pieces after Ross rushed out on another one of his business trips. I started by asking John what *he'd* heard from Ross on a particular assignment, or how I should proceed on a particular project.

"Gradually John and I developed the 'information exchange' I should have had with Ross. John, because he was a junior member of the staff, needed all the information he could get, and so did I. Our mutual support system greatly benefited both of us."

Be careful not to try this with someone who's at a higher level than your boss in the organization, or you'll have him wondering what you're up to.

READ YOUR BOSS'S MAIL

I'm always surprised by secretaries who claim they don't read the mail their bosses get or the correspondence their bosses write ("I don't read it; I just type it"). There's a tremendous amount of information flowing across your desk. Read it.

Don't crank back in your chair and read your boss's mail line for line, but scan one letter while you're opening the next. Your boss assumes you do anyway.

Again, discretion is important. You can mention to your boss that you noticed something in the mail you could handle for him, but never relay information you found in the mail to anyone else. It's just as confidential as information your boss *tells* you.

12. Office alliances—the right ones and the wrong ones

The right professional relationships are critical to breaking the secretary barrier. It's a world of "whom you know," and unless you have extraordinary and exceptional talent, the personal factor is an absolute necessity in business. Who you associate with and how you associate with them can make or break your career.

THE CONCEPT OF PROFESSIONAL ALLIANCES

Executives form alliances for a variety of reasons:

To bolster each other politically: "Back me up on this, Norm, and we'll generate all the business your department can handle."

To get better cooperation: "Let's talk about this order processing problem over lunch, Craig—I'm sure we can work something out that will satisfy both of us."

To promote themselves or their pet programs: "I'm playing golf with the president Saturday morning—it'll give me a chance to push my ideas about expanding our acquisition efforts."

When executives get together, it's for business reasons, a way of accomplishing business goals. They form *alliances* in the office, not personal friendships, and they keep these alliances loose. They want to cozy up to the company winners, but not too tightly—they want enough distance that they can break loose if those winners make a misstep and suddenly become the company losers.

HOW FRIENDSHIP WORKS AGAINST SECRETARIES

To most secretaries, though, personal relationships are an important part of work. A close friendship with another secretary provides emotional support—somebody to share your problems with, somebody to confide in, somebody to turn to when the going gets too tough. An emotional support structure is comforting, but openly displaying it in the office creates the wrong image:

Promptly at noon, Becky and Sarah, secretaries in the sales department, leave for lunch together—every day, just the two of them. Once in awhile they include Sandy, the vice president of sales' secretary, but this is just an occasional courtesy—Sandy is a little too close to the executives for their taste. Practically arm-in-arm, they head out the door together to have lunch or go shopping or run errands. Then precisely at 1:00, they stroll back in the door, exchange a few last whispered comments, and return to their respective desks.

Becky and Sarah not only lunch together every day, but they spend coffee breaks together, leave together at the end of the day, and sit together at company meetings. They're both hard workers, conscientious, and very productive, but they can't seem to get promoted. They think management has a bad attitude about promoting secretaries.

At 11:45 a.m., all six secretaries in the purchasing department begin rounding up for lunch. A lot of giggling, laughing, talking, making sure that everybody is ready to go, stalling to kill those last few minutes before noon, so they don't want to be accused of leaving early. With all those people, it always seems to take longer than expected to get served and sort out who owes what on the check, so at 5 or 10 minutes after one o'clock, they return en masse and rush back to their desks.

STOP BEING ONE OF THE "GIRLS"

You can't have it both ways. You can't be part of the secretary buddy system and be on the career track to management. The two are mutually exclusive.

If you ally yourself with the other secretaries, you give the impression that you want to continue to be a secretary. When an executive sees a tightly knit group of employees, he assumes they want to stay that way. He doesn't assume that one of them wants to break out and get promoted.

You give management the impression that:

1. *You are not "mature" enough for a management job.* A close friendship with another secretary gives you a schoolgirl appearance. In high school, you and your best friend ate lunch together, sat next to each other in study hall, and tried to schedule your classes together. In the business world, some secretaries behave the same way. Afraid to be independent, they cling to each other for support and companionship. The result is an image of weakness.

2. *Promoting you would create problems.* Becky and Sarah work together, so a promotion in the same department would put one reporting to the other. Their boss is convinced that friendship would take priority over business, so neither Becky or Sarah is considered when a management or sales position opens up in the department. Someone else gets the job.

3. *The secretarial level is where your true interests lie.* Why else would you spend so much time with the other secretaries?

GOING IT ALONE

To be one of the "boys," you have to stop being one of the "girls." That's a cold, hard fact of life. To be accepted into the mostly male management ranks, you have to disconnect yourself from the mostly female secretaries.

Management regards a secretary who is promotable as an exception. Those occasional exceptions, they will tell you, are women who shouldn't have been secretaries in the first place. They are promotable, because they're not really secretarial material. They're untapped management material—they just got off on the wrong foot.

This line of thinking, backward as it is, opens the door for you if you make yourself the exception, the outstanding secretary, the one that is obviously different from the rest. If you allow yourself to blend in with the rest of the group, you can't get noticed.

It's going to be difficult, but you have to:

- Stop going to lunch with the same secretary, the same group of secretaries, or any secretaries at all.

- Don't go for drinks after work with the secretaries unless managers are included in the group.

- Keep social conversation in the office with other secretaries to a minimum. Don't spend the first and last 15 minutes of every day chatting with them.

- Avoid the appearance of having an office "best friend."

- Don't involve yourself in secretarial group discussions of any kind in the office.

HOW TO MAKE THE BREAK

For many of you, this is a radical departure in your daily routine. Pulling it off without hurting someone's feelings (including your own) won't be easy. You can't simply say to your friends, "I know we've been having lunch together every day for the past two years, but starting tomorrow, I will be eating alone. I also won't be spending the first fifteen minutes every day finding out who Cheryl's dating, or if Anna is still fighting with her kids, or whether Bobbi is going to start using acrylic nails. From now on, ladies, it's strictly business for me. I'm on my way to the top if it kills me."

If it doesn't kill you, they will.

How you handle this depends on how close your office friends are. Be up-front with your true friends—the ones you'd go on seeing if they left the company or became Moonies or moved to Bulgaria. For everybody else, all the casual friends, acquaintances, and lunch companions, a subtler approach is wiser.

For Intimate Friends Only—Cards on the Table. Tell your close friends what you're up to. Explain that it would be best, for both of you, if your friendship carried a lower profile in the office. Suggest that you start getting together in the evenings or on weekends— either at home, or at a restaurant or bar where you're not likely to run into the rest of the office. (Don't meet at the favorite office watering hole.) Work hard to maintain your friendship, but do it outside of work.

Ideally, your friends, if they are real friends, will encourage or even share your desire to get ahead and will enthusiastically aid your efforts. But don't be surprised if they don't understand, or if they see your move toward success as a threat. They may decide they don't want to be your friend after all. If that happens, be consoled by the fact that they weren't the good friends you thought they were, and you probably haven't lost that much.

For Everyone Else—the Mirage. With all the other secretaries, or anyone whose reaction you're not sure of, just gradually disappear. Begin to be too busy to spend as much time with them as you used to. Appear regretful that you can't join them for lunch or coffee or a chat, but steadily decrease the amount of time you spend with them.

THE EXCUSES YOU NEED

Don't ignore the other secretaries, have nothing but business-related conversations with them, or avoid being seen in the company of another secretary. Just slowly extricate yourself from the secretarial buddy system. Avoid leaving with the rest of the secretaries at the end of the day by pleading one more letter to type or one more phone call to make—"You go on without me—I've *got* to get this finished." If the secretaries always sit together at department or company meetings, come in after the meeting has started, then stand at the back of the room.

Lunch is often the most difficult commitment to get out of, and the best way to escape gracefully is to set up other activities for yourself:

Go home. If it's possible, spend the lunch hour in your own kitchen—it will save you money.

Go shopping. Window-shopping is an excellent way to do your wardrobe research, and lunch is an excellent time to do it.

Go to the library. Read the fashion magazines and the business magazines we've talked about. Libraries also give you peace and quiet time you can't get in the office.

Take a short lunch. Go out and grab a quick burger, then go back to work.

Go for a walk. A brisk walk is refreshing—mentally and physically.

Run business errands. Deliver that contract to the attorney's office or pick up office supplies, and earn some points for being a go-getter.

Schedule personal appointments. See your doctor, dentist, or insurance agent during your lunch hour.

Have lunch with people you don't work with. Eat with your husband, boyfriend, or friends who work for other companies.

Expect resistance from the secretaries you usually have lunch with. They'll try to talk you out of doing other things. But steadily increase the number of days a week you have something else to do, and they'll stop counting on you to join them.

SECRETARIAL SABOTAGE

Some of your friends won't understand your motives, even if you're up-front about it, and will stop being friendly to you. But some of them may go beyond that and actually try to sabotage your efforts to get ahead. They will ostracize you and try to keep other people from associating with you as well. They will tell other secretaries that you think you're too good for them; they will tell their bosses that you're lazy and incompetent; they will hint that you're having an affair with one of the executives; and they will use everything you do against you.

Here are some examples of how nasty it can get:

When Lee was assigned to research demographics for her boss's test market proposal, she began spending several hours a day at the library digging up the information. The secretary at the next desk, insulted that Lee had begun disassociating herself from the rest of the secretaries, complained to her boss that Lee was never at her desk, and that she had to cover for Lee during these unexplained absences. Then she told everyone who called or dropped by that Lee had left no indication where she was or when she was coming back.

Maria, secretary to a C.P.A., frequently worked evenings, then took part of the next morning off as comp time—with her boss's permission. It annoyed the senior partner's secretary that Maria was acting more like a manager than a secretary, so when Maria's boss left on a 2-week vacation, she decided to teach Maria a lesson. She informed the senior partner that Maria was frequently coming to work several hours late. The senior partner immediately called Maria in and reprimanded her. Though her boss later cleared up the problem, the damage had been done.

Shellie was asked to begin scanning magazines for articles of interest to her boss, a long-range planning analyst, to reduce his reading load. Because dozens of publications had to be surveyed, she spent up to an hour a day reviewing them. Another secretary, irritated that Shellie was getting more responsible assignments than she was, reported Shellie to the vice president of administration for "doing nothing all day but sitting around reading magazines."

That hurts—particularly if the snitches and complainers are former friends. Do your best to rise above this—keep smiling, keep working, and at least publicly, write it off as a misunderstanding.

Protect yourself:

- Constantly mention to the other secretaries what you're doing, why you're doing it, where you're going, and when you'll be back.

- Make specific arrangements for someone else to handle phones and visitors if you have to be away from your desk, to ward off claims that no one knew they were supposed to cover for you.

- Warn your boss that ill-feelings exist, and keep him informed of all your work activities so he can come to your defense if other managers complain.

- Maintain your professionalism, and it will be apparent who the real troublemakers are.

Don't give in to pressure, and above all, don't let your boss or any of the other executives think you want to give up your new assignments to placate the other secretaries.

ME, MYSELF, AND I

Secretaries complain that "it's not fair that management's attitude dictates who you should associate with and who you shouldn't. It's not fair that to get ahead you have to cut yourself off from your friends."

I agree. If you've been at your job for any length of time, you probably have an established network of friends—women you enjoy going to lunch with, having a drink with, relying on for moral support. The worst part of disassociating yourself from the other secretaries is the loss of this friendship and support on the job. You're all alone.

When you trade in your secretarial friends, don't expect to trade them in for high-powered lunches with executives or breakfast meetings at the city club. When you trade in the other secretaries, you trade them in on yourself.

The executives won't have anything to do with you, because you're a secretary. That includes your boss who, if he's a man, will also want to avoid any suspicion that your relationship is something more than personal. If your boss is a woman, she is even less likely to associate with you. She has enough trouble getting respect as a woman and a manager, without appearing to be overly interested in making friends with the secretaries.

A woman executive in the electronics industry talked about her difficulty in dealing with secretarial friendliness. "When I first joined the company, I was the first female manager in my division. The secretaries were very friendly. Every day they asked me to go to lunch with them, and every day I made an excuse. The excuses got flimsier and more transparent, but they wouldn't quit asking. They didn't realize that I *couldn't* go to lunch with them. The other managers were already looking down their noses at me because I was a woman. Lunching with the secretaries would have increased my identification by sex instead of by position. Maybe I should have come clean and given the secretaries the straight story. Maybe they would have understood. But I was afraid to. So I just avoided them socially, and the result, naturally, was that I got a reputation for being a bitch."

CULTIVATING THE EXECUTIVES

Executives have no desire to make a secretary part of their group, but that's no reason to be intimidated by them, and it's certainly no reason to give up trying to be included. Lay the groundwork now, so once you become a manager, being included will be a cinch.

Establish a casual, conversational relationship with every executive you come in contact with. Be on speaking terms with everyone from the supervisors to the chairman of the board. Don't hesitate to take the initiative—you're building a network of contacts you can use to further your career.

Here's an example of how to do that:

You race into the building out of a rainstorm, get on the elevator, and find yourself alone with the president of your division. You've never spoken to him, and you're convinced he has no idea who you are. With typical elevator etiquette, he smiles and nods—you look vaguely familiar to him—then he stares at the floor numbers over the door.

What do you do? Smile back, say nothing, and try not to drip on him when you get off the elevator? Ride past your floor because you're afraid to ask him to push your floor button for you? Say you forgot something, and get off the elevator altogether?

No! This is the perfect opportunity to make yourself known—to elevate (no pun intended) your image from a vaguely familiar face he sees in the hallway to a confident, outgoing, personable employee. So you say:

"This is some rainstorm, isn't it?" The weather is a safe, universal topic of conversation. Say it cheerfully—you're not complaining, you just find it interesting that it's raining this hard.

"Uh-huh," he says, followed by silence.

Is this a snub? Should you accept your station in life and shut up? Of course not. He doesn't really know who you are, and he may be deep in thought about whether the construction division can deliver on those forecasts they've made.

Don't let it drop—take a little more initiative. He obviously doesn't want to talk about the weather, so get to the point—you want him to know who you are.

"You're Peter Schulberg, aren't you?" You immediately have his undivided attention—you've said, hey, I know you. The "aren't you" lets him know you're pretty sure who he is, but you don't have his face, name, and title engraved on a plaque above your desk.

"Yes, I am," he says with mild surprise. What he means is who are you, why are you talking to me, and what do you want.

"I'm Judith Powell—I work in the marketing department. I don't believe I've ever had the chance to meet you." Sound a little uncertain about whether you've been introduced (as if you didn't know), and act pleased that you finally have the chance to meet him. Avoid mentioning you're a secretary.

He'll say something like, "Well, it's nice to meet you, Judith," whereupon you can smile graciously, and step off the elevator with a parting cheery comment like, "Have a nice, or at least a drier, day." Smile, smile, smile.

Bingo—you're on speaking terms with the president of the division. Every time you see him from now on, speak to him. Speak first, don't wait for him to say something. And say more than just hello. Add comments that leave the door open for a longer conversation: "Finally stopped raining, didn't it," or, "Can I give you a hand with those packages?" You never know, he might be in the mood to talk.

Above all, sound relaxed, and speak to him as an equal. You may feel it's appropriate to call him "Mr. Schulberg," but don't say it as if you're about to bow and kiss his ring. If it helps, try to imagine him being your father-in-law, a friend of your mother, or anything that brings him back down to an earthly plane.

EXECUTIVES ARE HUMAN BEINGS

Remember that deep down, executives are just as human as you are. They have good days and bad days; they fight with their spouses; they stub their toes getting out of bed; they stay up too late. The man who wears an $800 suit and makes multi-million-dollar deals on Monday is the same man who wears an old sweater and cleans his garage on Saturday. Keep that in mind when your heart starts racing at the mere prospect of speaking to him.

The human side of executives also gives you a basis for conversation. You can't make small talk about your department's budget proposal with a high level executive—that's a staff meeting topic, not an elevator or hallway topic. And it's a topic for your boss to discuss, not you. But you can make semi-personal comments like:

"That sounds like a nasty cold you've got there," to an executive who's noticeably sneezing and sniffling.

"I heard you hit a hole-in-one this last weekend. Congratulations!"

"I noticed the story in the newspaper yesterday about your wife. This city certainly needs that kind of commitment to urban development."

Treat casual conversations with high-level executives just like you would conversations with anybody else—calm, relaxed, friendly. Just keep them short, to the point, and *positive*.

Don't use casual encounters with an executive to:

Complain about anything. If things aren't perfect, you don't mind—you enjoy a challenge.

Fawn on him. Don't grovel and say things like, "Oh, thank you so much for giving us that extra day of vacation around Christmas. That's really nice of you." Remember the Big Picture—he didn't do it as a personal favor to you.

Pump him for information. He should think you talk to him because you're an outgoing person who likes people, not because you're after something. People ask him for money, favors, decisions, and information all day long. Don't be one of them.

Ask for help. Get your help from your boss or low-level supervisors and managers. Don't try to get *anything* from an executive who has any stature whatsoever in the company.

Make overly personal remarks. Don't mention the cut of his suit, the status of his marriage, or the fact that all the girls in the office adore him. Remarks like that are too personal for a business environment, and may lead him to the wrong conclusion about why you're being friendly.

Say anything stupid or naive. Don't make comments that show you're not thinking or that you don't know how the world works, like, "Gee, how did you ever get season tickets to the football game?" Of course he got tickets—he's one of the top executives in the city. Suppliers and hangers-on were lined up to give them to him.

GETTING ACCESS TO EXECUTIVES

Other than the hall and the elevator, make opportunities to come in contact with executives:

Hand-deliver memos after hours. Instead of sending memos and other information through the interoffice mail, deliver them yourself. Don't do it during regular working hours—wait until the executive's secretary has gone for the day. Then stick your head inside his door, and say, "Abby's apparently gone for the day," (hinting that Abby doesn't have as much on the ball as you do); "here's your copy of the new benefits package." Walk in unintimidated, and hand it to him.

If at all possible, give him some additional information: "In case you're not aware of it, the major change is in the retirement contribution. It's covered on page 127."

Voilà—you've spoken to him, you've pointed out that you're still there after hours, and you've given him information that will save him wading through the entire 200-page report. You're looking good.

Be in the office when the other secretaries are gone. Before work, lunch hours, after work, and weekends are times that executives will be in the office, but secretaries won't. Be there and get noticed.

Pass along pertinent information. Forward to executives anything you come across in your professional or personal reading that they probably won't see otherwise. Be sure to sign your name to it so they know where it came from. Invest in some note paper that says, "From the desk of . . ." It's an unobtrusive way to display your name when a formal memo would be too much.

If you find something worth sending, send it immediately, before someone else does. If it's just FYI, don't follow up. And don't mention it the next time you see him: "Did you get the article I sent you from *Power Transmission Design* magazine?" He got it— don't make a big deal out of a little article.

Attend corporate functions. Since you can't get into the executive lunch/cocktail party/golf circuit, make sure you show up for all organized corporate activities where you *can* associate with the executives. The company picnic and the senior bookkeeper's retirement party may not be your idea of a good time, but they're great places to do a little politicking, because you can socialize with executives freely. Don't stay in one corner with the rest of the secretaries. "Work" the room—mingle!

Attending these functions also shows the executives that you have team spirit.

Volunteer for corporate charity projects. If the company needs volunteers for the United Way campaign or a food drive at Christmas, be the first to offer your services. It gives you an opportunity to meet formally with all the executives to explain the program and ask for donations (no high pressure!). Be cordial and confident, and let them see you in action. Make sure, though, that you have your boss's approval before embarking on a project like this, and do as much after hours as possible.

Hold meetings just before lunch and quitting time. If you have a reason to meet with managers and executives, do so just before noon and 5:00 p.m., to increase the chance that you might be invited along for lunch or after-work drinks.

This ploy takes some intestinal fortitude, because more often than not, a group of managers will interrupt your meeting and say, "Hey, Tom, do you want to go to lunch with us?" Then Tom and the group will go off to lunch together and leave you sitting there. Very humbling. I did this for 6 months at Borden before someone finally had the good manners to ask me to join them. It didn't happen frequently after that, but gradually I became one of the lunch crowd.

The key to getting invited again is to be an interesting lunch companion. Don't be shy and retiring. If you've done your Big Picture reading, you have plenty to talk about.

A word of advice: the lower on the organizational chart the managers are, the more likely it is that you will be included in lunch. The CEO isn't going to ask you to tag along with him and the president for a bite to eat in the executive dining room.

Offer to help. Make yourself available to other executives if your boss is out of town and your workload has tapered off. Don't offer your services to the secretaries, go directly to their bosses: "Gary's out of town, and I can't proceed with the big project we're working on until I hear from him this afternoon, so I've got a couple of hours free. If you need help with anything, I'd be glad to pitch in."

Make it look like a temporary lull—you don't want to appear to be underworked—but show that you want to keep busy and that as a team player, you're eager to help wherever you can.

An important by-product of doing this is that it makes it easier to ask *his* secretary for help when *you* need it.

THE INEVITABLE SEXUAL ADVANCES

As you become more visible and interact more often with male managers and executives, expect to receive more sexual advances.

Before we talk about how to fend them off, let's define terms. Sexual advances are *not*:

Dirty jokes. Sexually oriented jokes circulate through almost every office. Because a man tells you a dirty joke does not mean he is coming on to you. He may be trying to shock you, or see how much "one of the boys" you really are, but in most cases, he simply thinks that it's a funny joke and that you'll get a laugh out of it.

Off-color remarks. The same goes for the guy who sees a sexual connotation in everything you say, or who makes statements himself that have double meanings. These guys are harmless—they're the self-appointed office wits, not the resident Don Juans.

Personal comments and compliments. A man who mentions that you have a great set of legs isn't necessarily inviting you to bed. While it's possible that he's looking for encouragement, it's more likely that he just appreciates shapely legs.

"BUT I WAS ONLY KIDDING"

In the old days, men watched everything they said. They made no sexual references, they apologized if they said "damn," and they were mortified if they said something worse. As they became accustomed to women being in the office, they reverted to talking like they did when it was just the "guys."

Hyper-conscious of their sex, women often feel insulted or demeaned by sexually oriented jokes or remarks. They don't realize that, in many cases, it simply means the man in question is relaxed around you and thinks you're adult enough to laugh at a good joke, even an off-color one. Most men who tell dirty jokes and make sexual comments don't mean anything by it.

It's a bad idea to actively discourage this rather routine office activity. A tight-lipped "I don't appreciate that kind of language and those kind of jokes" marks you as uptight and inflexible. If you really don't want to hear dirty jokes and suggestive remarks from well-meaning males, just ignore them. Don't laugh at the jokes, don't tell any yourself, and don't respond to the remarks. Act like you don't hear any of it, and go on about your business. But don't set yourself up as the guardian of morality around the office.

HANDLING THE OFFICE WOLVES

Active discouragement *is* necessary for the jerks whose intentions *are* less than honorable—you know, the ones who make obscene remarks to shock you. Some men enjoy making women uncomfortable, and they make vulgar comments, to try to reduce you to stammering speechlessness. Don't give a man like this the satisfaction of getting upset or flustered or angry, just deliver a withering glance that says he is repulsive and so is the comment he just made. Sigh as if you are marshaling all your tact, and say with exaggerated patience, "Harold, I appreciate your attempt at humor, but could we get back to business here?"

If obscene remarks escalate into a direct come-on or pass, add ridicule to your condescension. Look down your nose at him, and say haughtily, "With you?" Then laugh and walk off. Don't hesitate to shut him off with remarks like, "You certainly have a distorted impression of your attractiveness." Or the line a friend of mine uses: "Men who are richer, better looking and more talented than you are have tried and failed. What makes you think you have a chance?"

Then leave, so he's left talking to himself. Don't stay and trade barbs with him.

THE SINCERE SUITOR

Occasionally a man will be attracted to you and honestly interested in dating you. This is a compliment, not an insult, so let him down as gently as possible. Tell him that you're married, or seriously involved with someone, or that you never-but-never mix business with pleasure. Let him think that even though you might like to, you can't. That way, the two of you can stay friends and work comfortably together.

ELIMINATE THE OPPORTUNITIES

Your best defense against sexual advances is a consistently professional demeanor. It usually stops them before they ever get started. A woman who goes to work in a short skirt and a camisole with no bra is inviting sexual overtures. A woman wearing a business suit who talks about sales figures instead of *her* figure is sending a message that she's off limits. Men will think twice before chasing her around the desk.

Your second best defense is to carefully control social situations. Opportunity is half the battle when a man wants to make a pass. He obviously can't and won't proposition you during a staff meeting, but meeting for drinks to "discuss your promotion" is a different story.

Take these precautions:

Cut those after-work get-togethers short. When you go out for a drink with the office gang after work, have only one drink and be one of the first to leave. One drink gives you plenty of time to get across what a charming, professional person you are. Once that's accomplished, get out before too much alcohol gives someone the wrong idea. The same goes for the Christmas party, going-away parties, or any office occasion that mixes men and liquor.

Don't lunch one-on-one with men in the office. Even lunches with your boss—if he's male and it's just the two of you—should be limited to once a month or less. Lunch with a *group* of men is fine, though; go every chance you get.

Make separate travel arrangements. If you're invited along (in a professional capacity, of course) to an out-of-town meeting or convention, keep your travel arrangements as separate as possible from your boss's. Make airline reservations departing at different times and stay on different floors of the hotel (different hotels is going too far—it's inconvenient and makes you look paranoid). Don't eat every meal with your boss. Plead fatigue or work to do, and order room service. Make every evening a short one.

Give impersonal and inexpensive presents. If you buy Christmas, birthday, or special occasion gifts for men in the office, make them business-related and not very costly. Buy a desk accessory, not a silk shirt.

DON'T BURN ANY BRIDGES

You never know when one of those sexual jokers, or a man who has made a pass, is going to be in a position to help you. As disagreeable as it may seem, maintain a good working relationship with *everyone* in the office. Office alliances ebb and flow, and you need a baseline of cordial relations to work from. You can't afford to have the newly promoted department manager be someone you've refused to speak to for the past 2 years.

Give everybody a second, third, fourth, and sixty-fifth chance. No matter how they offend you, address the problem, then go back to being agreeable and good-tempered with them. Besides keeping your future options open, professional affability shows you have class, and that you can rise above personal prejudices for the good of the organization.

13. Turn your boss into an ally

Your boss can be your best friend or your worst enemy when it comes to getting promoted. He can clear the way for you to move ahead, or he can stop you dead in your tracks. In other words, you've got to get the boss on your side.

WHY YOUR BOSS DOESN'T WANT TO PROMOTE YOU

As a secretary trying to move up, you're caught in a Catch-22:

If your job performance is substandard, your boss doesn't want to promote you, because he feels that you aren't qualified for a more responsible job.

If your job performance is outstanding, your boss doesn't want to promote you, because he doesn't want to lose you as a secretary.

Managers who feel their secretaries aren't qualified enough for a promotion say things like:

- "I can't get my secretary to do what I ask her to. She loses things, forgets things. She'll have to show me that she can handle the job she's got now, before I'd even consider promoting her."

- "I've got a secretary who used to be a manager—she had to take this job when her husband was transferred here. All she does is complain about how menial her job is and how she should have more responsibility and more money. Meanwhile, every letter she does for me has six typos in it."

- "Promote her? You must be kidding. I mean she's nice and all, but she's hardly management material."

On the other hand, managers with highly qualified secretaries say things like:

- "I know my secretary is capable of more than she's doing, but where would I find someone who is as qualified as she is? And I don't have time to train someone new. I'd just as soon leave things the way they are."

- "Do you know how many rotten secretaries I've had during my career? Wendy's the first decent secretary I've ever had, and I'd do anything to keep her. I'd be lost without her."

- "Maybe my secretary's mother will buy her a copy of this book—I certainly won't. I don't want to lose her."

The only managers who wanted to promote secretaries were women who are former secretaries themselves, and even they have some reservations:

- "I made the mistake of promoting a secretary who hadn't actively sought a promotion, and it was a disaster. She couldn't refuse the bigger salary and fancier title, but she wasn't prepared for the real world. She still wanted to act like a secretary and rely on me to make all the decisions for her."

- "I had a mentor who was instrumental in my advancement. I attempted to be a mentor to a couple of secretaries, but one wasn't interested and the other said she'd be glad to move up provided her compensation was adjusted *before* she assumed more responsibility."

OVERCOMING YOUR BOSS'S RESISTANCE TO PROMOTING YOU

We're dealing with some serious resistance here—managers who don't believe their secretaries can handle a promotion; managers who don't believe *they* could handle it if their secretaries were promoted; and managers who no longer want to help their secretaries get ahead.

Changing your boss's mind isn't going to be easy, whichever category he's in, but you've got to convince him that:

1. You're ready to move on.

2. You're qualified to move on.

3. He will survive without you.

A strategic plan of persuasion is called for here—a publicity campaign designed to win your boss over. But it has to be subtle—no demands, ultimatums, or premature moves that might put him on the defensive.

BE A SUPERB SECRETARY

Being a poor secretary works against you much more than being a good secretary, so perform every aspect of your job with excellence. Be the consummate organizer, planner, typist, word processor, filer, receptionist, and everything else your job description calls for you to be. Prove to your boss that you've more than mastered your secretarial job and that it's time for you to take the next step.

CRITIQUE YOURSELF

Take a hard, objective look at yourself. What are your weaknesses? What critical remarks has your boss made, either in a performance review or just in passing? Those weaknesses may not seem significant to you (does it really matter that your desk is a mess?), but if they are important enough for your boss to mention them, correct them.

ESTABLISH A GOOD WORKING RELATIONSHIP WITH YOUR BOSS

Tension and bad feelings are deadly to your promotion prospects. If your relationship with your boss is rocky, start mending fences. Outstanding job performance and a noticeable effort to overcome your weaknesses can go a long way toward mending a poor relationship, but more than that may be needed. Actively pursue a better relationship:

Act as if there is no problem. First stop the negative behavior. Stop being cool to your boss, stop trying to irritate him, stop reacting if he tries to needle you. Be pleasant, be friendly, and be patient—it may take a while for your boss to adjust to your new amiable behavior.

Address the problem. If being persistently agreeable doesn't improve relations, bring the problem out into the open. Have a candid discussion with your boss. Tell him you're concerned that the two of you are not getting along as well as you should be, and that you want to see your relationship improve. (This forces him to cooperate—he can't very well say he *doesn't* want your relationship to improve.) Then put the burden on him by saying, "What can I do to improve this situation? Is there something I'm doing that bothers you? If so, please tell me, so we can work it out."

Be willing to take the blame. Soft-pedal criticism of your boss with diplomatic phrases like: "Maybe I'm misinterpreting this, but it seems like . . . ," or, "I may be oversensitive on this point, but . . . ." You can't get your boss on your side by accusing him of causing the problem.

Graciously imply that the problem must be your fault—which

lets him feel generous in resolving it. Your goal is to solve the problem, not place the blame.

Let yourself off the hook. The problem may not be you—it may be a personal problem, problems with *his* boss, or any number of things. Don't second-guess him. Take his explanation at face-value, and go on. Don't torment yourself by thinking that he really dislikes *you*, no matter what he says about being worried about making quota. Personal affection is not at stake here, a professional working relationship is.

PROVIDE FEWER PERSONAL SERVICES

Gradually reduce the amount of personal services you provide. Many bosses are reluctant to give up their secretaries, because their secretaries do all sorts of nonbusiness favors for them. Start changing that. Your image should be one of competent businesswoman, not office handmaiden. Begin expressing some hesitation and reluctance to fetch cigars, pick up laundry, and buy birthday presents for the boss's daughter.

A little tact goes a long way here. If you've always run errands for your boss, don't go in tomorrow and flatly refuse to ever do it again. The next time your boss asks you to buy a present for a member of his family, just hesitate. Say, "I really enjoy shopping for you, but I'm buried in work out here." (Review the "Consider the Consequences" Technique in Chapter 9.) If he insists or pleads, do it. But step up your resistance with each subsequent request—always, of course, begging off for business reasons.

At the same time, show an increased interest in your work and in the company in general, so your boss doesn't think your attitude is slipping. Sooner or later he'll get the idea that you're responsible for his business well-being, not his personal well-being.

MENTION YOUR INTEREST IN BETTER ASSIGNMENTS

At appropriate times, mention that you are interested in expanding your responsibilities and learning new skills. Your boss may not have been thinking about developing your talents, but he will if you encourage him:

Be specific. Give your boss specific suggestions that he can act on. Don't say you'd like to know more about something as vague as finance or sales—tell your boss that you're interested in learning more about net worth statements or how to make a sales presentation.

Make sure your interests dovetail with your department's activities. Don't express an interest in developing your data processing skills if your department is years away from computerizing. Work on skills that can be directly translated into a management job in your department.

Express your interest intelligently. When your boss mentions the upcoming computerization, don't say, "Whew—I know zero about computers, but I'm sure I could sure get into them." Do a little research and show that you have some basic knowledge to work from, that training you or letting you become involved wouldn't be starting from scratch. The next time he mentions computerization, say, "Will we be getting a modem so we can use the computer to communicate with the Tampa office? If there's anything I can do to help get the new system going, let me know. I'd really like to be involved."

Mention a specific task you could do. If you know enough to make a specific recommendation about how you could help, don't hesitate. Say, "If it would help, I'd be glad to work with the Tampa office to standardize our accounting reports, so that transmitting information will be easier."

Never put any pressure on your boss. Keep mentioning that you want more training or better assignments. Mention it whenever it's convenient and appropriate, but always do it good-naturedly— even if it's the 350th time you've brought it up. The goal is not to get an immediate commitment for more responsibility, but to change your boss's outlook, to get him thinking of you as a resource he can develop, a secretary who has the potential to become a knowledgeable assistant, and a secretary who's interested in moving ahead.

MAKE YOUR JOB MORE MANAGERIAL, EVEN BEFORE YOU GET PROMOTED

Don't wait for a promotion to start doing management work. If you take on managerial tasks now:

1. Your boss can picture you as a manager.

2. He can evaluate your management abilities.

3. You can build your own management job, as an assistant to your boss.

4. You can make it obvious that you're overqualified for your secretarial job.

TREAT YOUR RESPONSIBILITIES LIKE A MANAGER WOULD

A few of the tasks you perform are an end in themselves. You type a letter your boss writes, mail it, file a copy, and that's the end of it; or you answer the phone, take a message, give it to your boss, and that's the end of that. But many of the things you do are part of the management process. For example:

- Typing invoices is actually part of accounting.

- Reviewing trade publications is part of research.

- Calling around for price estimates is part of purchasing.

- Keeping track of vacation days is part of personnel.

View your duties in their managerial context, and perform them in a managerial fashion, to show that you know how to function like a manager.

THE SITUATION: Your boss asks you to make hotel reservations for a conference he's going to attend.

The Secretary Response: Call the hotel where the conference is being held and make a reservation.

The Future Manager Response: Since making hotel reservations is actually a purchasing function—you are buying lodging for your boss—put standard purchasing principles into action: researching what you want to buy, getting estimates from several suppliers, and buying at the best possible price.

Call the company's travel agent, and have her research all the hotels within a four-block area of the conference site (or do it yourself with a hotel or city guide). After some investigation, you are able to find a hotel two blocks from the conference site that will rent a room for 35 percent less than the conference site hotel.

Present both sets of lodging costs to your boss, including a small map showing the location of the other, less expensive hotel. Point out that he may be staying a little outside the mainstream activity of the conference but he'll save several hundred dollars on his hotel bill. Mention that this is particularly important because the company is cracking down on travel expenses.

It's his choice, but you viewed the assignment in a larger context, and showed that you have a managerial outlook on your work.

TAKE YOUR RESPONSIBILITIES ONE STEP FURTHER

Management activities consist of a set of steps. Step A is followed by Step B which is followed by Step C and so on. Most of what you do is a first step or an intermediate step within a larger management activity. You can do more managerial work by:

1. Performing both your assigned task and the next task up.

2. Performing your task, and *inventing* another managerial task that needs to be done with it.

Look beyond the assignment you were given, and see how you can expand it:

THE SITUATION: Your boss asks you to find projections on the size of the housing market over the next 5 years.

The Secretary Response: Dig up the information and give your boss a handwritten set of numbers.

The Future Manager Response: Dig up the information and give your boss:

1. The projection typed up in the same format as the report. Include appropriate textual description, polished and tailored to the tone and content of the report, so your boss can insert this section directly into the report, without having to write the text or set up the tables himself.

2. Photocopies of magazine articles that you found during your research, which have a bearing on your boss's report. Highlight key sentences so your boss can review the article quickly, find the major points, and decide which parts of the material to use.

3. A note that mentions other publications or areas that might be worth investigating—and asks if there is any additional research you can do for him.

It's important, in taking these additional steps, to make sure your boss is aware of your extra efforts. Always engineer a way to bring them tactfully to his attention. Don't hide your light under a bushel basket—when you shine, shine publicly.

TARGET AREAS OF YOUR BOSS'S JOB FOR TAKEOVER

Most managers do work that could be easily delegated to a subordinate, if they'd just let go of it. Examine your boss's job for tasks you could handle:

1. *Break your boss's job down into specific activities.* It's not enough to say that you could handle customer service—customer service is a broad area that covers a multitude of tasks: communicating with customers by phone or by mail, talking to sales personnel, taking orders, sending them to the warehouse for fulfillment, invoicing, handling complaints, processing re-

turns, generating daily order/sales reports, and more. If your boss is the customer service manager, his duties might include:

- Supervising the order processing staff.
- Handling customer complaints for key accounts.
- Preparing daily sales reports.
- Conducting weekly staff meetings.
- Meeting with the vice president of sales to eliminate problems and improve service.
- Meeting with the vice president of production about inventory levels and problems.
- Preparing semi-monthly tallies of customer complaints for the sales and production managers.
- Visiting production locations and sales offices around the country.

2. *Reduce the list to activities that you have the ability to handle.* If listening to people complain makes you crazy, cross off "Handling customer complaints." If you have two small children you can't leave, or have a fear of flying, cross off "Visiting production locations and sales offices around the country."

3. *Cross off activities you don't have the political clout to handle.* That eliminates meeting with the vice president of sales and the vice president of production. They won't meet with a secretary.

4. *Eliminate tasks that your boss won't let you do.* He's not going to turn supervision of the customer service staff over to you— that's the heart of his job. The weekly staff meetings are his territory, too.

5. *Establish your takeover list.* Your list is now down to:

- Prepares daily sales reports.
- Prepares semi-monthly tallies of customer complaints for the sales and production managers.

Both are areas you could handle, and both are areas you should target for immediate takeover.

If your own list isn't long enough, go back over the "can't do/ wouldn't be allowed to do" items one more time. Are there *portions* of those tasks you could do? Keep subdividing your boss's duties until you find areas you could take over.

If you don't find any, get your creative juices flowing and develop new ways that your boss could do his job faster and more efficiently—ways that *you* could handle for him. You may not be able to, or allowed to, travel the country visiting the sales reps and production personnel, but you can still get involved. Recommend that you develop a monthly newsletter to get information out to the plants and sales offices, to help lighten up your boss's travel schedule. Offer to prepare the first draft of each issue, or write the whole thing outright, and be sure to put your name on it.

ASK FOR MANAGERIAL RESPONSIBILITIES

Unless you anticipate some resistance, ask your boss directly if you can take over responsibility for the targeted areas. If you think he'll say "no" ("No, I enjoy doing those," "No, you're too busy," or, "No, they're too important—I have to do them myself"), put your request more diplomatically, time it more carefully, and leave little or no reason for him to refuse:

- "You seemed really swamped today; why don't I put together a rough draft of the complaint report? It will give you something to work from."

- "While you're out of town next week, I'd be glad to fill out the 'Daily Sales' report for you. Mr. Jones is always over here looking for it when you're away. Since you call in every morning, I can go over the report with you on the phone before I distribute it to anyone—just to make sure it's right."

Who could refuse? You haven't said, "Step aside, Frank, I'll handle that from now on." Instead, you've offered to help.

With most bosses, this approach works just fine. But some bosses are very paranoid—they see a usurper behind every filing cabinet. Circumvent their paranoia by pampering their ego (and their usually inflated sense of their own position and abilities), with statements like:

- "Since you've got a meeting with the *vice president of the division* this afternoon, would it help if I . . . ?" (What an important guy he is—he meets with vice presidents.)

- "I know you're *terribly busy*, particularly with the *new responsibilities they've given you*. Wouldn't it save you some time if I . . . ?" (They just keep piling it on a talented guy like him, don't they?)

- "I'd be glad to help out with the leg work on that project—you know, the more menial stuff *you shouldn't be bothered with*." (Bosses with weak egos are terrified of doing work that is beneath them. They'll hand over the "small" stuff to you in a heartbeat.)

That may seem a little cold-blooded, but manipulation is part of office life. Don't forget that your number one priority is your own success.

MAKE THOSE ASSIGNMENTS YOUR OWN

Once you start doing something like the "Daily Sales" report, keep doing it. Don't quit just because your boss comes back to town. On his first day back, do the report before he has a chance to. Act as if he turned it over to you permanently, and don't stop doing it unless he specifically tells you to stop.

Delegated work stays delegated if the subordinate does a competent job and expresses an interest in continuing to handle the assignment. Do both.

Once it becomes an established part of your responsibilities, add it to your formal job description. Always keep your job description up-to-date, so that if the need arises, you can show your boss, or anyone else for that matter, what your real responsibilities are, and how they've exceeded the ones you were originally hired to do.

STAY ON TOP OF YOUR WORKLOAD

The danger in taking on these extra, albeit better, assignments is that you will find yourself with an 80-hour work week. Under that kind of workload, the natural reaction is to slack off on the less exciting tasks. Don't do that, or before too long, you'll hear your boss grumbling, "You write a great report, but why is the filing system such a disaster?" Or, "Before you help me develop next year's budget, why don't you go update our address file, so I can call customers without dialing six wrong numbers first?"

Don't unilaterally decide that some of your work doesn't need to be done, or you'll be setting yourself up for a fall. What you regard as unimportant may be *very* important to your boss, and if you stop doing it, he won't be happy.

Remember that a genuine overload is the best ammunition for getting a promotion. When your job becomes too big for one person to handle, a second person is needed. You can become a full-fledged assistant, and that second person can be a secretary who reports to *you*.

In the meantime, maintain your sanity by taking these steps to manage your growing workload:

1. *Streamline your job.* Scrutinize your activities for time-wasters.

   - Do you have a junk pile of papers on your desk that you sort through day after day looking for things? Sort those papers out, file them or throw them away, and get them off your desk.

   - Do you run errands you don't need to? Mail papers instead of delivering them by hand—even if their destination is only a mile or two away. It takes much less time to type and stamp an envelope than it does to get in your car and drive six blocks. Use suppliers with free pick-up and delivery, or ask your boss to approve delivery costs. A supplier with higher prices but free delivery is more economical than a lower-priced supplier who makes you pick up your merchandise.

   - Do you have an overcomplicated filing system? Simplify. A wonderful color-coded, cross-referenced, indexed system

may be eye-pleasing, but it's a waste of time if it's hard to
set up and maintain.

- Do you start and stop projects instead of persevering and
getting one done before you start another? Discipline yourself—and your boss, if necessary, if he frequently interrupts
your work and changes your priorities.

Read time management books and office management publications to find new ways to save time and make yourself more
efficient.

2. *Develop priorities with your boss.* Explain that you're stream-
lining your job to increase your efficiency, and go over all your
activities with your boss. Are there tasks that can be eliminated? Tasks that can be postponed? Ask for *his* suggestions on
how you can increase your efficiency.

3. *Computerize.* Any office that has not installed word processing
is behind the times. For as little as $5,000, your department
can have computerized word processing, bookkeeping, invoicing, and payroll. After the initial learning phase, those
systems will save you time and money.

DELEGATE—BUT TO WHOM?

Routine typing, filing, and other office procedures can be handled
by someone else, but secretaries often dismiss delegation as an option because they "have no one to delegate to."

That's not necessarily true. Depending on cooperation from your
boss, and possibly other executives in the office, you may be able to
delegate work to a variety of people:

Other secretaries. This requires some diplomacy, but it's certainly
possible. If Ellen down the hall seems to have frequent slow peri-
ods, mention to your boss that perhaps you and he could take
advantage of that. Have *him* talk to Ellen or her boss, and ask if
she'd be interested in helping out with your workload.

I tried this maneuver twice while I was a secretary. The first secretary threw a fit—how dare I tell my boss she wasn't busy? How dare my boss tell *her* boss she wasn't busy? (This from a woman who spent an hour a day cleaning her desk.) The other secretary was happy to help; she was bored and had too little work to do. I treated this as the big favor it was, heaped thank-you's and even an occasional lunch on her, and we didn't have a problem.

When trying this yourself, pick a secretary who *wants* to be busier, who has offered to help you in the past, or who indicates she wouldn't mind pitching in.

Students. A high school or college student can lighten your workload by working afternoons or full-time during the summer and holidays. It's easier to convince your boss to hire a student than a regular full-time employee, because students aren't as permanent or as expensive. Just make sure you hire a hard-worker who's eager to learn your business.

Typing pools. Typing pools have gotten a bad reputation for slow response and poor quality, but they're not all like that. It's to your advantage to try your company's again, even if you had a bad experience in the past. On long typing projects, they can free you up for more important things.

Secretarial and other office services. Farm out projects like typing or envelope stuffing to secretarial services or mail processing companies. Although they're expensive, these services can be justified if you have a large project or a short deadline. Get some estimates and talk to your boss.

PROMOTING YOU IS YOUR BOSS'S ONLY CHOICE

Your boss may not be thrilled that you're ready to charge up the corporate ladder, but sooner or later, as you take on more responsibility, he'll recognize it as inevitable. He'll also realize that:

If he doesn't promote you, he'll lose you as a secretary anyway.
Your boss knows that if he doesn't promote you, you'll go somewhere else where you can get promoted. Either way, your days as
his secretary are numbered.

If he does promote you, he doesn't have to lose you altogether. An
outstanding secretary may be an even better assistant. If your boss
promotes you to *his* assistant, he'll get to keep you, and you'll be
around to train your replacement. And he'll realize that promoting
you is in his best interest after all.

14. | Making your move

You may not need this chapter. After all this preparation, hard work, and image building, your boss—or someone else in the organization—may offer you a better job before you ever get around to asking for one.

But if no one's shown up yet with the keys to your new office, let's go after them.

Your first shot at getting promoted should be the best effort you can make it. Good planning is even more important now than it was before. A premature move or a badly executed one can turn your boss into an adversary and leave you with a defeated feeling that's hard to get over. If this is your second, third, or forty-seventh try, it's that much more important that *this* effort be skilled and successful.

ARE YOU READY?

When you make your move is just as important as *how* you make it. You are ready to go for it if you have:

1. *A managerial appearance.* Are you dressed as well as or better than any of the female managers in your organization? Do you look like you're ready for a promotion?

2. *Developed a confident attitude.* Are you acting like an equal member of the business team? Do you refuse to be intimidated?

3. *Demonstrated your problem-solving abilities.* Are you solving problems instead of passing them on to someone else?

4. *Management-level communication skills.* Are you talking and writing like a manager? Do you exhibit the proper emotional control in the office?

5. *A Big Picture perspective.* Do you understand both the organization as a whole and the work of the department you are directly involved in? Do you have an industry-wide perspective?

6. *Established the right office relationships.* Have you disassociated yourself from the other secretaries, and established contact with as many executives as possible?

7. *Your secretarial job firmly under control.* Have you eliminated any possibility of criticism in the way you handle your current job responsibilities?

8. *Expanded your responsibilities.* Have you grabbed every new management responsibility you could get your hands on?

9. *Prepared your boss for your promotion request.* Does your boss suspect you're about to pop the question—how about a better job?

10. *Held your present job for a reasonable time.* Have you been in your current job long enough that a request for a promotion is appropriate now?

If all these bases are covered, you're ready to go. If they aren't, get them covered before you ask for a promotion. A secretary who goes into her boss's office in a sleeveless dress and clogs, who has an 8-week backlog of work on her desk, or who had to reschedule her performance appraisal so she could leave early, is fighting a losing battle.

WATCH YOUR TIMING

Timing, as any actor can tell you, is crucial. Don't schedule a meeting to discuss your future when you've just sent the wrong report to the wrong branch office. Don't ask your boss for a promotion when he's just been called on the carpet by *his* boss for mismanaging the inventory. And don't walk into your boss's office and hit him cold with: "Have you got a minute? I want to talk about getting promoted."

All of these situations are guaranteed to get you a big "no." Pick your time carefully, and avoid any crisis situations—if one occurs just before your meeting, reschedule. Discuss your promotion either:

1. *During a performance appraisal.* Your boss expects to discuss your future plans then. If you have a performance appraisal coming up in the next month or two, you can wait for it to discuss your promotion plans. Use the intervening time to keep polishing your image and expanding your responsibilities.

2. *In a specially scheduled meeting.* If your appraisal is many months down the road, or if an attractive opening in another department comes up suddenly, set up a meeting with your boss by saying:

   > "I'd like to talk to you about my current position and my future prospects with the company. There are several ideas I'd like to discuss with you. When would you have an hour or so to meet with me?"

   There's no point in surprising your boss with the meeting topic in the hope that he won't have a counterargument developed. If he's going to say no, he'll say no—how much notice he gets has nothing to do with it. And if he wants to put you off, not knowing what the meeting was going to be about is the perfect excuse.

   It's also bad manners to spring a surprise meeting or topic on someone.

   Arrange the meeting at a time convenient *for him*—early morning, after work, or even Saturday afternoon if that's necessary to pin him down.

ARE YOU PREPARED?

Like any presentation, your promotion proposal needs careful preparation. Don't go in cold, hoping you'll say the right thing when you get there. You won't. Write down your pitch—either in outline form or in speech form, whichever you're more comfortable with— then get a tape recorder and practice until you can make your presentation clearly and calmly.

Sell your boss on the idea of promoting you, instead of just asking him for a better job. Your pitch should include:

Your excellent past performance. Point out that you've handled your job very competently. Emphasize improvements you've made in efficiency or productivity.

Your expanded responsibilities. Outline the additional responsibilities you've assumed. Stress the management nature of those duties and how beneficial it's been for your boss and the department/ company as a whole to have you handle them.

Be specific—these are your bargaining tools. Don't assume that your boss remembers how much time it used to take him to prepare the financial reports—tell him you've cut 10 hours a month off his workload by taking care of them. Have a current job description with you.

Your enjoyment of your job. State your pleasure in your job—as far as it goes—and your working relationship with your boss. Make sure he understands that your desire for promotion doesn't stem from a problem with him or your job.

Your need for greater professional development. Express your desire for more responsibility and more interesting assignments. Indicate that you want to plan a career, not just discuss a job.

Specifically what you want. Tell your boss what you're after—a management position in his department, a transfer to another department (either to a management position or to a secretarial position with more possibility for advancement), or simply his permission to apply for other jobs in the company.

THE BASIC PITCH

Until you get to this last item—what you want—the pitch is basically the same. Whether you want a promotion within your department or a transfer, the first part of your pitch should go like this:

- *Start friendly.* An intentionally scheduled meeting may have your boss wondering if you're going to hit him with a list of demands, so begin your meeting with a friendly, relaxed nonthreatening hello:

  "Thanks for taking the time to talk to me, Phil. I know how busy you are." (Smile.)

- *Get down to business.* Don't waste your boss's time with chit-chat about the weather or the fact that the copier's broken again. Get to it:

  "As I mentioned to you when I set this meeting up, I'd like to talk about where I am with the company and what my future prospects are."

- *Use an open, cooperative approach.* Make this session a give-and-take—here's what I think, do you agree with me, that's a good point you're making. Give your boss frequent opportunities to agree with your assessment of the situation.

  Watch his body language—is he getting defensive or showing resistance? If he says nothing, doesn't nod or smile, you may have a tough road ahead of you. If so, don't get strident or pushy, get more relaxed. Start using more specifics and examples to prove your points.

  Remember, whether you see eye-to-eye or not, this is a friendly meeting between two business associates. Keep it low-key and low-pressure. Build your case in a nonbelligerent way, leading your boss step-by-step through your arguments until he arrives at the conclusion you want him to reach.

- *Give him the bad news first.* Mention your dissatisfaction with your current position early in the conversation, so your boss isn't distracted throughout the meeting, wondering when you're going to deliver the bad news.

"I've worked for you for almost two years now, and I've been quite happy here. You're great to work for, and of course, this is a company I can personally be supportive of. I like the way they do business and the products they offer, which makes for very pleasant working conditions. But frankly, I need more of a challenge than I can get from being a secretary."

There. The other shoe, which your boss has been waiting to hear drop since you scheduled this meeting, has indeed been dropped. Now you can both get down to the nuts-and-bolts of whether, when, and how this promotion is going to take place.

- *Explain that being a secretary is no longer a challenge.* Let your boss know that you can do your current job with one hand tied behind your typewriter.

  "I feel like I've got the secretarial portion of my job well under control. You may have noticed that I've completely revamped our filing system—retrieval is substantially easier than it used to be. I've gotten more aggressive with purchasing, and I estimate I've cut 20 percent to 30 percent off our office supply and travel expenditures."

- *Show that you've already moved beyond your secretarial job.* Describe how you are already functioning in a quasi-management capacity and that you're doing it quite admirably:

  "In the past year—as you know—I've taken on quite a few new responsibilities. You were nice enough to let me try my hand at doing the financial reports, and that's now become a regular part of my responsibilities. I'm also handling all the routine customer correspondence, and writing first drafts of most of your project proposals.

  "In fact, here's a copy of the original job description you gave me when I first interviewed for this job, and here's my current one. You can see how much I've expanded my job. The current one is unofficial, of course, but I think it accurately reflects what I'm doing now.

  "I feel like I'm handling all these responsibilities quite well."

Don't go over the job descriptions line-by-line with him—you've already pointed out how you've expanded your job. But do leave both copies with him so he can review them later.

The reference to your current job description being "unofficial" is a hint that what you're doing now isn't being matched by your title and salary. You're officially a secretary, but unofficially, you're much more than that.

TELL YOUR BOSS WHAT YOU WANT

Now make your request—that you want to become his assistant or apply for a job in another department or whatever you're after. Make a well-developed presentation that describes in detail:

1. What you see as your next step.
2. Why that step is the most logical and feasible.
3. How that next step can be implemented, what the transition will be like.
4. The cost—if it involves hiring new people.
5. How much time the transition will take.
6. The effect on day-to-day operations during the transition period.

HOW TO CREATE AN ASSISTANT'S POSITION

If your goal is to become your boss's assistant and have a secretary reporting to you (or you and him), make sure you can justify adding another person to the payroll. Develop two job descriptions—one for your new job and one for the new secretary. Don't skimp on job descriptions, make both as fully developed as possible. Show your boss how the responsibilities would be divided, and make sure he can see that there really are two jobs worth of work to be done.

In building a job description for your assistant's position, you can work from your boss's job description (if you can get a copy). Where his says, "Manages corporate relations with national media," yours can say, "Assists in managing corporate relations with national media." Don't forget one of the most important items on your job description: "Supervises secretarial and clerical personnel."

Type up both job descriptions in official format, and have them ready when you say:

> "I've made a number of improvements in our operations to improve my efficiency and maintain control of my workload. But as you've probably become aware by now, this job has gotten too big for one person to do.
>
> "I'd like to recommend splitting my job into an assistant's position and a secretarial position. Hiring someone to handle my lower end responsibilities—typing, filing, phone answering—and making my job into an actual assistantship. I've drafted up job descriptions for each position so you could see what they'd look like.
>
> "As you know, I'm really already functioning in an assistant capacity on a day-to-day basis. By handling many of the customer relations and financial duties, I've been able to free you up for more important things. I think you'll agree that writing financial reports and working with customers is a better use of my talents than typing form letters and filing.
>
> "As far as replacing me, I'd be here to provide training and supervision, so I think we could hire an entry-level secretary/receptionist—at several hundred dollars a month less than you're currently paying me."

Always pitch the cost-savings factor—the cheaper it is to implement your plan, the more likely your boss will go along with it.

Now shut up. Smile expectantly, as if you expect your boss to jump up and shout, "Damn fine idea—I wish I'd thought of it myself!" Even if you sense he's gearing up for a fight, appear pleasantly hopeful that he'll see it your way. Sit back, relax, and see what he has to say. This is his chance to talk, to react to your proposal. Whatever he says next will give you a lot of information, so don't interrupt. Let him have his say.

DEALING WITH OBJECTIONS

Every good salesperson makes a list of objections he might hear from his customers, then works out responses to those objections. Do the same. Develop your own objection/response list to suit the circumstances in your department. Here are some common ones:

Objection	Response
"I'm not sure there are really two jobs here. Couldn't we eliminate some of what you're doing now?"	"When we met three weeks ago, we went over all of my responsibilities and cut out quite a few of them. I think we're down to the bare minimum now. The only alternative would be to give you back some of the administrative and management work I've been handling for you." *That's the last thing he wants—his delegated work back.*
"You know how tight money is around here right now. I don't see how we could afford another employee."	"That's one of the reasons I thought an entry-level secretary— with a lower salary—would be best."
"Even an entry-level secretary would add $X,000 a month to our budget. I don't think we can do it."	"Ellen down the hall seems to have quite a bit of extra time. In fact, she's been helping me out on a fairly regular basis. Perhaps we could consolidate secretarial positions, and she could function as secretary for her boss and you and me. If we gave Ellen $100–$200 a month more, I'm sure she'd be more than willing to handle the extra responsibility."

OR

"Perhaps we could hire a part-time secretary—just mornings or afternoons. That would cut the salary outlay, and because she's part-time, we wouldn't have to pay fringe benefits like medical, dental, and retirement.''

"Money's still going to be a problem.''

"I'm interested enough in this promotion, that if it's really necessary, I'd take less of a salary increase myself.'' *A tough step, but one that may be necessary to swing this.*

"I'm not sure I can justify an assistant for myself.''

"Look at what you're *not* getting done because you don't have one. Just yesterday you mentioned that you're way behind on developing a five-year capital investment plan, because there's just too much else to do. Besides, Hal Sommer in production has an assistant, and they are nowhere near as busy as we are.'' *A cheap shot—"Hal's got an assistant and you don't"—but what's a cheap shot or two when we're talking about your future.*

"What about physical space? We're wall-to-wall people around here now as it is.''

Have a new floor plan sketched out if this is a possible objection.

"We're in the middle of a hiring freeze—it's out of my hands.''

"Can we formalize my promotion now, and make arrangements to hire a new secretary when the hiring freeze is lifted? In the meantime, I'll handle both jobs.''

Make your list as comprehensive as possible. Brainstorm until you've generated every conceivable objection and a response to it. With luck, you won't need them, but as they say, better safe than sorry.

HOW TO HANDLE THE SALARY ISSUE

If you don't need your objection/response list because the boss says "yes"—congratulations! But don't jump up and start shouting. Take this joyous news calmly—you knew all along (didn't you?) that he'd agree with your flawless, well thought out, professionally presented recommendation. Smoothly move on to the next step: how soon does he want to implement this, can you start advertising for a new secretary immediately, are the job descriptions fine as they stand or are modifications needed, and most importantly, what will your new title and salary be?

Lead into a salary discussion by discussing what to pay the new secretary. Make a definite salary recommendation—you probably know more about what secretary salaries are in your area or industry than your boss does. Say:

> "I think we can get a decent secretary/receptionist for $X,000 a month. That's a little low, but it should be acceptable if we offer a review and raise at the end of three months. And it saves you $300 a month compared to what you're paying me to do that job. While we're talking about salary, what do you think is a reasonable salary for *my* new position?"

Getting the promotion is the primary goal, but get as much money as you can, too. Executives always negotiate their salaries, so show you have executive savvy and use these negotiating tactics:

1. *Let your boss make the first offer.* Secretaries are generally unaware of management salaries, so let your boss tell you what the ball park is.

2. *Find out what the range is.* Large corporations have pre-set salary ranges for most positions. If your boss responds to your salary question with "How much of a raise do you think you should get," say:

> "I'm sure the company has an established salary range for a position like this. Why don't I call the personnel depart-

ment and find out what it is? We can just set my salary at the midpoint."

If you have any connections at all in the personnel department, find out *beforehand* what the range is. Your boss may try to lowball you, figuring you won't know what you're worth.

But keep in mind that where salary ranges exist, so do limits on how large a raise corporate guidelines will let you have. At Borden, when I was promoted from marketing research assistant (which had originally been a secretarial position) to assistant product manager, corporate guidelines didn't allow for the salary jump I should have gotten. Instead, I got a 20 percent raise every 6 months—which was itself such an exception to corporate policy that the president of the entire Borden conglomerate had to approve it, every 6 months.

3. *Ask for up to a 50 percent increase.* In the absence of corporate guidelines, ask for a 30 percent to 50 percent increase. If your boss boxes you into a corner and insists that you tell him what salary you want, start at a 50 percent increase and if necessary, work your way down. While that may sound outrageous, you won't lose the promotion by asking for a high salary. You may not get it, but at least you won't have undercut yourself.

When I went to work for Kentucky Fried Chicken (though this was a change of company, which usually generates greater increases than internal promotions), my prospective boss demanded that I tell him what I was "going to cost him." I broke down and named a figure 33 percent higher than I was currently making. He laughed, and I knew I'd made a mistake. His starting offer, when it finally came, was even 8 percent higher than what I'd even asked for. If I'd been smarter, I could have gotten much more.

4. *Respond to any offer with hesitation.* That is, unless your boss offers to double your salary on the spot. In all other cases, pause, sigh reflectively, think about it for a minute (during

which time he may up the offer, thinking you're going to refuse), then say skeptically, "Is that the best you can do? I was hoping for . . . ," and name a slightly higher figure.

Then stop—don't say anything else until he responds. Don't say, "Is that the best you can do? I mean, if it is, that's okay, because I really want this job, but if you could give me more money, I'd really appreciate it." One key to being a strong negotiator is knowing when to *stop talking*.

If he doesn't come up, you haven't lost anything—he's not going to change his mind because you asked for more money. If anything, he'll admire your spunk. And you may be surprised when he throws another $100 a month onto his offer.

HOW TO APPLY FOR A MANAGEMENT JOB OPENING IN YOUR DEPARTMENT

If a management job opens up in your department that you think you could handle, go after it—but go after it the right way. Treat it as if it were a job in another department or a job in another company. Don't feel like you can do less because you already work in the department—because you're a secretary, you have to do more.

When a management job opens up in your department:

1. *Tell your boss you're interested.* Don't wait for your boss to approach you, because he may never do it. Get to him first:

   "I understand that one of our claims representatives is leaving. I'm very much interested in that position. Can we set aside some time to talk about it?"

2. *Find out about the job.* Talk to the person vacating the job or to other people in the company who have held that position. Get an in-depth understanding of the job requirements.

3. *Write a letter outlining your qualifications.* A résumé is too formal for your boss. A letter or written description of how you are uniquely qualified to handle the job is a better way to go. Don't be shy—describe exactly how your particular talents would benefit the job.

4. *Prepare an objection/response list.* Just like you did for creating an assistant's position.

5. *Interview for the job.* When you meet with your boss to discuss the job, deliver the Basic Pitch, then, using your list of qualifications, sell yourself as the perfect person for the job. Leave your list of qualifications behind for your boss to study.

6. *Follow up.* Don't badger him to death, but follow up periodically to find out if your boss has made a decision and to let him know you're still interested.

APPLYING FOR A JOB IN ANOTHER DEPARTMENT

If you work in a large company, and a job opens up in another department—either a management job or a secretarial job with more potential—deliver the Basic Pitch to your boss, but follow it up with:

"If you'll look at my recent activities, you'll see that I've been developing my management skills and have been building my job into more of an assistant's position. My goal all along had been to become an assistant in this department—I enjoy the work here, and I especially enjoy working for you. *However,* something else has come up."

Your boss's first thought will be that you've found another job. And he's not far off. If you had actually been offered another job, either from a different department in your organization or from a different company altogether, you would have this exact same conversation with your boss—because you're about to give him a chance to bid for you.

> "Martha in the contracts department told me they are looking for an assistant contracts administrator." (Or the personnel department posted the job or however else you found out about the job.) "As I said, my goal is to remain here in a more responsible position, but if that's not possible, I'd like your permission to apply for the job in the contracts department."

WHY YOU NEED TO ASK FOR PERMISSION

Some secretaries get indignant at the thought of asking their boss's permission to look for a better job, but I think it's an absolute necessity for several reasons:

1. You look like a sneak if you don't.

2. A boss who finds out after the fact that you've applied for a transfer may take it as a personal rejection. Then you'll have a soured relationship to patch up if the transfer doesn't come through.

3. You may need a recommendation from your boss to get that transfer. If your attempted defection takes him by surprise, his recommendation may be less than enthusiastic.

4. Your boss may actually promote you rather than lose you—if you're up-front about looking around. Approach him first to find out if he's got a job for you.

5. If you don't tell him, someone else will—the personnel department, the person you're interviewing with, or someone on the office grapevine (remember those vindictive secretaries?).

Here's what can happen if you don't tell your boss first:

Lois was the secretary to the industrial relations manager in a large personnel department. She was very capable, and when the vice president's secretary resigned, the VP approached Lois about taking the job.

Instead of talking to her boss first, Lois worked out a deal with the VP—including a relatively quick start date. After the deal was finalized, Lois went and broke the news to her boss. He was surprised, then furious. He thought Lois had been politicking behind his back, that their good working relationship had been a sham, and the final insult, that the VP had "stolen" Lois without the slightest regard for *his* needs.

He couldn't very well tell the VP off, so he took it out on Lois. He told her what he thought of her, then never spoke to her again—he'd walk away if she joined the group he was in. His actions were childish, vindictive, and made him, not her, look bad, but it cast a shadow over Lois's promotion. Instead of celebrating, she was embarrassed and hurt.

HOW TO DEAL WITH THE STALL

If your boss does offer to promote you within his department, grab it. A bird in the hand and all that. But be sure it is indeed a bird in the hand and not an attempt to stall you until the other opening has disappeared. Don't get trapped by vague promises from a boss who wants to hang on to you:

You: "I'd like to apply for the assistant's job that's opened up in the contracts department."

The Boss: "Well, now, don't get hasty. I know you want to get promoted, but I think there's something we can do for you here. Why don't you hold off on applying for that transfer?"

You: "Staying here in a better job would be terrific—just what I want, in fact. What type of position did you have in mind?"

The Boss, getting uneasy: "This is kind of sudden, so I don't really know. But I'm sure we can do something."

You, friendly but persistent: "Do you think an assistant manager position would be feasible?"

The Boss, getting more uneasy: "Hard to say. But you just be patient, we'll get you something here."

You, still friendly and still persistent: "What kind of time frame are we talking about? This month?"

The Boss, getting irritated: "Listen, I can't make any commitments right now."

You, still friendly, but changing course: "Oh, I understand that, and I don't want to rush you. I know you've got plenty of other things to work on right now. You know, of course, that there's no assurance I will get this transfer, even if I apply for it. So just to keep my options open, why don't I go ahead and apply for it, and hopefully you and I can work something out here in the meantime. Can I count on you for a good recommendation if the contracts administrator wants to talk to you?"

The Boss, seeing the handwriting on the wall: "Sure, sure, have her call me."

If you suspect he may be less than impassioned in his recommendation, warn the contracts administrator when you interview with her: "I told my boss I was applying for this job, and I'm afraid he's not very happy about the prospect of losing me. While I take that as a compliment, you may find him somewhat reluctant to talk to you when you call." Then if your boss gives you a lukewarm recommendation, the contracts administrator will think it's just sour grapes.

HELP YOUR BOSS RECOVER FROM THE SHOCK

Be prepared for almost any reaction from your boss when you tell him you want to apply for another job. Some bosses are hurt, no matter how much you say you enjoy working for them, and like Lois's boss, their reactions can be unpredictable. They may get mad, they may act like they're losing their best friend, or they may get condescending and insulting. Keep your professional demeanor, regardless of what they say, and don't burn any bridges.

They'll get over it—if you help them:

1. *Tell your boss you enjoy working for him.* Assure him that your motivation is not to get away from him, but to advance your career.

2. *Assure him that the transition will be a smooth one if you leave.* Let your boss know that you will get your current job in shape to be turned over to someone else *before* you leave. Offer to help hire that someone else. Promise to ask your new boss to "loan you back" for a few hours a day to train your replacement.

3. *Maintain a low profile about your application.* Don't give your boss a running play-by-play of how your attempt to get another job is going. Don't let him catch you discussing it with other people in the department either. Remember that his ego's involved, because you want to leave his department.

4. *Keep him informed of interviews.* Tell your boss as far in advance as possible if you have to be gone for an interview—*then make up the time*. Let him know, too, if someone will be calling him for a reference.

If you get the job, tell him regretfully—let him think you hate to leave. Save your celebrating for outside the office. Inside the office, downplay the transfer and refer to it only as an excellent opportunity you couldn't afford to pass up.

If you don't get the job, act somewhat relieved (even if you're crushed). Let your boss think your heart's really in his department, but do mention that you hope to eventually have a chance at a management job there. Don't give him the impression that you've given up trying to get ahead.

MAKE A FORMAL APPLICATION FOR THE TRANSFER

Treat applying for a job in another department just like you would treat applying for a job in another company. Submit a résumé, with a cover memo outlining your qualifications. (See Chapter 3 for a review.) Prepare carefully for the interview—your prospective boss knows you as a secretary, so you may have to overcome some prejudices.

CONDUCTING A COMPANY-WIDE JOB SEARCH

You may decide to survey the company for other opportunities, even though there are no definite openings right now. Do this informally, if you can, by casually mentioning to people in other departments that you'd like a more responsible position and if they hear of anything to let you know. Don't worry about notifying your boss that you're looking around. By now he knows you want a better job, and there's no reason everybody else shouldn't know it, too.

Launching a formal job search is a different ball game—enlisting the aid of the personnel department and scheduling meetings with the heads of other departments. It's a good idea only if:

1. You've tried, but you can't get a good working relationship established with your boss—you'd rather be a secretary in another department than be a vice president working for him.

2. You're convinced there's no place to move up in your department.

Now it becomes imperative to inform your boss that you want to look around and *why*.

BEWARE OF THE PERSONNEL DEPARTMENT

In a large organization, a formal job search means getting the personnel department involved. Never, ever go to the personnel department about a transfer without telling your boss first. And never tell the personnel department anything negative. You want a transfer because you want a greater professional challenge, *not* because you can't stand your boss.

The personnel department's loyalty is to the executives, not the secretaries.

> Annette's boss, a high level executive with a Fortune 500 company, was a monster. He treated her like dirt, had her constantly running personal errands, and blamed her when anything went wrong.
>
> When she'd finally had enough, she went down to the personnel department, told them what an S.O.B. this guy was, and demanded to be transferred to another department. The personnel manager was very sympathetic and promised she would look into other openings and try to place Annette in a more congenial atmosphere. Annette left the meeting feeling relieved.
>
> It was an eight-floor elevator ride from the personnel department back up to Annette's department. When she got back to her desk, her boss was just finishing a phone call. He hung up and angrily ordered her into his office. The personnel manager had called, *while Annette was on the elevator,* and told him every word she had said—including the S.O.B. part.
>
> In less than a month, her boss had a replacement for her, and Annette was fired.

"WE JUST DON'T GET ALONG"

Had Annette advised her boss ahead of time that she wanted to look around, she might have kept her job. She could have said:

> "You and I seem to have very different opinions of what my true job responsibilities are, and I'm not sure we'll be able to resolve that. I feel like you're not happy with my job performance, and it makes me uncomfortable that I can't live up to your expectations. It might be better for both of us if I were working in another department. That way, you'd have an opportunity to get a secretary that you'd be more comfortable with. Would I have your support if I talked to the personnel department about a transfer?"

Her boss would have been very supportive—he wasn't any happier with Annette than she was with him. A transfer would have solved both their problems. He could have gotten a more servile secretary, and Annette could have kept a job with the company.

"THERE'S NO OPPORTUNITY FOR ME HERE"

When relations are fine, but there's just nowhere for you to go in the department, get your boss to tell *you* that, instead of telling him. Deliver the Basic Pitch, then ask:

> "What's your assessment of my abilities, and what are the chances of my getting promoted in this department?"

Your boss will probably give you the straight story. If he hesitates or beats around the bush, ask him to be straight with you. Tell him you don't want any unrealistic expectations, that he's doing you a favor by being as honest as possible. Then, if no promotions are on the horizon, tell him what you need to do:

> "I appreciate your being candid with me—it will help me make an informed decision about where I'm going with this company. Since it unfortunately looks like a promotion is unlikely in this department, I think it would be in my best interests to look around the company for opportunities in other departments.
>
> "I'd like to talk to the personnel department and the heads of some of the other departments, but naturally, I wouldn't want to do that without your approval and support. Your recommendation would mean a lot in helping me get a transfer or a promotion in another department. Will you help me?"

Actively solicit help from your boss in securing that transfer or promotion. Ask him to let you know if he hears of any openings, and ask him to recommend you as a possible candidate for those openings.

OPPORTUNITIES OUTSIDE YOUR ORGANIZATION

When you decided to get promoted, you in essence put yourself on the job market. You are job-hunting. Whether it's inside or outside your company, you're looking for a new job. Act like it:

Read the want-ads every Sunday. And apply for any management job that you are even marginally qualified for. If you have to fudge your qualifications a little, do it. Changing your title to something more prestigious than secretary—like sales coordinator or production assistant—is fair play as long as you don't overdo it.

Besides the possibility of finding another job, keep tabs on the job market to get a feel for overall opportunities in your area and the going salary rates.

Put the word out that you're looking for a better job. Make everyone you know aware that you want a more responsible position. Your friends can be told directly to be on the look-out for you, but be more cautious with suppliers, customers, and other people that you have a strictly business association with. It's bad form to have the company's best customer tell your boss that you asked him to help you find a better job.

Express your interest in something better in a more subtle way. When a supplier makes a comment like, "It sounds like you've got your hands full," or, "You've been with Ben a long time," that's an opening for you to say:

> "Yes, there's always something to do—never a dull moment. I just wish it was more challenging. Ben gives me as much authority as he can—he's really great to work for—but this job is rather limited. I need something with more responsibility—but with all this work I don't have time to look for it!" (Laugh, indicating that you aren't actively job-hunting, but making the point that you wouldn't turn down a better offer if you got one.)

If you're ready to bail out right now, go ahead and be as direct with outside business associates as you are with your friends. Just ask them to be discreet—you don't want your boss to find out any sooner than necessary.

LET YOUR BOSS BID FOR YOU

When that better job offer does come along, don't rush into your boss's office and hand in your resignation. Give him a chance to keep you by upping the ante. Without going into details like salary, tell him you've had a fantastic job offer:

> "Promotions Unlimited has made me a very attractive offer. They want me to start as assistant public relations manager. I haven't given them an answer yet, because frankly I'd rather stay here— though obviously not in a secretarial position. I've mentioned several times in the past that I'd like more responsibility—is there any chance we can do something about that now?"

Having another, better offer is the best bargaining position in the world. Use it for all it's worth.

SURE-FIRE WAYS TO GET PROMOTED

There are a couple of ways that make all this maneuvering unnecessary, but they're much harder to come by:

THE BIG SCORE

A major contribution to the corporation is a guarantee of a promotion. If you come up with an idea that saves the company a bundle of money, you'll get a promotion. If you meet someone while on vacation in Hawaii and convince them to place a $250,000 order for your

company's products, you'll get a *big* promotion. If you ask for it, that
is. Go directly to your boss and say:

> "I'm obviously too qualified for a secretarial job. Let's discuss the
> promotion I've earned."

Don't settle for anything less.

MENTORS

In the old days, a woman couldn't get promoted without a mentor.
An executive woman was such a rarity that without a high-powered
man to bring her along, she was soon crushed by the opposition.

Times have changed, and mentors, though a blessing if you have
one, are no longer a necessity. That's fortunate, because you can't go
out and find a mentor. Mentors find you.

Because mentors do the choosing, your role in the relationship is
to recognize when you've been chosen. Some managers try to be
mentors, only to be rebuffed, intentionally or otherwise, by the very
people they're trying to help. Watch for signs that someone is considering you as a protégé:

> *They talk to you about their past.* Listen for stories that begin
> "when I was your age," "when I was in your position," or, "when
> I was starting out like you are." Those stories mean you bring back
> memories of that person's early career. He or she can identify with
> you and may be willing to help you advance.

> *They respond enthusiastically to your requests for help.* Mentors
> are help-oriented. They spend the extra time and effort a neophyte
> needs. An executive who does that is making an overture that says,
> "I can help you get ahead. Are you interested?"

> *They help you get better assignments.* A prospective mentor may
> request your help with a special assignment or recommend to your
> boss that you be given additional responsibility.

> *They are genuinely interested in your career.* You can spot a men-
> tor by his continual questions about your future—where you want

to go in the company, what areas of business interest you, what you see as your next step.

Your responsibilities to a mentor, once you get one, are:

Don't mistake professional interest for personal interest. A mentor wants to improve your professional standing, not mend your broken marriage, fix your car, or hear about the bowling trophy you won. Keep it on a business level.

Don't flaunt the relationship. Mentors work in mysterious ways— usually discreet and behind the scenes. Don't offend yours by bragging to other people in the office that you've got somebody powerful in your corner.

Don't let your mentor down. Once you have a mentor working for you, live up to his or her expectations. A mentor gives you one of the best shots you'll ever have at getting ahead—don't let him, or yourself, down.

15. The unofficial promotion and other tactics

Your move may not work. You may be refused, put off, stalled, or dismissed with the ultimate insult: "Oh, you don't want a managerial job. Look at me—I've got migraines and an ulcer from being a manager. Stay where you are, you'll be happier." Poor, but happier.

THE POWER OF POSITIVE PERSISTENCE

Don't let one failure stop you from applying for other promotions. Each time you fail, pick yourself up and try again. Earn a reputation for never giving up. Make your boss and other executives realize that it's just a matter of time before you get the promotion you want.

You're starting from a tough spot, probably the toughest in the organization—but that's no reason to give up. Don't be a quitter. Show them you've got guts.

Successful people, in any field of endeavor, all have three qualities in common—talent, desire, and determination. They have the necessary ability, but talent alone can't move you up in the world—you have to *want* to be successful. And even more than that—you have to work at it. The strength of spirit to persevere, despite setbacks and defeats, is the stuff that success is made of. The secretary who gives up after her first attempt justifies her rejection. Management looks at her and says, "See? She didn't really want to get promoted. She only tried it once. She doesn't have what it takes."

A setback only means that you have to be more persistent, more determined, and more clever. Because "no" isn't the end, it's just the beginning.

"NO" IS THE BEGINNING OF NEGOTIATIONS

If trying for a promotion in your own department doesn't work, you still have plenty of room to maneuver. You're right on the scene— you can manipulate the players, the rules, and the whole game so they go your way. In other words, if you can't get an official promotion, arrange an unofficial one.

When your boss turns you down, that's not the end of the discussion, it's the beginning of negotiations. And like any good negotiator, have a list of secondary demands in case you don't get your primary one. That list could include:

- A new title.
- More money.
- A bonus plan.
- More training.
- Assignment to a special project.
- Better equipment/furniture/accessories.

A NEW TITLE—THE UNOFFICIAL PROMOTION

If you can't get a full-blown promotion, with a huge salary increase and your own secretary, a better title is the next best thing. Once you have the title and establish yourself in the position, you can negotiate for the other amenities.

Tell your boss:

"If we can't do a full promotion now, can we at least do something about my title? The title of "secretary" has some negative connotations, and I believe it hinders my job performance. A more managerial title would . . ."

Depending on your position in the company, you can finish that sentence with one or more of the following statements:

- ". . . help me deal more effectively with people outside the company. Our suppliers and customers are often reluctant to work with a secretary."
- ". . . help me deal more effectively with people *inside* the company. They're also reluctant to talk to a secretary."
- ". . . more accurately reflect the work I'm doing. I may do all the typing, but I'm really functioning as your assistant."
- ". . . not cost you a cent."

YOU ARE WHAT YOU'RE CALLED

Make a specific recommendation on what your new title should be. The most desirable title is your boss's title with "assistant" in front of it, because it puts you squarely in the promotional path. An assistant manager is the logical person to replace the manager when he leaves or is promoted.

Your Boss's Title	Your Title
Coordinator	Assistant Coordinator
Supervisor	Assistant Supervisor
Manager	Assistant Manager

But at the director level and above, tacking on "assistant" doesn't work. No one's going to let you call yourself assistant vice president.

If your boss is a high-level executive, derive your title from the department or division you work in:

Your Boss's Title	Your Title
Director of Sales	Sales Coordinator
Director of Research & Development	Research & Development Assistant
General Manager, Food Products Division	Assistant Manager of Administration, Food Products Division
Vice President, Corporate Communications	Publicity Specialist

Use your imagination. Don't assume that a manager's position has to exist for you to become an assistant manager. In our Food Products Division example, the secretary became the assistant manager of administration, even though there was no *manager* of administration. She told her boss that an assistant title was commensurate with her present experience, and that as she gained more managerial experience, she would earn the full manager's title and position. She not only arranged one promotion for herself, she set up a second one.

TITLES TO AVOID

Some titles aren't much better than "secretary:"

Administrative assistant became another name for secretary years ago. It has no prestige whatsoever.

Assistant to means personal assistant, glorified flunky, someone who steps 'n fetches for a top corporate executive. Refuse it.

Office manager is an effective title if you're managing a staff of secretaries, receptionists, and clerks—not if you're managing yourself and the filing cabinets. Through overuse and misuse, "office manager" is becoming as meaningless as "administrative assistant."

SALARY INCREASE—AN END OR A MEANS?

More money is often a secretary's top priority—which is understandable, because secretarial wages in some parts of the country are criminally low. Raises are also criminally low—sometimes a meager $50 or $100 a month, which taxes and inflation reduce to nothing. But concentrating on money when you should be concentrating on getting into management is short-sighted and in the long run, self-defeating.

What would happen if you refused that $100 a month raise? What if you traded it for an unofficial promotion, a more prestigious title, tuition for data processing classes, or field training with the sales force? What would you lose—a paltry $38 take-home on your semi-monthly check?

But think of what you could gain—an entrée into management.

Look at it this way: a raise could put you at the end of the secretarial salary bracket, with nowhere left to go. But if you trade that raise in on an assistant's title, you are on the threshold of the vast *executive* salary range. And there's everywhere to go from there.

Since many bosses see salary as the only "reward" they can give a secretary, you may have to re-educate them:

> "I appreciate your offer of a $100 a month raise, but what I'm really looking for is more responsibility. I want to evolve my job into a more managerial position, and I'm more interested in how we can do that than just becoming a better-paid secretary. What I'd like is an assistant manager title, and if necessary, I'd be willing to apply some of that raise to my career development—seminars, classes, professional publications, perhaps some field work with the sales force."

The most important point to remember about salary is that with success comes money, not the other way around. When you become a manager, more money will follow naturally. Don't demand a raise before you'll agree to accept more responsibility. Take the responsibility, prove yourself, and the raises will come automatically. (Even if they don't, a managerial title makes it much easier to find a management job in another company. Instead of being a secretary looking for a job, you're an assistant, a supervisor, or a coordinator looking for a job.)

A word on salary increases: a raise is not a gift, it is an offer. It is negotiable. *How* negotiable depends on what you've done since your last raise. You have a good reason to ask for a raise, or more of a raise if you're offered a small one, if you have:

- Taken on new assignments.

- Handled special projects.

- Worked a large amount of unpaid overtime.

- Saved or made the company money.

- Made innovations in your job.

You don't have a good reason to ask for a raise, just because:

- You can't afford your car payment.

- You don't think it's fair to pay anybody as little as they pay you.

- With two kids, you can't live on what you're making.

- Your husband lost his job.

The only acceptable reasons for a raise are *business* reasons. Your personal situation has nothing to do with it, and you show an embarrassing lack of business acumen by bringing it up.

THE BONUS PLAN

If you can't get a promotion, you may be able to get a bonus plan, particularly if you're willing to take it instead of a raise. Some managers are fond of giving bonuses, or at least *promising* bonuses—the old, "If you put in the extra effort we need to make our forecast, you can count on a fat bonus in December." One secretary who fell for this line worked nights and weekends and found her "fat bonus" was a whopping $150.

A bonus plan should be a bonus *plan*, not a vague bonus promise. It should include:

Controllable circumstances. The plan must be based on something you can control. A bonus plan is pointless if it's based on production quotas, but you have no way to affect the level of production. A bonus plan that is contingent on a reduction in travel expenses does make sense if you are the one who makes the travel arrangements.

Measurable results. The plan must have quantifiable, measurable results, so that you know exactly what you need to accomplish to earn the bonus. "A reduction in travel expenses" isn't specific enough. How much of a reduction—5 percent, 20 percent?

Realistic goals. Is it possible to achieve the results asked for? You won't be able to reduce travel expenses by 25 percent if your department has six new people who travel all the time. One manager of a profit center said ruefully:

"Every year I turn in an increase in sales—sometimes as high as 15 percent. But every year they set 20 percent as the goal needed to earn the bonus. A 20 percent increase in this business would be a miracle. The bonus package is very lucrative—but I can't remember the last time I got one."

A time limit. When are the results to be achieved by—the end of the quarter, the calendar year, the fiscal year? Set a definite date.

A written agreement. Formalize the plan in a written agreement that both you and your boss sign. You don't want your boss to "forget" exactly what the bonus was when you try to collect it.

For most secretaries, the attempt to nail down these specifics shows the bonus plan for what it really is—more fluff than substance.

But that's okay. Once the offer has been made, you can trade it off for something else—a better title, a regular raise, or more training.

MANAGEMENT TRAINING

To counteract the complaint that you have no experience in finance or data processing or sales or general management or whatever, negotiate for additional training—at the company's expense, of course. Develop a list of training options, and present it to your boss. That list could include:

Seminars. Not secretarial seminars, but seminars on finance or data processing or sales or any area you need more experience in.

Trade shows, conferences, and conventions. Every industry is loaded with trade shows and conferences, ranging from small local events to international exhibitions. They generally include product exhibits, seminars, speeches, and social functions. For a quick overview of your industry, trade shows and conventions can't be beat.

College courses. Ask for tuition reimbursement from the company, and take classes that will directly improve your chances for promotion.

Professional publications. Ask your boss to pay for trade books, workbooks, tapes, magazines, or newsletters that will help develop your skills.

Don't get training activities approved without getting a budget approved. Without it, you'll have to ask every time you want to order a magazine—giving your boss a chance to renege on his commitment. Make some rough estimates, add 20 percent for contingencies (everything always costs more than you think it's going to), and ask that those dollars be set aside specifically for your training.

SPECIAL ASSIGNMENTS

If you can't get promoted to a particular position, try to at least get an assignment in the same area:

"Even though I wasn't promoted to data processing coordinator, I would like to be assigned to work more with the new coordinator. My lack of data processing experience obviously hurt me in trying to get this promotion, and I'd like to gain the background I need to qualify for future promotions. I would like to be the liaison between you and the DP coordinator and be responsible for the administrative end of our relationship with that department. What do you say?"

MORE MANAGERIAL TRAPPINGS

If you absolutely can't get a managerial title or any managerial responsibilities, make one last try for an office, partitions to make a cubicle, a location out of the "bull pen," a word processor, or any physical thing that will improve the professional ambiance in your area or help you do your job better.

Your justification is:

- You need a private office, because of the confidential reports you do.

- You need partitions to reduce the noise level, so you can get more work done.

- You need nicer furniture to make a better impression on the many customers who visit the office.

- You need more sophisticated office equipment to increase your productivity.

DON'T WALK AWAY EMPTY-HANDED

A performance appraisal or a meeting about your future with the company is a negotiating session. The only defeat is walking away with no concessions whatsoever from your boss. Stay friendly and stay positive, but don't give up until you get *something*.

DEALING WITH FAILURE HEAD-ON

When you get turned down or passed over, find out why. Not some superficial, tactful excuse why you were turned down, but the *real* reason, so you can start making some changes.

Meet with the person who stalled your attempt at success, and have a frank discussion about why you didn't get the job. Tough as that may sound, it has several benefits. You can:

1. *Demonstrate your professionalism.* Failure is not the end of the world—it's part of the reality of business. Those who can deal with it and are willing to work hard to overcome it are well respected.

2. *Maintain and strengthen your relationship with the person who turned you down.* Turning someone down is difficult. Your boss (or prospective boss) may fear that you'll be hurt, resentful, and difficult to deal with. Make the first move and assure him there are no hard feelings—it was a business decision, you understand his position, and you hope he'll consider you for another promotion in the future. Make rejection a way of acquiring a supporter.

3. *Improve your opinion of yourself.* Rejection, no matter how justified or how diplomatically put, hurts. A conversation which reviews your strong points as well as your weak points can shore up your battered ego. It's comforting, even motivat-

ing, to find out you were an extremely close second, not dead last.

GET TO THE PERSON WHO MADE THE DECISION

Determine who made the decision not to promote you. It's probably your boss, but if you've applied to another department for a promotion, the decision-maker could be anyone from a first-line supervisor to a divisional vice president. Don't assume that whoever *told* you you didn't get the job is the same person who turned you down. Ask the person who gave you the bad news to also tell you who made the final decision. Then call the decision-maker and request a meeting:

> "This is Bonnie Sanders. I wanted to thank you for interviewing me for the assistant technical writer position. I'm sorry I didn't get the job, but I appreciate the opportunity to talk to you about it. Because I'm still very interested in getting ahead here at Promotions Unlimited, I wondered if you could spare me a half-hour sometime this week. I'd like to get your suggestions on how I can improve my presentation for future interviews and what steps I can take to better prepare myself for a promotion."

Make it clear that this is a self-improvement session, not a bitch session. Don't let the decision-maker think you're coming over to tell him off, or he'll become very unavailable.

KEEP IT POSITIVE

Start your meeting by smiling and expressing your gratitude. Come on warm, friendly, and appreciative of the executive's willingness to counsel you. Eliminate all suspicion that you're there to complain:

> "Thank you for seeing me. I don't want to take up too much of your time, but I do want to get some feedback on my recent interview with you. I especially wanted to ask your advice on what I should do to improve my chances for promotion."

If the interviewer and final decision-maker was your boss, this kind of formality isn't as necessary, but the procedure is. You've got to find out what's holding you back.

This conversation is difficult. If the executive plays it straight with you, you'll hear all about your weaknesses, inadequacies, and faults. You may hear negative generalizations about secretaries that don't apply to you. You may hear comments about yourself that you don't believe are true. And the worst part is that you can't get upset, become defensive, or tell the executive he's totally off-base.

Right or wrong, what the executive tells you is, in fact, his perception of you, and it has to be dealt with. If he sees you as someone who has trouble getting along with people, don't ignore his perception because you're convinced you get along fantastically with everyone in the office. His perception still exists, and it has to be corrected.

You need to ask yourself, "If I'm so great with people, why does he think I have a problem in that area?" Maybe *your* perception needs a little work.

A postmortem interview on a promotion works only if you use it to get information. If you use it to berate the interviewer, defend yourself, or beg for another chance at the job, you fail a second time.

Keep your meeting positive by *not* saying things like:

- I don't think you evaluated me fairly.

- Did I lose this promotion because I'm a woman?

- Is it because the people in this department don't like me?

- What does a person have to do around here to get promoted?

- I demand to know why I didn't get this job.

- This looks like discrimination to me.

"WHAT CAN I DO TO GET AHEAD?"

During your meeting, cover these topics:

- *Interview style.* Ask for a critique of your interviewing ability. Don't ask how well your interview went or for an *opinion* of your interviewing skills—that sounds like you're looking for an ego massage. It also lets the interviewer give you a general: "Oh, I think you did fine." *Fine* doesn't give you any information. Ask *how* you can improve, and ask for specific answers, not generalities.

Throughout the meeting, avoid asking questions that can be answered by a simple "yes" or "no"—they don't elicit much information. Ask open-ended questions that begin with "how much," "in what ways," or, "would you describe." (Think of it as the difference between a true/false test and an essay test.)

- *Professional credentials*. Did you lose the promotion because you're a secretary? Ask that question diplomatically, so you don't appear to be accusing the interviewer of discriminating against secretaries:

  "How much did my lack of managerial experience hurt me in trying to get this job?"

- *Ways to improve your professional credentials*. Get suggestions on how you can overcome your professional deficiencies:

  "As a secretary, it's sometimes hard to get experience in the areas you mentioned. Do you have any recommendations on how I can get that background?"

- *Personal qualifications*. Even though it appears you lost out because of your business background, don't neglect to ask about your personal qualifications. "We need someone with more experience" is an easy answer to give a secretary—easier than telling you the truth if the real problem is personal.

  Nobody wants to say, "Every time I see you you're goofing off with the other secretaries. In my opinion, you're too lazy for this job." But if that's the case, you need to know. Ask:

  "How much of a factor were my personal skills—communication skills, management skills, general people skills—in your decision not to hire me for this job?"

  Do a little prompting if you have trouble getting a straight answer:

  "How would you rate my level of motivation compared to what was required for this job?"

Show genuine interest in correcting the difficulty—particularly if you didn't realize you had a problem in that area:

> "I'm surprised, and frankly I'm concerned, to hear you say that I don't seem to get along well with people. I've always prided myself on my relations with my co-workers, but apparently I'm not doing as well as I thought I was. Could you elaborate—perhaps give me some specific examples—because this is an area I feel very strongly about working on."

Your concern shows that if this is a problem, it won't be one for long.

DON'T THREATEN TO QUIT

Meeting failure head-on does not mean threatening to quit. People don't like being threatened, and they won't stand for it if they don't have to. Unless you've caught him with his hand in the till (or worse), no boss has to yield to demands issued by a secretary. Ultimatums simply don't work—you either get your way and offend your boss, or you don't get your way and you're out of a job.

> One very successful salesman I worked with threatened to quit every time things didn't go his way. He was going to quit because his new office wasn't big enough, his bonus wasn't big enough, he didn't like the direction the division was taking, and on and on. Because he generated so much income for the corporation, he thought he could bully everyone and get away with it. And he did—for awhile.
>
> During one memorable meeting, he was making his usual noises about being approached by the competition and how he didn't know if he could continue with us if certain conditions weren't met, when the president of the division suddenly said in a deadly quiet tone of voice, "I think it might be a good idea if you didn't continue with us."
>
> All the begging in the world didn't save his job. The president had had enough.

The moral of this story is that if a highly successful salesman can blow his job by threatening to quit, what chance do you, as a secretary, have?

Threaten to quit only if:

1. You already have another job lined up (in which case, you're in a very strong bargaining position).

2. You are prepared to walk out the door in the next 5 minutes.

3. You can afford to be out of work while you look for another job.

NO BITTERNESS ALLOWED

Don't let a setback ruin your attitude. The minute you get bitter, start complaining, or let your work slide, you've lost the war. Not just one of the battles, but the entire war. Your image degenerates from potential executive to problem employee. You're seen as temperamental, emotionally immature, and at the limit of your potential with the company. It will be a long, uphill battle for another chance.

When you've given up all hope of ever getting a promotion where you are, don't get mad, get another job. The world is full of organizations searching for capable people who want to take on responsibility. Don't let a bad experience with one company or one boss destroy your faith in your ability to get ahead.

A stiff upper lip is essential equipment for a secretary—there's always another day and another opportunity.

THE CAREER DEVELOPMENT PLAN

If you can't get an official or even an unofficial promotion, don't back off—step up the offensive by creating a career development plan for yourself.

Some companies (albeit very few) have development plans for secretaries. Ask your boss if such a thing exists, and if it doesn't, tell him that you want to build one with his help:

"I don't seem to be considered qualified for any of the promotions I've applied for, and I want to start correcting that. First, I'd like for us to establish some realistic goals for my professional advancement, then I'd like to work out a plan that will help me achieve those goals."

Your plan should be a written document that includes:

A statement of your professional goals and objectives. Where do you want to go? Do you want to become a sales representative, an auditor, or a land surveyor? Be specific and realistic.

A time frame in which to accomplish those objectives. Where do you want to be 6 months, a year, 2 years from now? What rate of advancement is feasible?

An honest appraisal of your strengths and weaknesses. Insist that your boss be frank about your limitations. You can't correct them if you don't know what they are.

Specific development activities. What's the best way to get the experience and training you need? A seminar on how to handle customers? Special schooling? Will your boss delegate assignments that will help you grow?

Progress evaluation. When will your progress be evaluated? And how will it be evaluated? How will you know you're succeeding and that you're on the right track?

Real progress. What assurance do you have that, given acceptable development, you will get the promotion you seek? Will your efforts result in a promotion, or is this just make-work designed to pacify you and get you off your boss's back? Get a commitment.

Third-party involvement. Request that the personnel department or your boss's boss receive a copy of this plan, so that your boss is publicly committed to it. Diplomatically tell your boss that you want to keep everyone informed to avoid any misunderstandings about your activities (the vindictive secretaries may strike again).

THE SECRETARY AS MANAGEMENT TRAINEE

Think of yourself as a management trainee. You are one—you're learning how to become a successful business executive. Absorbing all this knowledge and taking on all this responsibility is your way of training to be a manager. Your boss may not know it, the other executives in the office may not know it, the personnel department may not know it, and even the other secretaries may not have figured it out. But inside, you know you're going to be a manager one day. And with your guts, skill, and determination, that day may very well be tomorrow.

16. The view from the other side

You made it. You've been promoted. You've captured the management job you had your sights set on, and it feels wonderful. You've got a great career ahead of you, one that's filled with challenges, excitement, and rewards.

LOOKING AHEAD

Everything you did to get promoted to a management job—creating the right image, tackling problems, assuming responsibility, pushing for what you want—is everything you need to do to keep getting promoted. Because you've done it once, you can look forward to the next promotion being easier. No barrier will be as tough as the one you've just broken. Just give the next promotion the same intense effort you gave this one, and you are well on your way to the top.

YOU EARNED YOUR SUCCESS

Many women who break the secretary barrier attribute their success to "luck" and having been "in the right place at the right time."

That's undue modesty. All of them worked very hard to be ready for opportunity when it arrived.

Right places and right times aren't accidents or flukes, they happen over and over again—they just don't always get noticed. When an assistant's position opens up in the next department, that's a right place and right time. If you're ready, if you've worked hard and prepared yourself for a promotion, you'll hear about the job and you'll get it. If you're not ready, if you haven't done the necessary preparation, someone else gets the job, and you may never know the opportunity occurred. It's a matter of being prepared.

Don't shortchange yourself and give "luck" all the credit for your success. Luck and being in the right place at the right time take a lot of effort and hard work.

SHEDDING YOUR SECRETARIAL REPUTATION

The biggest problem you will face as a new manager is still being treated like a secretary. Your transition from secretary to manager is so major that many people will have trouble adjusting to it. Re-orient them tactfully but firmly:

- When your boss asks you to type a letter or place a phone call for him, immediately turn the request over to your replacement. Say, "I'll have Mandy do that for you right away." Don't embarrass yourself or your boss by loudly reminding him that you are no longer a secretary and you don't type his letters or place his phone calls anymore.

- Don't hesitate to turn responsibilities over to your replacement. You are a manager now—learn to delegate.

- If someone calls you "Mr. Brown's secretary," don't let it go by. Politely correct them by saying, "I'm an assistant account executive now."

- Be ready to deal with the inevitable few who will take pot shots at you—the ones who will refer to you as "Mr. Brown's former secretary," "a glorified secretary," or as I was once called after my promotion to assistant product manager, "the girl who helps out in the office." People who do this don't like the fact that you were promoted, but that's their problem, not yours. Maintain a businesslike manner, and don't let them bother you. Deliver an innocent: "I must have forgotten to tell you what my new title is. It's assistant account executive—isn't that fabulous?" Or "I'm sure I told you about my promotion. In fact, I've mentioned it three or four times. You seem to keep forgetting it."

The farther up you go in any organization, the more detractors you will have, the more people who will criticize you, and the more intense the competition becomes. It's part of the game.

- On the other hand, don't regard every comment on your promotion with suspicion. Some people will tease you just because your promotion is something new to talk about. Don't be hypersensitive and assume everyone is trying to insult you.

ON TO GREENER PASTURES

If the people you work *for*, however, can't seem to forget you're a "former secretary," you may have to consider going elsewhere—to a different company where people see you only as a manager, not as someone with a typewriter in her past. One secretary who changed jobs after being promoted said:

"I was so surprised when I left the company where I had been a secretary. I had been promoted to assistant purchasing manager, but I couldn't seem to get beyond that. After a year and a half, I could do my job with my eyes closed, but the head of the division said I needed at least two more years as an assistant before I would even be considered for another promotion.

"I started job hunting and landed a job as the head of purchasing for a small firm. I couldn't believe the difference in attitude. People in the new company regarded me as an expert—they didn't think of me as someone who used to be a secretary. For the first time in my career, I was treated with respect. I hadn't realized what I was missing."

EDIT YOUR RÉSUMÉ

It's a good idea to "edit" your résumé when you decide to change jobs. When I left Borden, I dropped the "secretary" off my résumé altogether. I think it's only fair to show yourself as an assistant on your résumé *for as long as you had assistant-level responsibilities—* even if you didn't get the title right away.

Suppose your job history looks like this:

July 1985–December 1985	Assistant Account Executive, Promotions Unlimited
April 1981–July 1985	Secretary, Sales Department, Promotions Unlimited
October 1979–April 1981	Receptionist, Promotions Unlimited

Your résumé shows you've had the assistant title for only 6 months, but in reality you functioned as an assistant for almost 2 years before the official promotion came through. So revise your résumé to show your real experience:

March 1984–December 1985	Assistant Account Executive, Promotions Unlimited
April 1981–*March 1984*	Secretary, Sales Department, Promotions Unlimited
October 1979–April 1981	Receptionist, Promotions Unlimited

Your job-hunting efforts will be more productive if you show more time as an assistant. An assistant with 1½ years' experience is ready for a manager's job. An assistant with only 6 months' experience is questionable.

Don't overdo it and show that you've been an assistant for 6 or 7 years. You'd have to explain why you couldn't get promoted to manager in all that time. Just try to show a steady upward progression without too little or too much time in any one position. As long as you are employed, you can ask prospective employers not to call for verification of your current position. On the excuse, of course, that your boss doesn't know you're looking for another job.

LOOKING BACK

The world looks different from a manager's office. You find yourself doing things you swore you'd never do as a manager. You give your secretary a rush proposal to type at 4:45 on a Friday afternoon. You forget to tell her that you'll be out of the office. You get angry because you can't find a certain file.

For the first time, you have some sympathy for the managers you used to work for. You see the problems they had, and the reasons for some of the unreasonable things they did.

But you're lucky, and your secretary's even luckier, because you've been on the receiving end of those unreasonable things. So you know to explain to your secretary why the proposal didn't get done until 4:45; you know to offer her some comp time or overtime pay for staying late; and you know how to let her help you so the unreasonable doesn't happen very often.

You have a tremendous advantage over a manager who's never been in the "trenches." Because you've been there, you know how to make a secretary's job more productive, more challenging, and more fun.

The days of pounding out letters for $950 a month should make you a more considerate, more compassionate boss. Never forget them.

EXTEND A HELPING HAND

It was a struggle to get your management job. And it will be a struggle for every secretary coming up behind you. Don't turn your back on them. Help them achieve what you've achieved for yourself. Delegate responsibility to other secretaries, assign special projects to them, advocate higher salaries, and encourage career development programs.

Make the way easier for those who come after. Because your success is doubled if you pass it on.

Appendix: Recommended reading

Of the many books I reviewed or read while writing *Breaking the Secretary Barrier*, the following are the ones I think will be most helpful in your move for the top. Many of the others were excellent, but won't do you much good until you are a full-fledged manager. Others were good in their day, but have now become outdated.

This list is by no means exhaustive—and good new books are being printed every day. But here are some that are worth investing in now:

APPEARANCE

Dressing to Win: How to Have More Money, Romance, and Power in Your Life!, Robert Pante, Doubleday & Company, Inc., Garden City, New York, 1984.

A motivational guide to dressing that can catapult you into the big leagues, both professionally and personally. You can't read this book and not want to get ahead.

Executive Style: Looking It . . . Living It, Mary B. Fiedorek and Diana Lewis Jewell, New Century Publishers, Piscataway, New Jersey, 1983.

Specifically for women, this is advice on how to dress for conservative occupations, both in the office and on the road. Even those in nonconservative fields can pick up some tips on office-style and lifestyle.

The Professional Image, Susan Bixler, G. P. Putnam's Sons, New York, New York, 1984.

A practical guide to developing a business wardrobe and a marketable business image. Down-to-earth advice on how to buy a suit, how to choose the right fabrics and accessories, and a section on proper business body language.

ATTITUDE

Giving Away Success: Why Women Get Stuck and What to Do about It, Susan Schenkel, Ph.D., McGraw-Hill Book Company, New York, New York, 1984.

If you have trouble taking the steps you need to take to become successful, this book will tell you what's holding you back and how to overcome it.

GENERAL JOB SKILLS

Games Mother Never Taught You: Corporate Gamesmanship for Women, Betty Lehan Harragan, Warner Books, Inc., New York, New York, 1977.

A must-read on corporate politics for any woman in business. Harragan examines all the subtleties of the business world that men know so well and most women don't understand, and provides advice on how women can learn to be masters of the game.

No-Nonsense Management Tips for Women, Jeannette Reddish Scollard, Wallaby Books, Simon & Schuster, New York, New York, 1983.

Somewhat mistitled, this book is actually the definitive work on how an executive woman should act in any situation—from making a presentation to the board of directors to knowing the right executive small talk. Indispensable!

1000 Things You Never Learned in Business School: How to Get Ahead of the Pack and Stay There, William N. Yeomans, McGraw-Hill Book Company, New York, New York, 1985.

Across-the-board advice on developing your business skills, taking control of your career, and moving up in the organization.

Paths to Power: A Woman's Guide from First Job to Top Executive, Natasha Josefowitz, Ph.D., Addison-Wesley Publishing Company, Reading, Massachusetts, 1980.

All the phases of a woman's career are covered here, from leaving the kitchen to entering the board room. Josefowitz focuses on obstacles, attitudes, and the unique conditions of each stage of a woman's progress through the business world.

The Promotable Woman: Becoming a Successful Manager, Norma Carr-Rufino, Van Nostrand Reinhold Company, New York, New York 1982.

This management primer for new women managers, or women aspiring to be managers, covers everything from stress to operating budgets. Very valuable for women making the transition to management.

The Six-Figure Woman (and How to Be One), Lois Wyse, Linden Press/Simon & Schuster, New York, New York, 1983.

A concise collection of tips for getting ahead and staying ahead for women in three salary categories—under $25,000, $25,000 to $75,000, and the six-figure woman—but women in any stage of business will find valuable information here.

Skills for Success: A Guide to the Top, Adele M. Scheele, Ph.D., William Morrow and Company, New York, New York, 1979.

Dr. Scheele identifies and describes six "career competences" that lead to professional success. Excellent examples on how to improve your chances for advancement.

Strategies for Women at Work, Janice LaRouche and Regina Ryan, Avon Books, New York, New York, 1984.

LaRouche identifies over 100 problem situations at work and provides concise, to-the-point solutions. Topics include boss problems, problems in moving up, and problems you'll have when you get there.

You're the Boss, K. K. Wallace, Contemporary Books, Chicago, Illinois, 1982.

Whether you are a subordinate or a boss, Wallace believes you're in charge of your career. She covers how to understand office relationships so you can get promoted.

SPECIFIC JOB SKILLS

About Time! A Woman's Guide to Time Management, Alec Mackenzie and Kay Cronkite Waldo, McGraw-Hill Book Co., New York, New York, 1981.

Mackenzie, author of the time management classic *The Time Trap*, extends those principles to cover a woman's problem of time management at home and at the office. Some good tips for secretaries.

Finance for Nonfinancial Managers, Neil Seitz, Ph.D., Reston Publishing Company, Reston, Virginia, 1983.

Unless you're a finance freak, this book is not an evening's casual reading. But it's an excellent reference that gives you a clear, concise description of financial topics.

How to Get Control of Your Time and Your Life, Alan Lakein, Signet/New American Library, New York, New York, 1973.

One of the great classics in time management, this book will give you a new perspective on making the most of the time you've got.

The Résumé Kit, Richard H. Beatty, John Wiley & Sons, New York, New York, 1984.

One of the best of the many résumé how-to books on the market. It's directed at managers, but secretaries can use it to develop a managerial-looking résumé. Includes information on dealing with the "problem" résumé—too little experience, lack of education, gaps in employment, etc.

JUST FOR FUN

The Executive Woman's Coloring Book—or You've Come a Long Way, Person, Martin A. Cohen and Mary McDonald Horowitz, Price/Stern/Sloan, Los Angeles, California, 1983.

A final case history

When Janet Dight graduated from Ohio State University, she had no idea what she was going to do about a job—or a career, for that matter. She'd earned a bachelor of arts degree in English, which left her unprepared for any business career whatsoever. Her only real experience was two summers as a girl Friday in a small advertising agency.

One day shortly after graduation, Janet got a tip that the Borden, Inc.'s Chemical Division was looking for an assistant in its marketing research department. It wasn't really an assistant's job—the title was marketing research assistant/secretary—and it didn't pay very much, but during the interview, the marketing research manager told her that the position was expanding and that they were looking for someone who could handle more than just secretarial responsibilities. The job sounded like it had possibilities.

Janet worked hard, worked long hours, and took on every new responsibility she could get. Her efforts quickly attracted the attention of the director of marketing (her boss's boss), who took an interest in her career and began channeling more managerial assignments her way. Her boss soon agreed to make her a full-fledged assistant and hire a new secretary.

Janet continued to expand her responsibilities wherever she could, and only 6 months later, the director of marketing promoted her to assistant product manager on the Krylon Spray Paint brand. Since then, she has held several marketing management positions, including manager of merchandising and promotion for the Equipment & Supplies Division of Kentucky Fried Chicken.

Today Janet Dight is a marketing consultant in Colorado Springs, Colorado. She specializes in developing marketing and advertising programs for new products and new businesses in the data processing field. She has written several articles for data processing magazines and has just published her first book, which is called *Breaking the Secretary Barrier: How to Get Out from Behind the Typewriter and Into a Management Job.*

Index